T0214039

Lecture Notes in Computer Science 12604

More information about this subseries at http://www.springer.com/series/7409

Asbjørn Følstad · Theo Araujo ·
Symeon Papadopoulos ·
Effie L.-C. Law · Ewa Luger ·
Morten Goodwin · Petter Bae Brandtzaeg (Eds.)

Chatbot Research and Design

4th International Workshop, CONVERSATIONS 2020
Virtual Event, November 23–24, 2020
Revised Selected Papers

 Springer

Editors
Asbjørn Følstad ⓘ
SINTEF
Oslo, Norway

Theo Araujo ⓘ
University of Amsterdam
Amsterdam, The Netherlands

Symeon Papadopoulos ⓘ
CERTH-ITI
Thessaloniki, Greece

Effie L.-C. Law ⓘ
University of Leicester
Leicester, UK

Ewa Luger ⓘ
University of Edinburgh
Edinburgh, UK

Morten Goodwin ⓘ
University of Agder
Grimstad, Norway

Petter Bae Brandtzaeg ⓘ
University of Oslo
Oslo, Norway

ISSN 0302-9743   ISSN 1611-3349 (electronic)
Lecture Notes in Computer Science
ISBN 978-3-030-68287-3   ISBN 978-3-030-68288-0 (eBook)
https://doi.org/10.1007/978-3-030-68288-0

LNCS Sublibrary: SL3 – Information Systems and Applications, incl. Internet/Web, and HCI

This Springer imprint is published by the registered company Springer Nature Switzerland AG
The registered company address is: Gewerbestrasse 11, 6330 Cham, Switzerland

Preface

Introduction

Chatbots see continued uptake in a range of application areas. Spurred by interest from industry and service providers, chatbot research is a rapidly growing field with an exponential increase in scientific publications in the last few years. Research areas span from the examination of evolving patterns of use and user experience (UX) to conversational design and studies about the technologies underpinning chatbots such as natural language processing and machine learning. Research also increasingly addresses specific application areas and use cases. For example, research on social and relational chatbots is receiving growing attention; so are chatbots in areas such as customer service, education, health, and commerce. Research is also addressing the potential social implications of chatbots, exploring how chatbots impact individuals' patterns of technology use, how chatbots can provide information and support in challenging situations – such as the ongoing COVID-19 pandemic – and how to facilitate compliance with ethical norms or avoid ethical and normative pitfalls in chatbot development and applications.

In consequence of the increased interest in chatbot research, and the potential social and industrial impact of conversational technology, there is a need to establish arenas for chatbot researchers and practitioners to share, discuss, and collaborate. This is particularly important given the interdisciplinary nature of this field of research, spanning disciplines within the humanities, social sciences, human-computer interaction, technology research, design, and management.

Motivated by this need, we established an international workshop series for chatbot researchers to share work and experiences with fellow researchers, students, and practitioners. CONVERSATIONS 2020 (https://conversations2020.wordpress.com/) was the fourth event in this series, held on November 23-24, 2020. The University of Amsterdam hosted the workshop, in collaboration with SINTEF, CERTH, University of Leicester, University of Edinburgh, University of Agder, and University of Oslo. This year the workshop was organized as a fully virtual online event due to the COVID-19 pandemic. In total 150 participants from 31 countries registered for the online workshop.

Paper Invitation, Review, and Revision

We distributed the workshop call for papers to researchers in the field of chatbot research, and to relevant general mailing lists within fields such as human-computer interaction and information systems research. In the call for papers, three submission categories were outlined: Full papers, position papers, and demos. In total, 36 submissions were made to the workshop: 26 full papers, eight position papers, and two demos. A rigorous double-blind review process was conducted with three independent reviewers from the program committee providing detailed feedback on each submission. In addition, each paper was appointed a review lead from the group of workshop organizers coordinating the review process for the paper, proposing a decision recommendation, and providing meta-reviews for accepted papers. Acceptance decisions were made in a dedicated workshop organizers meeting.

Fourteen of the papers were accepted as full papers. Two were accepted without changes, eight followed requests for minor revision, and four followed requests for major revision. Revised papers were checked for compliance with change requests prior to final acceptance. When necessary, a second round of revisions was requested. The acceptance rate for full papers was 54%, which is lower than for previous editions of the workshop.

For submissions authored by a workshop organizer, review and decision making was conducted by other organizers and blinded to the authoring organizer.

Workshop Outcomes

Over the two days, the workshop program included two keynote speakers, three groupworks, and six paper sessions. The workshop keynote speakers were Q. Vera Liao, IBM research AI, and Björn Schuller, Imperial College London and University of Augsburg. The three workshop groupworks addressed different topics: *chatbot development*, led by Raphael Meyer von Wolff and Sebastian Hobert, University of Göttingen, *chatbot concept co-creation*, led by Federica Tazzi, Assist Digital, and *chatbot ethics*, led by Symeon Papadopoulos, CERTH, Asbjørn Følstad, SINTEF, and Effie L.-C. Law, University of Leicester. The paper sessions included full papers and position papers. The final versions of the full papers are included in these proceedings.

The papers in the proceedings are structured in four topical groups: Chatbot UX and user perceptions, social and relational chatbots, chatbot applications, and chatbots for customer service. The papers provide new knowledge through empirical, theoretical, or design contributions.

Under the topic of *chatbot UX and user perceptions* five papers addressed the impact of chatbot self-presentation and communication style, as well as users' perceptions of chatbots and guidelines for chatbot design. De Cicco et al. presented an empirical study on how chatbots disclosing themselves impact trust, social presence, and attitudes towards online retailers. Liebrecht et al. studied how varying levels of formality in chatbot communication affect social presence, brand attitude, and quality of interaction. Ruane et al. showed how variations in chatbot and user personality can affect user experience. Etzrodt presented findings concerning users relating to chatbots as things, as persons, or as something in between – personified things. Finally, Crovari et al. discussed a set of guidelines on how to design for chatbots applied in a multimodal context.

Three papers addressed *social and relational chatbots*, a topic of substantial current relevance following recent work on open-domain chatbots from Google and Facebook as well as the increased uptake of companion chatbots such as Replika. Croes and Antheunis presented a study comparing users' willingness to disclose information about themselves to chatbots or human conversation partners, van Wezel et al. surveyed the literature on social support in chatbots, and Löw et al. presented a design case of using a chatbot to strengthen social relations among university freshmen as part of a scavenger hunt.

Six of the papers addressed different applications for chatbots. Three of these are included in the general topic *chatbot applications* and three are included in the more specific topic of *chatbots for customer service*. In the first cluster of papers, Höhn and Bongard-Blanchy presented a timely study on current chatbots providing information and support on COVID-19, Klopfenstein and Di Lorenzi presented a prototype chatbot design for presenting interactive narratives, and Catania et al. presented a prototype chatbot for teaching bodily concepts to children. In the cluster on chatbots for customer service, Janssen et al. presented a review of chatbots for business-to-business support, van der Goot et al. presented a study of users' perceptions of chatbots as part of a customer journey, and Kvale et al. presented a study exploring customer satisfaction scores as a source for insight into chatbot user experience.

New at this year's CONVERSATIONS workshop was a best paper award. Three papers with the highest review score were nominated for the award. Of these, one was selected as best paper based on rankings made independently by the workshop organizers. The best paper award was granted to Antje Janssen, Davinia Rodríguez Cardona, and Michael H. Breitner, for the paper *More than FAQ! Chatbot Taxonomy for Business-to-Business Customer Services*. The other best paper nominees were: Roberta De Cicco, Susana Cristina Lima da Costa e Silva, and Riccardo Palumbo, for the paper *Should a Chatbot Disclose Itself? Implications for an Online Conversational Retailer* and Margot van der Goot, Laura Hafkamp, and Zoë Dankfort, for the paper *Customer Service Chatbots: A Qualitative Interview Study into Customers' Communication Journey*.

The presented papers, along with the groupworks and keynote speakers, made CONVERSATIONS 2020 a successful venue for sharing and discussing chatbot research. Through these proceedings, a key outcome of the workshop – the presented full papers – are made available for a broader audience of chatbot researchers and practitioners, as a basis for future chatbot research. Motivated by the success of this year's workshop, we look forward to the continued sharing of chatbot research also in the coming editions of CONVERSATONS.

November 2020

Asbjørn Følstad
Theo Araujo
Symeon Papadopoulos
Effie L.-C. Law
Ewa Luger
Morten Goodwin
Petter Bae Brandtzaeg

Organization

General Chairs/Workshop Organizers

Asbjørn Følstad   SINTEF, Norway
Theo Araujo   University of Amsterdam, The Netherlands
Symeon Papadopoulos   Centre for Research and Technology Hellas, Greece
Effie L.-C. Law   University of Leicester, UK
Ewa Luger   University of Edinburgh, UK
Morten Goodwin   University of Agder, Norway
Petter Bae Brandtzaeg   University of Oslo & SINTEF, Norway

Program Committee

Alexander Mädche   Karlsruhe Institute of Technology, Germany
Amela Karahasanovic   SINTEF, Norway
Ana Paula Chaves Steinmacher   Northern Arizona University, USA
Arkaitz Zubiaga   Queen Mary University of London, UK
Carolin Ischen   University of Amsterdam, The Netherlands
Christian Löw   University of Vienna, Austria
Christine Liebrecht   Tilburg University, The Netherlands
David Kuboň   Charles University, Czech Republic
Despoina Chatzakou   Centre for Research and Technology Hellas, Greece
Eleni Metheniti   Saarland University, Germany
Emmelyn A. J. Croes   Tilburg University, The Netherlands
Fabio Catania   Politecnico di Milano, Italy
Federica Tazzi   Assist Digital, Italy
Frank Dignum   Umeå University, Sweden
Fréjus Laleye   CEA, France
Frode Guribye   University of Bergen, Norway
Gaël de Chalendar   CEA, France
Guy Laban   University of Glasgow, UK
Jasper Feine   Karlsruhe Institute of Technology, Germany
Jo Dugstad Wake   NORCE & University of Bergen, Norway
Konstantinos Boletsis   SINTEF, Norway
Lara S. G. Piccolo   The Open University, UK
Lea Reis   University of Bamberg, Germany
Leigh Clark   Swansea University, UK
Margot van der Goot   University of Amsterdam, The Netherlands
Marita Skjuve   SINTEF, Norway
Massimiliano Dibitonto   Link Campus University, Italy
Patrick McAllister   Ulster University, UK

Raphael Meyer von Wolff   University of Göttingen, Germany
Rricha Jalota   Paderborn University, Germany
Sebastian Hobert   University of Göttingen, Germany
Stefan Schaffer   DFKI – German Research Center for Artificial
                             Intelligence, Germany
Stergios Tegos   Aristotle University of Thessaloniki, Greece
Sviatlana Höhn   University of Luxembourg, Luxembourg
Ulrich Gnewuch   Karlsruhe Institute of Technology, Germany
Zia Uddin   SINTEF, Norway

Contents

Chatbot UX and User Perceptions

Should a Chatbot Disclose Itself? Implications for an Online Conversational Retailer

Roberta De Cicco[1,2(✉)], Susana Cristina Lima da Costa e Silva[3], and Riccardo Palumbo[1,2]

[1] Department of Neuroscience, Imaging and Clinical Sciences,
University of Chieti-Pescara, Chieti, Italy
roberta.decicco@unich.it
[2] CAST, Center for Advanced Studies and Technology,
University of Chieti-Pescara, Chieti, Italy
[3] Católica Porto Business School–Universidade Católica Portuguesa, Porto, Portugal

Abstract. Today many consumers prefer interactions with companies via chat and instant messaging, however, although in most cases it is now a virtual agent to handle the interactions, many of them feel it would be eerie if a chatbot pretended to be human. The present study aims at disentangling this sort of ambivalence people have for chatbots through an investigation on how the explicit disclosure of the chatbot identity, before the interaction, influences consumers' perceptions. Specifically, this study compares the effects that the explicit disclosure of the chatbot identity has on social presence trust and users' attitudes toward the online retailer. Findings from an online experiment with 160 participants show that interacting with the chatbot whose identity has been primed through a disclosure leads to less perceived social presence, trust, and attitude toward the online retailer, compared to interacting with the chatbot whose identity has not been disclosed before the interaction. The study further analyses a causal chain among the variables, proving that social presence and trust mediate the relationship between the chatbot identity disclosure and the attitude toward the online retailer.

Keywords: Chatbot · Disclosure · Social presence · Trust · Attitude toward the online retailer

1 Introduction

The spread of digital services and digital marketing channels offer companies new opportunities to satisfy customers [4]. Among these channels, considerable interest has been addressed to conversational touchpoints. Today conversational systems in the form of chatbots have become a reality on social media and messaging apps [2]. Chatbots are programs that simulate human conversations through voice commands or text chats and serve as virtual assistants to users [25]. These systems are designed to carry out tasks as simple as sending airline tickets or as complex as giving health, financial, or shopping advice [2] depending on the resources invested in terms of artificial intelligence. Human-chatbot interactions usually take place within the context of the so-called "conversational

A. Følstad et al. (Eds.): CONVERSATIONS 2020, LNCS 12604, pp. 3–15, 2021.
https://doi.org/10.1007/978-3-030-68288-0_1

marketing" that, among its multiple facets, involves conversational commerce, which is messaging with consumers and allowing them to make purchases [41] over platforms like Facebook Messenger.

According to Hubspot, the main reasons for the spread of chatbots lies in the fact that they help consumers find solutions anywhere, anytime and with any device, and that with chatbots, users do not need to fill bottomless forms, cluttered inboxes and waste time searching and scrolling through content. Chatbots raise interest because they seem to express the future of user-provider interactions [22]. On a firm-level, they are increasingly applied for marketing purposes such as customer relationship management (CRM), pre and post-purchase support [33] and customer service [14], as they represent a potentially cost-effective solution offering between 15–90% cost reduction opportunity depending upon the characteristics of the functions selected for the automation [7]. Many market research companies that provide advice on the existing and potential impact of technology are ahead in expressing optimism toward the future of this technology. As reported by Gartner, over the next ten years, AI will be infused in most technologies. The main factors that will contribute to this trend will be the augmentation in computational power, big data, and the development of deep neural networks. It is expected that in the next years, Messenger users will be more often talking to chatbots than to a partner every day, and 25% of interactions between a client and a brand will not be based on direct contact with a human [12]. These expectations are supported by the quick projected growth of the chatbot market size from $250 million in 2017 to over $1.34 billion in 2024 [25].

More than 21% of U.S adults and over 80% of Generation Z use voice/text bots for information search and shopping [27]. Many brands such as American Eagle Outfitters and Domino's Pizza have turned to chatbots to take orders or recommend products, and major platforms such as Amazon, eBay, Facebook, and WeChat are starting to adopt chatbots for conversational commerce. Despite the potential benefits offered by chatbots, a key challenge this technology has to face is the potential customers' pushback. In fact, many people still feel uncomfortable talking and chatting with computer programs to reveal personal needs or purchase decisions [25]. Many companies adopting chatbots face the dilemma of whether disclosing the artificial nature of this channel to customers as, if doing so, companies might go through negative effects due to the perception of the bot as a less knowledgeable and empathetic entity [25]. In the future, however, disclosing the artificial identity of the bot may not be an option anymore. The California Consumer Protection Act (CCPA) has started inviting all companies using machine/AI bot in customer services to disclose the bot identity in the conversation.

In light of the above, a few questions arise: what are the implications for explicitly disclosing the artificial identity of the chatbot at the beginning of the interaction? Is transparency helpful or does users' resistance queen it over?

As suggested in a very recent work by Luo et al. [25], disclosing the artificial identity of the conversational agent can have a strong influence on consumers' overall perceptions. According to the authors, to be successful companies must understand whether, when, and how to best introduce the identity of the artificial agents to consumers. On this premise, our research sheds light on a promising topic in Human-Computer Interaction

(HCI) and media psychology, that is the disclosure of the artificial nature in human-chatbot interaction. In so doing, the present work extends earlier research by analyzing the effects of disclosing the chatbot's identity on three crucial variables in online transactions that are social presence, trust, and attitude toward the online retailer. The study further disentangles the relationships among these variables by explicating a causal chain that identifies social presence and trust as serial mediators between the effect of chatbot identity disclosure on attitude toward the online retailer.

2 Theoretical Framework and Hypotheses Development

2.1 The Effect of Chatbot Disclosure on Social Presence, Trust and Attitude Toward the Online Retailer

Humans and chatbots have different capabilities [37], consequently, humans differ in how they perceive the interaction and how they interact with a chatbot compared to another human [19]. This makes transparency in the nature and limitations of this technology somehow an important issue for academics and practitioners studying human-chatbot interactions. Some scholars argue that chatbots should be upfront about their machine status [28] because this is beneficial to limit users' expectations in the system and avoid negative implications from users failing to realize the limitations in chatbots. According to a recent study, however, there are some negative effects in disclosing artificial agents that seem to be driven by a subjective human perception against machines [25]. Studies show that people prefer replacement of human employees by other humans as opposed to by machines/robots/new technologies, which negatively influences their overall attitude towards AI [15] that can be defined as an evaluative response, including both cognitive and affective components [30]. Moreover, compared to trust towards humans, prior research has argued that people tend to have less trust towards AI by default, so, according to the definition of trust, less belief in the competence, dependability, and security of the system, under the condition of risk [21], which may partly be explained by the high media attention on instances in which AI went wrong [36].

A prejudice many people have is that chatbots lack personal feelings and empathy and are less trustworthy [10] and less pleasant [37] compared to humans. So, on the one hand, if companies decide to explicitly disclose the artificial agent identity, they might not gain the full business value of AI chatbots due to customer resistance [25]. On the other hand, however, customers should have the right to know whether it is a bot or a human that handles their communications because of moral and ethical concerns, especially if such differentiation leads to disagreeing perceptions and outcomes.

A recent study tested the causal impact of a voice-based bot disclosure on customer purchases and call length [25]. The results of the study show that when customers know the conversational partner is not a human, they are brusque, short the conversation length, and purchase less. Kim and Sundar [20] were among the first to argue that if an agent is presumed to be operated by an artificial agent, users are more likely to evaluate the quality of the agent's performance based on their pre-existing perceptions, regardless of the agent's actual performance quality. In the years, other studies investigated the different perceptions users have when they chat – or believe they are chatting – with a human or rather with an artificial agent. These studies confirmed the preference for humans, even when the other (believed to be a human) is a bot [6, 31]. More specifically, Murgia et al. [31] found that a bot that answered users' questions on a social website was regarded more positively when posing as a human than when explicitly revealing its bot identity. In Corti and Gillespie [6], users were more likely to expend effort in making themselves understood when the agent's chat content was conveyed through a human than through an artificial text-based interface. Similarly, Sundar et al. [39] showed that participants were more willing to recommend a website to others when it provided a human chat agent compared to a chatbot agent, despite in both conditions the chatting protocol to communicate with all the participants was the same.

According to some authors [e.g. 2], perceptions about the conversational agent may be influenced by how the agent is introduced before the conversation.

Making users believe that they are engaging with a fully-autonomous agent when, in reality, the agent is human-controlled, or priming users to believe that they are engaging a real person when they are in reality interacting with an agent are common practices in experimental studies in HCI [6]. This priming effect was found to considerably influence subsequent general perceptions about the agent and, particularly, social presence, a construct at the heart of the HCI literature (Human-Computer Interaction) representing the *"degree of salience of the other person in the interaction"* [35 p. 65]. According to Etemad-Sajadi and Ghachem [8], social presence is particularly relevant in online business contexts because it creates the feeling of the employees' presence and improves the customer experience in a retail interaction.

From these premises, in line with past studies where the explicit disclosure of the artificial agent identity was shown to negatively affect users' perceptions of the interaction and the system, we expect that participants will perceive lower levels of social presence, trust and attitude toward the online retailer in the disclosed chatbot condition than in the undisclosed chatbot condition.

H1. *Users perceive lower levels of social presence in the online retailer when the chatbot identity is disclosed compared to when the chatbot identity is undisclosed.*
H2. *Users perceive lower levels of trust in the online retailer when the chatbot identity is disclosed compared to when the chatbot identity is undisclosed.*
H3. *Users perceive a less positive attitude toward the online retailer when the chatbot identity is disclosed compared to when the chatbot identity is undisclosed.*

2.2 Social Presence and Trust Mediate the Relation Between Disclosure of Chatbot Identity and Attitude Toward the Online Retailer

Social presence represents the feeling of being with another in a mediated environment [3]. This construct is of great value for the human-chatbot interaction, especially in the business domain where it is found to be a positive predictor of trust and attitude not only when considering overall evaluations of the artificial agent [44] but also when evaluating outcomes related to e-service interactions [e.g. satisfaction with the service, 42] or the emotional connection with the company [2].

In the online environment, social presence is one of the most influential predictors of trust [32], which represents a crucial construct in online interactions because it influences a customer's willingness to accept the information provided and to follow suggestions [16]. Trust is often based on familiarity [24], hence, in order to reduce the social uncertainty in a new environment like that of conversational commerce, people may naturally seek peripheral cues that enhance their sense of familiarity. A higher perception of social presence in the interaction should help the user to experience more familiar elements compared to when the social presence perceived is low. In keeping with this, we believe that priming users with the notion of acting with artificial intelligence should increase eeriness and resistance due to pre-existing negative perceptions toward the artificial agent [20], thus enhancing the perceived ambiguity and decreasing the familiarity regarding the expected behaviours of the medium and the online retailer. The more are the uncertainty and ambiguity related to the conversational vendor system, the more trust should be hindered, while the opposite should occur when the chatbot identity is not explicitly disclosed.

Previous research offered consistent and strong support for the effect of trust on the overall consumers' responses in terms of attitudinal experience with a system [40]. The attitude represents a valuable construct to be assessed in new forms of transactions (i.e. conversational commerce) as it explains a significant amount of variation in consumers' patronage intention (i.e., the likelihood to use and recommend the service) [45]. Past studies relying on the Theory of Reasoned Action (TRA) [9] and Theory of Planned Behavior (TPB) [1] agree in defining trust as salient beliefs capable of influencing consumer attitudes [23]. This effect was confirmed in many studies investigating different technologies or business elements. In a study on Internet banking users, Suh and Han [38] found that trust positively affects customers' attitudes toward using e-commerce for trade transactions. Macintosh and Lockshin [26] showed that customers' trust in a store is positively related to their attitude toward the store, concluding that attitude is also a major component of loyalty. So, based on the evidence from past studies, we expect social presence to positively predict trust and, in turn, attitude to be positively influenced by trust. In few words we expect social presence and trust to serially mediate the relation between the chatbot identity disclosure and the attitude toward the online retailer.

H4. *Social presence and trust serially mediate the relation between the disclosure of the chatbot identity and attitude toward the online retailer.*

3 Research Method

3.1 Design, Experimental Procedure, and Measures

A single factor experimental design was adopted for the study. Participants were randomly assigned either to the group interacting with the chatbot whose identity was introduced by the disclosure *"you are going to try a conversational service provided by an artificial agent"* and explicitly reinforced with the bot itself (*"I am a chatbot"*) or the group interacting with the chatbot whose artificial identity was not primed neither by the disclosure nor by the chatbot itself. The interaction in this case directly starts with the phrase *"Hi [Name], welcome! I am here to guide you through your purchase"*. Aside from the first block of text where the chatbot presents itself as such (in the disclosure condition), the rest of the conversations (or rather the scripts) are exactly the same for both conditions. The interaction with the chatbot was designed to guide users through a set of products from which they had to choose. An example of chatbot interaction is displayed in Fig. 1.

Translation: Hi Roby, welcome! I'm a chatbot and I am here to guide you through your purchase. Swipe left to view all the products and choose the one that better suits you!

Fig. 1. Example of human-chatbot interaction (identity disclosure condition)

An a priori analysis was conducted for sample size estimation (using GPower 3.1). With an alpha = .05 and power = .80, the projected minimum sample size needed to detect a medium effect size of 0.5 is n = 128 for a between-groups comparison (T-test: difference between two independent means).

We recruited participants through a snowball sampling by sharing the link on Facebook and inviting users to do the same with their contacts. The recruitment text briefly informed participants about the data collection and how it would be conducted, in addition to listing requirements for participation. The participants had to be at least 18 years and possess a Facebook account to interact with the chatbot. Participants' task was to look for food products and virtually buying the desired ones. Participation in the study was voluntary. According to the ethical standards of the 1964 Declaration of Helsinki, participants were informed about all relevant aspects of the study, e.g., institutional affiliations of the researcher, data protection and privacy (GDPR) before they became involved in the experiment. They were apprised of their right to refuse to participate in the study or to withdraw their consent to participate at any time during the study without fear of reprisal.

A total of 160 participants of Italian nationality took part in the study. Participants ranged from 18 to 45 years in age (M = 22.1, SD = 3.38), 59.4% of participants were women.

The questionnaire consisted of a first part designed to acquire demographic insights on the use of messaging apps and online purchases experience and a second part consisting of statements regarding the constructs.

As expected, respondents reported a daily use of messaging apps, as only 3.1% indicated to have no or very little use of messaging apps. The survey recorded the online purchasing behaviour of the respondents. Only 1.9% of them indicated they have never made online purchases. More specifically 88.1% declared to make online purchases between one and four times per month. At the end of the questionnaire, participants were asked if they had ever interacted with a chatbot to interact with companies and to make purchases. Overall, 89.4% have experienced interactions with chatbots, while only 24.4% of participants declared to have experienced an AI conversational chat-based retailer.

Previous research was reviewed to ensure that a comprehensive list of measures was included. The responses were recorded on a seven-point Likert scale (1 = "*strongly disagree*"; 7 = "*strongly agree*").

The measures for social presence was taken from Gefen and Straub [13] (five items, $M = 3.86$; $SD = 1.53$; Cronbach's alpha = .93), trust was assessed accordingly to Pengnate and Sarathy's [34] (four items, $M = 5.00$; $SD = 1.24$; Cronbach's alpha = .89), attitude toward the online retailer (four items, $M = 4.82$; $SD = 1.42$; Cronbach's alpha = .87) was measured accordingly to Moon and Kim [29]. The items are displayed in Table 1.

Table 1. Constructs' items and correlations

Constructs	1	2	3
1 Social presence			
There is a sense of human contact in the online retailer			
There is a sense of personalness in the online retailer			
There is a sense of sociability in the online retailer			
There is a sense of human warmth in the online retailer			
There is a sense of human sensitivity in the online retailer			
2 Trust	.50***		
I believe that the online retailer keeps its promises and commitments			
I trust the online retailer keeps customers' best interests in mind			
The online retailer is trustworthy			
The online retailer will not do anything to take advantage of its customers			
3 Attitude	.54***	.68***	
The online retailer is good			
The online retailer is wise			
The online retailer is pleasant			
The online retailer is positive			

Note: *** p < .001

4   Results

First of all, we run a bivariate Pearson correlation analysis to examine the relationship between the key variables (Table 1). As expected, results show that social presence was positively associated with trust (b = .50 $p < .001$) and attitude toward the online retailer (b = .54 $p < .001$). Trust was also positively related to attitude toward the online retailer (b = .68 $p < .001$). To test for H1, H2, and H3 we relied on a normal-model based ANOVA. Specifically, we performed three ANCOVAs controlling for age, gender, past experience with chatbot and awareness of the artificial nature of the system (these two questions were asked at the very end of the questionnaire as not to interfere with the overall responses) adjusting the p-values for Bonferroni significance tests for pairwise comparisons. In line with H1, the analysis revealed a significant main effect of chatbot identity disclosure on social presence ($F(1, 156) = 7.836, p < .01$, partial $\eta2 = .05$), indicating that participants reported lower social presence in the disclosed chatbot identity condition than in the undisclosed chatbot identity condition. In line with H2, the analysis showed a significant effect of chatbot identity disclosure on trust ($F(1, 156) = 5.720, p < .05$, partial $\eta2 = .04$), indicating that participants reported lower trust in the disclosed chatbot identity condition than in the undisclosed chatbot identity condition. Finally, in line with H3, the analysis revealed a significant main effect of chatbot identity disclosure on attitude toward the online retailer ($F(1,156) = 23.181, p < .001$, partial $\eta2 = .13$), indicating that participants reported lower attitude toward the online retailer in the disclosed chatbot identity condition than in the undisclosed chatbot identity condition. Means and Standard Deviations for the disclosure conditions are reported in Table 2.

Table 2. Means and Standard Deviations for the chatbot disclosure conditions

Construct	Chatbot identity disclosed	Chatbot identity undisclosed	p-value
Social presence	3.57 (1.46)	4.18 (1.59)	$p < .01$
Trust	4.82 (1.31)	5.26 (1.16)	$p < .05$
Attitude twd the online retailer	4.35 (1.29)	5.34 (1.39)	$p < .001$

4.1   Mediation Analysis

We expected that social presence and trust would mediate the relationship between chatbot identity disclosure and attitude toward the online retailer (H4). To examine this hypothesis, we relied on PROCESS, the SPSS macro developed by Hayes and Preacher [17], a method that employs observed variable OLS regression path analysis and allows for the estimation of direct and indirect effects of multiple mediators. We used model 6 with 5000 bootstrapping resamples to compute 95% confidence intervals, knowing that confidence intervals that do not contain zero denote statistically significant indirect effects. We examined the mediation model with chatbot identity disclosure (-1 = disclosed; 1 undisclosed) as predictor. The overall equation was significant ($R^2 = .55$, F(3, 156) = 63.49, $p < .001$), confirming that social presence and trust are serial mediators between chatbot identity disclosure and attitude toward the online retailer. In line with H4, the results show the hypothesized causal chain is significant (b = .07, confidence interval [95% CI] = [.0135, .1459]). As displayed in Fig. 2, when the chatbot identity is undisclosed, social presence increases ($\beta = .30$, p < .05) and has a positive influence on trust ($\beta = .49$, $p < .001$), which in turn, positively predicts attitude toward using the online retailer ($\beta = .57$, $p < .001$). We found that the remaining direct effect of chatbot identity disclosure on attitude toward the online retailer was still significant ($\beta = .23$, $p < .001$) thus, suggesting a partially mediated effect. Table 3 reports direct and indirect effects of chatbot identity disclosure.

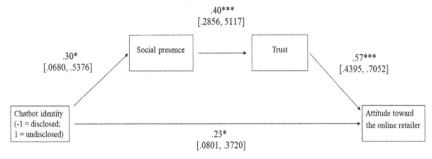

*p < .05, **p < .01. ***p < .001

Fig. 2. Mediation model with values indicating unstandardized path coefficients.

Table 3. Other direct and indirect effects

Chatbot Identity (CI): disclosed vs. undisclosed
N = 160

	b (SE)	Lower 95% BCBCI	Upper 95% BCBCI
Direct effects	.40 (.06)	.2856	.5117
SP → Trust	.26 (.06)	.1442	.3753
SP → Attitude	.54 (.07)	.4006	.6823
Trust → Attitude	−12 (.05)	−2350	−0265
Indirect effects	−08 (.04)	−1555	−0156
CI → SP → Trust	−06 ns (.05)	−1540	.0375
CI → SP → Attitude	.23 (.05)	.1398	.3491
CI → Trust → Attitude	.06 (.03)	.1395	.0119
SP → Trust → Attitude			
CI → SP → Trust → Attitude			

Note. Unstandardized b coefficients (with *boot SE* between parentheses). BCBCI = bias corrected 5,000 bootstrap confidence intervals.
ns = not significant.

5 Discussions, Implications and Future Studies

Many customers in the world retain that chatbots can offer great value for their quickness, personalization, and entertainment, but despite this, still few academic studies confirmed the possibility of using chatbots as a means of securing new customers and launching new services such as conversational commerce [18].

Although few studies show important insights on users' behavior and experiences with chatbots, little is known about how online retailers leveraged by artificial agents are perceived and what variables determine chatbots' effectiveness [45]. In this perspective, the present study enriches literature in HCI and more specifically in human-chatbot interaction for business purposes. The main caveat of the study concerns the disclosure of artificial agents' identity, a timely and managerially relevant topic since regulators are increasingly concerned about customer privacy protection and transparency and that the Federal Trade Commission (FTC) itself has already started encouraging companies to be transparent on chatbot applications during customer communications [11]. This study aimed to provide useful implications on the effects of such transparency on chatbots applied for conversational commerce to give a substantial contribution to the literature investigating chatbots for business purposes. This objective has been pursued through an experimental study testing the effects that the disclosure of the chatbot identity has on social presence, trust, and attitude toward the online retailer. In so doing, this study provides a basis for understanding the implications that priming users with an explicit disclosure of the chatbot identity has for the business.

This study extends early research on HCI and more specifically on the effect of priming participants with a disclosure indicating the artificial nature of the system. The first key result of the study suggests that, in line with Araujo [2], priming consumers with a specific frame introducing the conversational online retailer has a significant impact on users' perceptions. Keeping with Luo et al. [25], where disclosing the chatbot identity at the beginning of the call causes worse results when it comes to perceiving the system as being sociable and warm, our results show that priming participants with the notion of interacting with a company's artificial agent reduces their perceptions of social presence, trust and overall attitude toward using the online retailer. The most reasonable explanation for these findings is probably due to the prejudice people have developed toward chatbots in terms of expectations, lack of personal feeling, and empathy [25], which is recalled after priming users of the artificial nature of the system.

In line with earlier research on artificial agents [6, 31], this study confirms the preference for a non-artificial interface, further translating this preference in terms of social presence, trust, and attitude. The study also addresses the role of social presence and trust as serial mediators in the relation between the chatbot identity disclosure and the attitude toward the online retailer. The mediation hypothesis was supported, thus confirming the centrality of social presence and trust, for assessing the users' overall feelings toward the online retailer. The causal chain underlines that when users interact with a chatbot whose identity is explicitly disclosed (compared to when it is not disclosed), they perceive a lower degree of social presence, which induces less trust and less positive attitude toward the online retailer.

In light of the results of this study, we expect that practitioners should be aware of the consequences of disclosing artificial agents' identity and start focusing on how to best disclose chatbots.

Due to the increasing ability of chatbots to be humanized to such an extent that customers may not realize the machine identity in the conversation, major concerns about customer privacy protection and business ethics are rising. In view of this, it cannot be excluded that in near-future new government policy regarding the machine identity disclosure in chat conversations may become the norm. In this perspective, our results represent interesting insights that highlight the necessity to find ways to mitigate the negative effect of chatbot identity disclosure. With this in mind, practitioners will need to identify new cues that could positively affect social outcomes [5]. In the same way, we believe just as important that the chatbot identity disclosure was not to represent a limit but rather to act as a lever. As an example, a clear communication aligned to the user in terms of conversational cues (e.g. tone of voice) could help in strengthening the users' experience and limit skepticism and mistrust. Similarly, a clear communication on the actual capability on what the chatbot can do or cannot do for the user could help meeting the consumers' expectations and increase the level of social presence and trust in the interaction.

The present research may undergo possible improvements that call for future studies. The majority of participants (93.8%), regardless of the condition they were exposed to (disclosure vs not disclosure), declared to be aware of the artificial nature of the online retailer. Such insight is very important because it highlights that the simple priming effect derived by the explicit disclosure of the artificial agent's identity can activate different and not always positive associations among various consumers [43]. In this perspective, future works may consider proving how different text disclosures - for example in terms of communication style or timing (before, during, and after the interaction) -, impact consumers' attitudes. Future research may look for effects within different framings in the introduction of the chatbot. For instance, in order to limit users' mistrust, future studies might consider chatbots that introduce themselves by briefly illustrating the technological benefits they offer, such as reducing customer costs in terms of less time to waste waiting for the answers. Moreover, new relevant constructs could be examined in a more detailed model using real company data, or rather it would be interesting for future research to extend similar data collections to markets where the levels of digital technology uptake are different.

References

1. Ajzen, I.: The theory of planned behavior. Organ. Behav. Hum. Decis. Processes **50**(2), 179–211 (1991)
2. Araujo, T.: Living up to the chatbot hype: the influence of anthropomorphic design cues and communicative agency framing on conversational agent and company perceptions. Comput. Hum. Behav. **85**, 183–189 (2018)
3. Biocca, F., Harms, C., Burgoon, J.K.: Toward a more robust theory and measure of social presence: review and suggested criteria. Presence Teleoperators Virtual Environ. **12**(5), 456–480 (2003)

4. Calantone, R.J., Di Benedetto, A., Rubera, G.: Launch activities and timing in new product development. J. Glob. Scholars Mark. Sci. **28**(1), 33–41 (2018)
5. Chattaraman, V., Kwon, W.S., Gilbert, J.E., Ross, K.: Should AI-based, conversational digital assistants employ social-or task-oriented interaction style? a task-competency and reciprocity perspective for older adults. Comput. Hum. Behav. **90**, 315–330 (2019)
6. Corti, K., Gillespie, A.: Co-constructing intersubjectivity with artificial conversational agents: people are more likely to initiate repairs of misunderstandings with agents represented as human. Comput. Hum. Behav. **58**, 431–442 (2016)
7. Deloitte: Chatbots Point of View. Retail. Retrieved October 2, 2019, from https://www2.del oitte.com/content/dam/Deloitte/nl/Documents/deloitte-analytics/deloitte-nl-chatbots-mov ing-beyond-the-hype.pdf (2018)
8. Etemad-Sajadi, R., Ghachem, L.: The impact of hedonic and utilitarian value of online avatars on e-service quality. Comput. Hum. Behav. **52**, 81–86 (2015)
9. Fishbein, M., Ajzen, I.: Belief, Attitude, Intention and Behavior: An Introduction to Theory and Research. Addison-Wesley, Reading, MA (1975)
10. Forbes: AI Stats News: 86% Of Consumers Prefer Humans To Chatbots. Retrieved November 20, 2019, from https://www.forbes.com/sites/gilpress/2019/10/02/ai-stats-news-86-of-con sumers-prefer-to-interact-with-a-human-agent-rather-than-a-chatbot/#15216c922d3b (2019)
11. FTC: Privacy & Data Security Update (2016) | Federal Trade Commission. Retrieved November 15, 2019, from https://www.ftc.gov/reports/privacydata-security-update-2016 (2017)
12. Gartner: Gartner Says 25 Percent of Customer Service Operations Will Use Virtual Customer Assistants by 2020. Retrieved December 17, 2019, from https://www.gartner.com/en/new sroom/press-releases/2018-02-19-gartner-says-25-percent-of-customer-service-operations-will-use-virtual-customer-assistants-by-2020 (2018)
13. Gefen, D., Straub, D.: Managing user trust in B2C e-services. e-Service **2**(2), 7–24 (2003)
14. Gnewuch, U., Morana, S., Maedche, A.: Towards designing cooperative and social conversational agents for customer service. In: ICIS (2017)
15. Granulo, A., Fuchs, C., Puntoni, S.: Psychological reactions to human versus robotic job replacement. Nat. Hum. Behav. (2019). https://doi.org/10.1038/s41562-019-0670-y
16. Hancock, P.A., Billings, D.R., Schaefer, K.E., Chen, J.Y., De Visser, E.J., Parasuraman, R.: A meta-analysis of factors affecting trust in human-robot interaction. Hum. Factors **53**(5), 517–527 (2011)
17. Hayes, A.F., Preacher, K.J.: Statistical mediation analysis with a multicategorical independent variable. Br. J. Math. Stat. Psychol. **67**(3), 451–470 (2014)
18. Heo, M., Lee, K.J.: Chatbot as a new business communication tool: the case of naver talktalk. Bus. Commun. Res. Pract. **1**(1), 41–45 (2018)
19. Hill, J., Ford, W.R., Farreras, I.G.: Real conversations with artificial intelligence: a comparison between human–human online conversations and human–chatbot conversations. Comput. Hum. Behav. **49**, 245–250 (2015)
20. Kim, Y., Sundar, S.S.: Anthropomorphism of computers: is it mindful or mindless? Comput. Hum. Behav. **28**(1), 241–250 (2012)
21. Kini, A., Choobineh, J.: Trust in electronic commerce: definition and theoretical considerations. In: Proceedings of the thirty-first Hawaii International conference on System sciences, vol. 4, pp. 51–61. IEEE (1998)
22. Knijnenburg, B.P., Willemsen, M.C.: Inferring capabilities of intelligent agents from their external traits. ACM Trans. Interact. Intell. Syst. (TiiS) **6**(4), 1–25 (2016)
23. Lien, C.H., Cao, Y.: Examining WeChat users' motivations, trust, attitudes, and positive word-of-mouth: evidence from China. Comput. Hum. Behav. **41**, 104–111 (2014)
24. Luhmann, N.: Familiarity, confidence, trust: problems and alternatives. Trust Making Breaking Coop. Relat. **6**(1), 94–107 (2000)

25. Luo, X., Tong, S., Fang, Z., Qu, Z.: Frontiers: machines vs. humans: the impact of artificial intelligence chatbot disclosure on customer purchases. Mark. Sci. **38**(6), 937–947 (2019)
26. Macintosh, G., Lockshin, L.S.: Retail relationships and store loyalty: a multi-level perspective. Int. J. Res. Mark. **14**(5), 487–497 (1997)
27. Mastercard: Conversational commerce: A new opportunity for card payments. Retrieved November 6, 2019, from https://newsroom.mastercard.com/documents/conversational-commerce-a-new-opportunity-for-card-payments/ (2018)
28. Mone, G.: The edge of the uncanny. Commu. ACM **59**(9), 17–19 (2016)
29. Moon, J.W., Kim, Y.G.: Extending the TAM for a World-Wide-Web context. Inf. Manage. **38**(4), 217–230 (2001)
30. Mou, J., Shin, D.H., Cohen, J.F.: Trust and risk in consumer acceptance of e-services. Electron. Commer. Res. **17**(2), 255–288 (2017)
31. Murgia, A., Janssens, D., Demeyer, S., Vasilescu, B.: Among the machines: human-bot interaction on social q&a websites. In: Proceedings of the 2016 CHI Conference Extended Abstracts on Human Factors in Computing Systems, pp. 1272–1279 (2016)
32. Ogonowski, A., Montandon, A., Botha, E., Reyneke, M.: Should new online stores invest in social presence elements? The effect of social presence on initial trust formation. J. Retail. Consum. Serv. **21**(4), 482–491 (2014)
33. Paschen, J., Kietzmann, J., Kietzmann, T. C.: Artificial intelligence (AI) and its implications for market knowledge in B2B marketing. J. Bus. Ind. Mark. (2019)
34. Pengnate, S.F., Sarathy, R.: An experimental investigation of the influence of website emotional design features on trust in unfamiliar online vendors. Comput. Hum. Behav. **67**, 49–60 (2017)
35. Short, J., Williams, E., Christie, B.: The Social Psychology of Telecommunications. John Wiley & Sons, London (1976)
36. Schmidt, P., Biessmann, F., Teubner, T.: Transparency and trust in artificial intelligence systems. Journal of Decision Systems **29**(4), 1–19 (2020)
37. Skjuve, M., Haugstveit, I.M., Følstad, A., Brandtzaeg, P.B.: Help! is my chatbot falling into the uncanny valley? an empirical study of user experience in human-chatbot interaction. Hum. Technol. **15**(1) (2019)
38. Suh, B., Han, I.: The impact of customer trust and perception of security control on the acceptance of electronic commerce. Int. J. Electron. Commer. **7**(3), 135–161 (2003)
39. Sundar, S.S., Bellur, S., Oh, J., Jia, H., Kim, H.S.: Theoretical importance of contingency in human-computer interaction: effects of message interactivity on user engagement. Commun. Res. **43**(5), 595–625 (2016)
40. Toader, D.C., et al.: The effect of social presence and chatbot errors on trust. Sustainability **12**(1), 256 (2020)
41. Tuzovic, S., Paluch, S.: Conversational commerce – a new era for service business development? In: Bruhn, M., Hadwich, K. (eds.) Service Business Development, pp. 81–100. Springer, Wiesbaden (2018). https://doi.org/10.1007/978-3-658-22426-4_4
42. Verhagen, T., Van Nes, J., Feldberg, F., Van Dolen, W.: Virtual customer service agents: using social presence and personalization to shape online service encounters. J. Comput.-Mediated Commun. **19**(3), 529–545 (2014)
43. Wheeler, S.C., Berger, J.: When the same prime leads to different effects. J. Consum. Res. **34**(3), 357–368 (2007)
44. Xu, K., Lombard, M.: Persuasive computing: feeling peer pressure from multiple computer agents. Comput. Hum. Behav. **74**, 152–162 (2017)
45. Zarouali, B., Van den Broeck, E., Walrave, M., Poels, K.: Predicting consumer responses to a chatbot on Facebook. Cyberpsychol. Behav. Soc. Networking **21**(8), 491–497 (2018)

Too Informal? How a Chatbot's Communication Style Affects Brand Attitude and Quality of Interaction

Christine Liebrecht[1]([✉]), Lena Sander[1], and Charlotte van Hooijdonk[2]

[1] Tilburg University, PO Box 90153, 5000 LE Tilburg, The Netherlands
`C.C.Liebrecht@tilburguniversity.edu`
[2] Utrecht University, Trans 10, 3512 JK Utrecht, The Netherlands
`C.M.J.vanHooijdonk@uu.nl`

Abstract. This study investigated the effects of (in)formal chatbot responses and brand familiarity on social presence, appropriateness, brand attitude, and quality of interaction. An online experiment using a 2 (Communication Style: Informal vs. Formal) by 2 (Brand: Familiar vs. Unfamiliar) between subject design was conducted in which participants performed customer service tasks with the assistance of chatbots developed for the study. Subsequently, they filled out an online questionnaire. An indirect effect of communication style on brand attitude and quality of interaction through social presence was found. Thus, a chatbot's informal communication style induced a higher perceived social presence which in turn positively influenced quality of the interaction and brand attitude. However, brand familiarity did not enhance perceptions of appropriateness, indicating participants do not assign different roles to chatbots as communication partner.

Keywords: Chatbots · Communication style · Social presence · Conversational human voice · Brand familiarity

1 Introduction

Conversational agents are artificial intelligent computer programs using natural language to engage in a dialogue with users (Følstad and Skjuve 2019; Laban and Araujo 2020). These agents are increasingly being deployed by organizations in customer service settings (Følstad and Skjuve 2019; Shawar and Atwell 2007) and are designed to perform simple tasks, such as sending airline tickets, as well as more complex tasks, such as providing shopping advice (Araujo 2018; Shawar and Atwell 2007). According to the Gartner Technologies in Service Bullseye 68 per cent of the service leaders expect conversational agents will become more important in the next years (Bryan 2019). The Gartner Hype Cycle predicts that by 2021, 15 per cent of all customer service interactions will be completely handled by AI.

However, organizations experience skepticism in adopting chatbot technology in customer service (Elsner 2018; Araujo 2018). Customers tend to perceive their conversations with chatbots as unnatural and impersonal (Drift, SurveyMonkey Audience,

A. Følstad et al. (Eds.): CONVERSATIONS 2020, LNCS 12604, pp. 16–31, 2021.
https://doi.org/10.1007/978-3-030-68288-0_2

Salesforce and Myclever 2018). A quarter of the chatbot users even indicate to refrain from using a chatbot because it was not able to chat in a friendly manner, and 43 per cent still prefer to communicate with a human assistant (Drift et al. 2018).

This skepticism highlights a challenge in designing chatbots for customer service purposes. For organizations and designers it is important to understand how a communication style influence users' perceptions about the conversational agent and their perceptions about the organizations using these agents. The current study investigates the effects of conversational agents using an (in)formal communication style on social presence, quality of interaction, and brand attitude. In line with Gretry et al. (2017), we also investigated the moderating effect of users' brand familiarity on the relation between an (in)formal communication style and perceived appropriateness. Gretry et al. (2017) found that an informal communication style in human customer service messages was perceived appropriate for familiar brands but inappropriate for unfamiliar ones. Our study extends the role of brand familiarity and examines whether this social norm in human-to-human communication also applies for human-to-chatbot communication. In summary, we propose the following research question:

RQ: To what extent does an (in)formal communication style in chatbot's customer service messages and participants' brand familiarity influence perceptions of social presence, appropriateness, quality of interaction, and brand attitude?

2 Theoretical Background

2.1 Customer Service Chatbots

Customer service plays an important role in providing information and assistance to customers, strengthening their engagement with an organization, and generating revenue (Følstad and Skjuve 2019). Organizations are increasingly deploying chatbots for customer service purposes because they can provide 24/7 service and save time and money by reducing the number of service employees (Gnewuch et al. 2017). For example, there are already more than 300,000 customer service chatbots available on Facebook messenger (Jovic 2020). These chatbots are designed to execute simple tasks, such as sending airline tickets, or more complex tasks, such as giving shopping advice (Araujo 2018; Shawar and Atwell 2007).

Research on users' motivations for engaging with chatbots showed that they mainly used customer service chatbots for efficiency reasons, i.e., quickly receiving information instead of searching for information themselves or waiting in line (Brandtzaeg and Føstad 2017; Følstad and Skjuve 2019). Another aspect which is highlighted in the literature is the adoption of humanlike qualities in customer service chatbots (Araujo 2018; Go and Sundar 2019; Liebrecht and van der Weegen 2019; Verhagen et al. 2014). Especially in service encounters consumers value personal interaction and a 'human touch' (Paluch 2012; Laban and Araujo 2019) which might be achieved by adopting a humanlike communication style (Liebrecht and van Hooijdonk 2020). However, customers tend to perceive their conversations with chatbots as unnatural and impersonal (Drift et al. 2018).

2.2 Social Reactions to Communication Technology

The Computers Are Social Actors paradigm (CASA; Nass et al. 1994) states users are likely to respond to computers in a social manner similar to their behavior towards humans. Even adults and experienced computer users seem to apply social norms and rules mindlessly to the interactions with computers (Nass et al. 1994; Nass and Moon 2000) which are triggered through social cues (Nass and Moon 2000).

A concept that is closely related to this perception in human-to-computer interaction lies in the field of human-to-human interaction and is coined as social presence. Short et al. (1976) defined social presence as the "degree of salience of the other person in the interaction" (p. 65). Lombard and Ditton (1997) distinguished two types of social presence: presence as social within medium and medium-as-social-actor presence. The former refers to people responding to the social cues presented by the characters within the medium (Lombard and Ditton 1997). This type of social presence originates from parasocial interaction (Horton and Wohl 1956). The latter refers to peoples' responses to the medium itself. When a medium itself presents social cues, people are likely to perceive it as a real person instead as an object. Applying the notion of medium-as-social-actor presence to chatbot communication implies that a chatbot with social cues stimulates users to perceive the chatbot as a social entity to which they react similar to as in human-to-human interaction (Lombard and Ditton 1997).

Two of the possible social cues chatbots could present are language output and the ability to respond to prior outputs of users (i.e., interactivity; Nass and Moon 2000). As chatbots typically have both cues, it may be expected that users respond to them socially. Indeed, previous research applying the CASA paradigm to chatbots (Araujo 2018; Go and Sundar 2019) found social presence, or perception of humanness, of the chatbot positively affects users' perceptions. In this study, we focus on one specific social cue, i.e., the communication style.

2.3 Communication Style

As chatbots often communicate rather machinelike, some researchers have already addressed the challenge of making chatbots appear more humanlike in a customer service context. They used visual and/or linguistic cues to enhance social presence which in turn affect several attitudinal and behavioral outcomes (Araujo 2018; Go and Sundar 2019; Liebrecht and van der Weegen 2019).

Go and Sundar (2019) created two versions of a chatbot that, amongst other variables, differed in visual cues: the humanlike chatbot contained a human avatar whereas the machinelike chatbot contained a dialog bubble figure. In both cases, the agent was introduced with the name Alex. The scholars found no direct effects on social presence nor an indirect effect on attitudinal and behavioral outcomes between the humanlike and machinelike avatar. Araujo (2018), on the other hand, only used linguistic elements to differentiate between the humanlike and machinelike chatbot. Participants interacted with either a humanlike chatbot named Emma that used informal language, or a machinelike chatbot named ChatBotX that used formal language, although it remains unclear how the difference in language use was operationalized. Also, in the humanlike condition participants started the conversation with 'hello' and closed with 'goodbye' while participants in the machinelike condition used 'start' and 'quit'. Results showed participants' emotional connection with the organization was higher after interacting with a humanlike chatbot. This effect was mediated by social presence. However, no direct effects were found between the two chatbot versions on social presence, attitude, and satisfaction with the company which could be explained by the operationalizations of the concepts (Araujo 2018).

Also, Liebrecht and van der Weegen (2019) used linguistic elements to differentiate between the humanlike and machinelike chatbot. The messages of the humanlike chatbot contained many elements of the Conversational Human Voice (i.e., CHV; Kelleher 2009; Kelleher and Miller 2006) including message personalization (e.g., personal greeting of the customer: 'Hello David'), informal language (e.g., mimicking sound and using emoticons: 'woohoo ☺'), and invitational rhetoric (e.g., showing sympathy and empathy: 'nice, have fun!') (van Noort et al. 2014). The humanlike chatbot also contained a personal name ('Booky') and avatar. The messages of the machinelike chatbot did not contain elements of CHV, had an impersonal name ('Bookbot') and the brand's logo was the avatar. Also, different scales than Araujo (2018) were used to measure social presence and brand attitude. Confirming their expectations, Liebrecht and van der Weegen (2019) showed participants' brand attitude was higher after interacting with a humanlike chatbot, which was mediated by perceived social presence.

Since Liebrecht and van der Weegen (2019) used 16 linguistic elements to operationalize the humanlike chatbot, it is unclear which linguistic element(s) caused the effects. Therefore, this study focuses solely on the (in)formality of the communication style in order to replicate their findings. According to Gretry et al. (2017) an informal communication style is easier to operationalize objectively than the concept of CHV. Citing McArthur (1992) they define an informal communication style as "common, non-official, familiar, casual, and often colloquial, and contrasts in these senses with formal" (p. 77). Since the humanlike chatbot of Liebrecht and van der Weegen (2019) also contained some elements of informal language, we expect a chatbot only adopting an informal communication style will enhance social presence which in turn positively affects brand attitude, compared to a chatbot using a formal communication style. This is reflected in Hypothesis 1a.

While investigating the effects on brand attitude gives insights into the consequences for brands, it does not give insights into perceptions of the conversation itself. For chatbot development, however, it is valuable to investigate whether the communication style matches the user's needs. Derived from Jakic et al. (2017) who investigated informal language in human customer service messages, we will also measure the impact of communication style on quality of interaction. Similar to brand attitude, we expect a chatbot with an informal communication style will enhance quality of interaction, mediated by social presence (Hypothesis 1b).

H1: Social presence will mediate the relation between chatbots adopting an informal communication style and users' positive evaluations of a) brand attitude, and b) quality of interaction.

2.4 Appropriateness and Brand Familiarity

Besides the positive effects, an informal communication style can also backfire, for example when perceived as inappropriate. This has been shown in Gretry et al.'s (2017) study. They illustrated that not only the communication style can be essential for the perceived appropriateness of the customer service message, but also the sender of the message, i.e., the brand (Gretry et al. 2017). The argumentation of Gretry et al. (2017) is grounded in Role Theory (Sarbin and Allen 1968). Based on this theory, evaluation and success of interactions depend on the appropriateness of the behavior of the interaction partner in regard to their social roles. If interaction partners are strangers, a formal communication style is considered appropriate compared to interacting with an acquaintance or friend. This theory explains the results found by Gretry et al. (2017): participants perceived an informal communication style as appropriate when they were familiar with the brand, but as inappropriate when they were unfamiliar with the brand.

Liebrecht and van der Weegen (2019) included brand familiarity as a factor in their chatbot study, but did not find a moderation effect on brand attitude. Although the scholars operationalized brand familiarity in a similar way as Gretry et al. (2017), they focused on the effects of message personalization, informal language, and invitational rhetoric together instead of solely focusing on the effects of the (in)formal communication style like Gretry et al. (2017). If people respond similar to a chatbot as to a human being, as stated by the CASA paradigm (Nass et al. 1994), and thus feel their interpersonal distance is violated if the (in)formality does not correspond to the social role in the conversation, as is suggested in literature on politeness (Stephan et al. 2010), one could assume that a closer replication of Gretry et al.'s (2017) study will result in similar outcomes. That is, we expect a chatbot's informal communication style can have a negative effect on brand attitude if people are unfamiliar with the brand, whereas it can positively impact brand attitude if people are familiar with the brand. This moderation effect will be mediated by perceived appropriateness. This expectation is reflected in Hypothesis 2a.

A similar effect will be expected with regard to quality of interaction, because Jakic et al. (2017) showed customers have expectations about the communication style of the brand. If customers' expectations about the language style align with the actual style used, quality of interaction will be perceived higher (Jakic et al. 2017). The same could be true for chatbot users and their familiarity with the brand. Our hypothesis 2b is therefore that brand familiarity will moderate the effect of communication style on quality of interaction, which will be mediated by perceived appropriateness.

H2: Brand familiarity will moderate the effect of communication style on a) brand attitude, and b) quality of interaction, which is mediated by perceived appropriateness.

3   Method[1]

3.1 Design

An online experiment following a 2 (Communication Style: Informal vs. Formal) × 2 (Brand: Familiar vs. Unfamiliar) between-subject design was conducted to test the effect

---

[1] Supplementary materials of the experiment, such as the survey and illustrative videos of the chatbots can be found here: https://doi.org/10.17605/OSF.IO/8TGNS.

of a chatbot's communication style on brand attitude and quality of interaction. Participants were randomly assigned to one of the four chatbot conditions in which they had three chatbot conversations about customer service topics. Afterwards, brand attitude, quality of interaction, perceived social presence, and appropriateness were measured.

3.2 Participants

Initially, 131 participants took part in the experiment. Nine participants were removed from the dataset because they did not consent, or did not succeed in any of the chatbot conversations. The final sample of 122 participants consisted of a quite balanced gender distribution (64.8% female participants) with a mean age of 26.48 ($SD = 7.93$) years (range 19–61 years). Most participants were highly educated with 66.4% participants holding a bachelor's degree or higher. The participants in the four conditions were comparable concerning gender (χ^2 (6) = 4.69, $p = .59$), age (Welch's F (3,59.90) = 2.16, $p = .10$), and education level (χ^2 (12) = 7.29, $p = .84$), see Table 1.

Table 1. Characteristics of participants per experimental condition.

Condition	N	Education			Gender		Age
		Sec. School/other	Bachelor degree	Master degree	Male	Female	M (SD)
Informal* Unfamiliar	29	10	12	7	10	19	24.34 (4.05)
Formal* Unfamiliar[a]	34	11	19	4	10	23	25.12 (4.02)
Informal* Familiar	33	11	16	6	10	23	28.94 (11.58)
Formal* Familiar	26	8	11	7	12	14	27.54 (8.74)
Total	122	32	58	23	42	79	26.48 (7.93)

[a]One participant in this condition did not prefer to indicate gender.

3.3 Chatbot Development

The chatbots were developed with Flow.ai, a platform with which conversation flows for chatbots for customer service or marketing contexts can be developed and implemented (https://flow.ai/, see also Liebrecht and van der Weegen 2019).

For each conversation, a conversation flow was created and trained on the most likely responses participants could give. Participants could send messages by typing their responses in the chatbot's text boxes (see Fig. 1). In order to avoid communication errors, the bots offered participants also reply buttons corresponding with the tasks that participants were asked to fulfil (see Fig. 2). To enhance the validity of the chatbot some filler buttons were added. Buttons are oftentimes used to direct users through the chatbot's tree structure (Pricilla et al. 2018).

Furthermore, the chatbots were able to lead participants back to a previous step of the conversation flow in case they deviated from the scenario instructions, for example by stating the chosen option was out of stock. After the development of these basic chatbots, the four conditions were created in which the communication style and brand differed. Illustrative videos of the chatbots can be found in the online appendix.

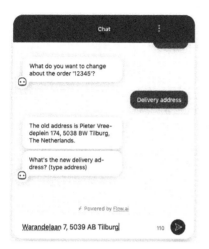
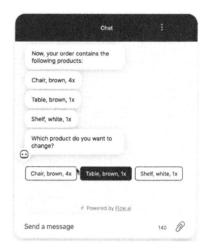

Fig. 1. Example of the chatbot asking users to type in the answer via the text box.

Fig. 2. Example of directing users through the conversation flow via reply buttons.

3.3.1 Communication Style

The operationalization of the informal versus formal communication style was based on a selection of different linguistic elements from Gretry et al. (2017), and the operationalizations of informal language in Liebrecht and van der Weegen (2019) and Jakic et al. (2017). In their literature review on the linguistic manipulations of CHV, Liebrecht, Tsaousi and van Hooijdonk (under review) divided informal language manipulations into non-verbal and verbal cues. Non-verbal linguistic cues are used to mimic non-verbal cues from face-to-face conversations, whereas verbal cues comprise the use of words in an informal way. Following their classification, the informal language manipulations used in the current study can be labeled into four non-verbal and four verbal cues (see Table 2). Figure 3 shows differences in communication style between the chatbot conditions. A manipulation check confirmed participants in the informal chatbot conditions rated the communication style as more informal than participants in the formal chatbot conditions (on a 7-point scale: $M = 5.48$, $SD = 1.04$, versus $M = 3.78$, $SD = 1.23$, $t(120) = 8.27$, $p = .001$).

Table 2. Manipulation of two different chatbot communication styles.

Linguistic element	Informal (example)	Formal (example)	Source
Non-verbal cues			
Emoticons	☺ ☹	-	Gretry et al. (2017); Liebrecht and van der Weegen (2019)
Capital letters	BYE, THANKS	-	Gretry et al. (2017); Liebrecht and van der Weegen (2019)
Sound mimicking	Aww, woohoo	-	Gretry et al. (2017); Liebrecht and van der Weegen (2019)
Informal punctuation	???, !!!	?, !	Gretry et al. (2017); Liebrecht and van der Weegen (2019)
Verbal cues			
Contractions and Shortenings	That's, ASAP	That is, as soon as possible	Gretry et al. (2017)
Active (versus passive) voice	Do you want to change something about your order?	Is there something to be changed about your order?	Gretry et al. (2017); Liebrecht and van der Weegen (2019)
Informal vocabulary	Great, awesome	-	Jakic et al. (2017); Gretry et al. (2017)
Present tense	Do	Would	Gretry et al. (2017)

3.3.2 Brand Familiarity

Brand familiarity was manipulated by using two different brands. Following the operationalizations of Gretry et al. (2017) and Liebrecht and van der Weegen (2019) an existing (familiar) and fictitious (unfamiliar) brand was used. Since the current study's context was furniture, we selected a well-known brand as familiar brand which was verified in a pretest. The fictitious brand was named Interiordreams.com.

Similar to Liebrecht and van der Weegen (2019), the brands were briefly presented prior to every chatbot conversation. To strengthen the presence of the brand manipulation, the companies were described as either a very successful and well-known seller of furniture or a recently founded online shop for furniture (Interiordreams.com). Furthermore, the brand logo and name were displayed in the scenario's and in the first and last message of the chatbot (i.e., 'Thank you for choosing [brand][2]') (see Fig. 3). A manipulation check revealed the manipulation of brand familiarity was successful. Participants

---

[2] Brand name for purpose of publication.

rated the well-known brand as a familiar brand compared to the fictitious brand (on a 7-point scale: $M = 5.89$, $SD = 1.26$ versus $M = 2.19$, $SD = 1.32$, $t(120) = 15.81$, $p = .001$).

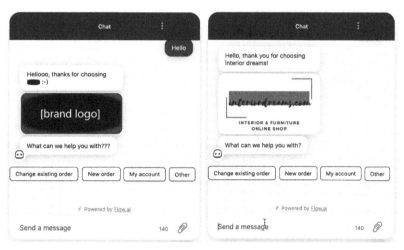

Fig. 3. Examples of brand manipulation when opening the chatbot conversation (informal*familiar (logo for publication) versus formal*unfamiliar).

3.4 Measures

All items were measured on 7-point Likert scales (1 = strongly disagree, 7 = strongly agree). Brand attitude was measured on an eight-item scale. Items were translated from the scale used by Liebrecht and van der Weegen (2019). Participants indicated whether they perceived [brand] as e.g., *likeable, uninterested (reversed item), and respectful*. The scale was found reliable (Cronbach's $\alpha = .84$, $M = 5.38$, $SD = 0.85$).

Quality of interaction was measured on a scale adapted from Jakic et al. (2017). The scale was adjusted, so participants evaluated the communication with brands based on three items, such as: *The interaction with [brand] is excellent*. The scale was found reliable (Cronbach's $\alpha = .93$, $M = 5.27$, $SD = 1.28$).

Social presence was measured, similar to Liebrecht and van der Weegen (2019), with five items. Participants were asked to indicate their feelings regading the conversation with the chatbot using items such as: *I felt a sense of human contact, human warmth, and sensitivity*. The scale was found reliable (Cronbach's $\alpha = .92$, $M = 3.87$, $SD = 1.39$).

Perceived appropriateness was assessed with a three-item scale, adapted from Gretry et al. (2017). An example of an item is: *The communication style of [brand] corresponds with how I expect to communicate with me*. The scale was found reliable (Cronbach's $\alpha = .90$, $M = 5.10$, $SD = 1.28$).

3.5 Procedure

After receiving approval through the Research Ethics and Data Management Committee of Tilburg University, data were collected between November 19th and December 2nd, 2019 through an online survey in Qualtrics. Participants were recruited through network sampling, i.e., mainly through social media posts and email requests of the researchers, and the survey exchange platform 'survey circle'. After giving informed consent, participants received a general introduction into the study and general instructions on the chatbot conversations.

Participants were asked to imagine themselves as customer of a furniture brand. Using three scenarios, participants interacted with one of the four chatbot conditions about customer service issues, such as ordering new furniture products, or changing details of an existing order. Participants accessed the chatbot through a link in the survey. After the three chatbot conversations, they filled in the survey that measured the dependent and mediating variables. Lastly, the participants were thanked and debriefed regarding the purpose of the study. It was disclosed that the chatbots were developed solely for the purpose of the experiment and the brands were not involved in the study. Participation took around 14 min, and participants did not receive any compensation.

4 Results

4.1 Communication Style and Social Presence

Two mediation analyses were conducted using Hayes' PROCESS model 4 (Hayes 2017) to test the effect of communication style on respectively brand attitude or quality of interaction, and the mediating effect of social presence.

The first mediation analysis revealed no significant total effect of communication style on brand attitude, $b = 0.13$, $SE = 0.15$, $p = .41$. This effect remained insignificant when adding social presence as a mediator in the model, $b = -0.08$, $SE = 0.15$, $p = .62$. However, a significant indirect effect of communication style on brand attitude through social presence was found, $b = 0.20$, $SE = 0.08$, 95% BCa CI [0.07, 0.37]. Overall, the model summary indicated that the mediation model was significant (see Fig. 4). Thus, an informal communication style leads to higher social presence which, in turn, results in higher brand attitude. This supports Hypothesis 1a.

The second mediation analysis investigating the effect of communication style and social presence revealed an insignificant total effect of communication style on quality of interaction, $b = -0.26$, $SE = 0.23$, $p = .26$. This effect became significant when adding the mediator of social presence in the model, $b = -0.48$, $SE = 0.23$, $p = .04$. Furthermore, the indirect effect of communication style on brand attitude through social presence was significant and positive, $b = 0.22$, $SE = 0.10$, 95% BCa CI [0.05, 0.46]. Overall, the model summary indicated the mediation model was significant (see Fig. 5). Again, informal communication resulted in higher social presence which, in turn, impacted quality of interaction. This supports Hypothesis 1b.

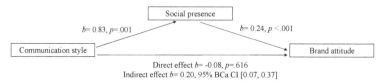

Fig. 4. Indirect effect of communication style (formal/informal) on brand attitude, mediated through social presence.

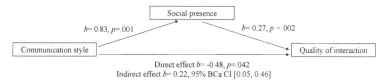

Fig. 5. Indirect effect of communication style (formal/informal) on quality of interaction, mediated through social presence.

4.2 Appropriateness of Communication Style and Brand Familiarity

To test Hypothesis 2, two moderated mediation analyses using Hayes' PROCESS model 7 (Hayes 2017) were conducted. In the first moderated mediation analysis appropriateness was the mediating variable between communication style and brand attitude and brand familiarity was the moderator. Figure 6 summarizes the model and its effects on brand attitude. The analysis revealed that communication style did not have a significant effect on appropriateness, $b = -1.02$, $SE = 0.73$, $p = .17$. Brand familiarity did not have a significant effect on appropriateness as well, $b = -0.70$, $SE = 0.74$, $p = .35$. Furthermore, there was no significant interaction effect of communication style and brand familiarity, $b = 0.47$, $SE = 0.47$, $p = .32$. There was also no significant direct effect of communication style on brand attitude when adding appropriateness as mediator and brand familiarity as moderator in the model, $b = 0.24$, $SE = 0.13$, $p = .08$. Furthermore, there was neither a significant indirect effect of communication style on brand attitude through appropriateness for the unfamiliar brand, $b = -0.19$, $SE = 0.12$, 95% BCa CI $[-0.45, 0.02]$ nor for the familiar brand, $b = -0.03$, $SE = 0.12$, 95% BCa CI $[-0.27, 0.20]$. However, a significant positive effect of appropriateness on brand attitude was found, $b = 0.33$, $SE = 0.05$, $p < .001$. Thus, Hypothesis 2a was rejected.

The moderated mediation analysis was repeated with quality of interaction as outcome variable (see Fig. 7). Again, there was no significant direct effect of communication style on quality of interaction when adding appropriateness as mediator and brand familiarity as moderator in the model, $b = -0.04$, $SE = 0.17$, $p = .83$. Furthermore, there was neither a significant indirect effect of communication style on brand attitude through appropriateness for the unfamiliar, $b = -0.37$, $SE = 0.24$, 95% BCa CI $[-0.87, 0.05]$ nor for the familiar brand, $b = -0.06$, $SE = 0.23$, 95% BCa CI $[-0.51, 0.41]$. However a positive effect of appropriateness on quality of interaction was found, $b = 0.67$, $SE = 0.07$, $p < .001$. Although no evidence was found for Hypothesis 2b, we did find a positive relation between appropriateness and brand attitude, and quality of interaction.

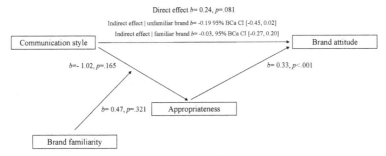

Fig. 6. Moderated mediation of the effect of communication style (formal/informal) on brand attitude.

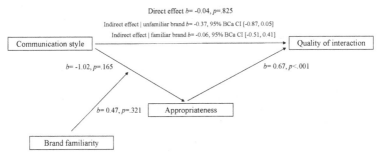

Fig. 7. Moderated mediation of the effect of communication style (formal/informal) on quality of interaction.

5 Conclusion and Discussion

Since customers tend to perceive chatbot conversations as unnatural and impersonal (Drift et al. 2018) and they value a 'human touch' in service interactions (Paluch 2012; Laban and Araujo 2019), the current study examined which mechanisms come into play if customer service chatbots use (in)formal language. Drawing upon the CASA paradigm (Nass et al. 1994) which states that users react similar to computers as to human beings, we expected to find similar positive and negative results of an informal communication style in a human-to-chatbot context as has been found in prior research in a human-to-human customer service setting (Gretry et al. 2017).

Our study revealed a chatbot's informal communication style positively influences quality of the interaction and brand attitude if participants perceived high levels of social presence (i.e., the perception of actually communicating with another human being; Short et al. 1976). These findings consolidate prior results in both a human-to-human (Park and Lee 2013) and human-to-chatbot context (Liebrecht and van der Weegen 2019). The findings furthermore indicate that it is relevant to investigate the (in)formal communication style of chatbots as an isolated factor (in contrast to Araujo (2018) and Liebrecht and van der Weegen (2019)) and to measure a chatbot's social presence by means of perceived warmth, intimacy, and sociability (similar as Liebrecht and van der Weegen (2019), but different from Araujo (2018)).

Building on Role Theory (Sarbin and Allen 1968), a negative effect was expected when the communication style was perceived inappropriate which could be moderated through brand familiarity. This effect appeared in a human-to-human context (Gretry et al. 2017), but our study did not replicate this result. The informal communication style of a chatbot was not considered inappropriate, and participants' familiarity with the brand did not influence this relation. Since Liebrecht and van der Weegen (2019) did not find evidence for this moderating effect of brand familiarity as well, it can be reasoned that in a human-to-chatbot customer service setting customers apparently do not assign different roles to chatbots as communication partner.

The current study contributes to our theoretical understanding how customers perceive a chatbot's communication style and the mechanisms that could explain the effects. Participants seem to react to a certain extent similar to computers as to human beings, as is stated in the CASA paradigm (Nass et al. 1994), and the usage of a humanlike communication style could strengthen this even more because users indicate to experience a higher level of social presence (Short et al. 1976). However, boundaries could appear in assigning social roles to computers compared to a human-to-human customer service setting. Since effects of brand familiarity and appropriateness are not confirmed in human-to-chatbot interaction, customers might have less expectations regarding the role and communication style of their programmed communication partner.

Based on the present findings, practical guidelines regarding the communication style of chatbots can be formulated. In order to design a 'human touch' in the messages of customer service chatbots (non)verbal elements of an informal communication style could be added. These linguistic cues enhance the perception of social presence which in turn can improve the quality of interaction and brand attitude. In turn, brands can profit from a high quality of interaction as it is partly contributing to the whole concept of service quality (Brady and Cronin 2001) and can furthermore increase brand trust and loyalty (Zehir et al. 2011). Although informal communication style did not influence the perceived appropriateness, brands could use the present insights by reflecting on characteristics of their target groups and their expectations on chatbot communication in a customer service setting to improve social presence, quality of interaction, and brand attitude.

5.1 Limitations and Directions for Future Research

In order to gain a deeper understanding of mechanisms behind customers' perceptions of humanlike chatbots, more research is needed that take the following limitations into account. First of all, the participants' existing experience with chatbots could influence their perceptions of the chatbot conversation. Our participants indicated to be moderately experienced with chatbots. Given their greater experience with human-to-human interactions, it is reasonable to assume they do have expectations about social roles and appropriate communication styles in this context (as stated by Role Theory), but not yet in a chatbot context. Furthermore, based on Social Learning Theory (Bandura and Walters 1977), people learn from the observation and imitation of other humans, yet it is possible to assume that this does not apply to chatbot conversations. In fact, users might not yet have engaged in a sufficient number of chatbot conversations nor observed enough human-to-chatbot interactions to judge whether the specific communication style of a chatbot is appropriate. Future research could investigate the perceptions of appropriateness concerning the chatbot's communication style between more and less experienced chatbot users.

Second, an additional measure in the manipulation check revealed that participants who interacted with the informal chatbots also perceived its communication style as more personalized compared to participants interacting with the formal chatbots. An explanation could be that some informal language manipulations were perceived as personal, i.e., active voice operationalizations oftentimes contained personal pronouns like 'you' and 'I' (compare: 'You ordered the item 'chair' four times' versus 'The item 'chair' was ordered four times') while in CHV research these linguistic elements are categorized as message personalization features (van Hooijdonk and Liebrecht 2018). On the other hand, this finding could indicate that informal language and message personalization are closely related, which consolidates the multiple strategies to operationalize the concept of CHV (Kelleher 2009; Kelleher and Miller 2006). Future research should therefore investigate to what extent personalization and informal speech are perceived as separated concepts.

Lastly, despite the improved manipulation of brand familiarity in the current study, no moderating effects of the brand were found, confirming Liebrecht and van der Weegen's (2019) findings. Before drawing the conclusion that brand familiarity does not affect customers' perceptions of a chatbot's communication style, it is highly recommended to take the customers' own experiences regarding the existing brand into account. After all, the brand's reputation or previous service encounter experiences with the brand could affect their perceptions of the chatbot's communication style. Furthermore, differences in brands' communication styles can be observed, both between industries and between competitors (Liebrecht et al., submitted), which could create consumers' expectations regarding the chatbot's communication style. For example, the well-known brand's communication style is rather informal in all communication channels, which rise expectations on the communication style of their chatbot. Besides alignment between the brands regular communication style and its chatbot's communication style, alignment with the customers' style could be important as well. Since Jakic et al. (2017) showed beneficial effects of language style accommodation in human customer service messages, and Liebrecht and van Hooijdonk's (2020) results are promising regarding automatization of language style accommodation, it is worthwhile to continue research that enables us to develop chatbots that tailor conversations in a human way.

References

Følstad, A., Skjuve, M.: Chatbots for customer service: user experience and motivation. In: Proceedings of the 1st International Conference on Conversational User Interfaces – CUI 209. ACM, New York (2019)

Laban, G., Araujo, T.: Working together with conversational agents: the relationship of perceived cooperation with service performance evaluations. In: Følstad, A. (ed.) CONVERSATIONS 2019. LNCS, vol. 11970, pp. 215–228. Springer, Cham (2020). https://doi.org/10.1007/978-3-030-39540-7_15

Shawar, B., Atwell, E.: Chatbots: are they really useful? LDV Forum **22**, 29–49 (2007)

Araujo, T.: Living up to the chatbot hype: the influence of anthropomorphic design cues and communicative agency framing on conversational agent and company perceptions. Comput. Hum. Behav. **85**, 183–189 (2018)

Bryan, J.: Service leaders expect use of AI and virtual customer assistants to gain importance in the future (2019). https://www.gartner.com/smarterwithgartner/bots-gain-importance-in-gartner-service-technologies-bullseye/. Accessed 24 Aug 2020

Elsner, N.: KAYAK mobile travel report: Chatbots in the UK (2017). https://www.kayak.co.uk/news/mobile-travel-report-2017/. Accessed 09 Nov 2020

Drift, SurveyMonkey Audience, Salesforce, Myclever: The 2018 State of Chatbots Report. How chatbots are reshaping online experiences (2018). https://www.drift.com/wp-content/uploads/2018/01/2018-state-of-chatbots-report.pdf. Accessed 01 Sept 2019

Gretry, A., Horváth, C., Belei, N., van Riel, A.: "Don't pretend to be my friend!" when an informal brand communication style backfires on social media. J. Bus. Res. **74**, 77–89 (2017)

Gnewuch, U., Morana, S. Maedche, A.: Towards designing cooperative and social conversational agents for customer service. In: Proceedings of the International Conference on Information Systems (ICIS) (2017)

Jovic, D.: The Future is Now – 37 Fascinating Chatbot Statistics. Smallbizgenius, 13 August 2020. https://www.smallbizgenius.net/by-the-numbers/chatbot-statistics/#gref

Brandtzaeg, P.B., Følstad, A.: Why people use chatbots. In: Kompatsiaris, I. (ed.) INSCI 2017. LNCS, vol. 10673, pp. 377–392. Springer, Cham (2017). https://doi.org/10.1007/978-3-319-70284-1_30

Go, E., Sundar, S.S.: Humanizing chatbots: the effects of visual, identity and conversational cues on humanness perceptions. Comput. Hum. Behav. **97**, 304–316 (2019)

Liebrecht, C., van der Weegen, E.: Menselijke chatbots: een zegen voor online klantcontact? Het effect van conversational human voice door chatbots op social presence en merkattitude. Tijdschrift voor Communicatiewetenschap **47**, 217–238 (2019)

Verhagen, T., van Nes, J., Feldberg, F., van Dolen, W.: Virtual customer service agents: using social presence and personalization to shape online service encounters. J. Comput.-Mediated Commun. **19**(3), 529–545 (2014)

Paluch, S.: Remote service technology perception and its impact on customer-provider relationships: an empirical exploratory study in a B-to-B-setting. Gabler Verlag, Wiesbaden (2012)

Liebrecht, C., van Hooijdonk, C.: Creating humanlike chatbots: what chatbot developers could learn from webcare employees in adopting a conversational human voice. In: Følstad, A. (ed.) CONVERSATIONS 2019. LNCS, vol. 11970, pp. 51–64. Springer, Cham (2020). https://doi.org/10.1007/978-3-030-39540-7_4

Nass, C., Steuer, J., Tauber, E.R.: Computers are social actors. In: Proceedings of the SIGCHI Conference on Human Factors in Computing Systems, pp. 72–78. ACM (1994)

Nass, C., Moon, Y.: Machines and mindlessness: social responses to computers. J. Soc. Issues **56**, 81–103 (2000)

Short, J., Williams, E., Christie, B.: The Social Psychology of Telecommunications. Wiley, Londen (1976)

Lombard, M., Ditton, T.: At the heart of it all: the concept of presence. J. Comput.-Mediated Commun. **3**(2), JCMC321 (1997)

Horton, D., Wohl, R.: Mass communication and para-social interaction: observations on intimacy at a distance. Psychiatry **19**(3), 215–229 (1956)

van Noort, G., Willemsen, L., Kerkhof, P., Verhoeven, J.: Webcare as an integrative tool for customer care, reputation management, and online marketing: a literature review. In: Kitchen, P.J., Uzunoglu, E. (eds.) Integrated Communications in the Post-Modern Era, pp. 77–99. Palgrave Macmillan, London (2014)

McArthur, T.: The Oxford companion to the English language. Oxford University Press, Oxford (1992)

Jakic, A., Wagner, M.O., Meyer, A.: The impact of language style accommodation during social media interactions on brand trust. J. Serv. Manag. **28**(3), 418–441 (2017)

Sarbin, T., Allen, V.: Role Theory. Addison-Wesley, Handbook of Social Psychology. Reading (1968)

Stephan, E., Liberman, N., Trope, Y.: Politeness and psychological distance: a construal level perspective. J. Pers. Soc. Psychol. **98**, 268–280 (2010)

Pricilla, C., Lestari, D.P., Dharma, D.: Designing interaction for chatbot-based conversational commerce with user-centered design. In: 5th International Conference on Advanced Informatics: Concept Theory and Applications (ICAICTA), pp. 244–249 (2018)

Liebrecht, C., Tsaousi, C., van Hooijdonk, C.: Linguistic elements of conversational human voice in online brand communication: manipulations and perceptions. J. Bus. Res. (under review)

Hayes, A.: Introduction to Mediation, Moderation, and Conditional Process Analysis: A Regression-Based Approach. Guilford Publications, New York (2017)

Park, H., Lee, H.: Show us you are real: the effect of human-versus-organizational presence on online relationship building through social networking sites. Cyberpsychol. Behav. Soc. Netw. **16**(4), 265–271 (2013)

Kelleher, T.: Conversational style, communicated commitment, and public relations outcomes in interactive online communication. J. Commun. **59**, 172–188 (2009)

Brady, M.K., Cronin, J.J., Jr.: Some new thoughts on conceptualizing perceived service quality: a hierarchical approach. J. Mark. **65**(3), 34–49 (2001)

Zehir, C., Şahin, A., Kitapçı, H., Özşahin, M.: The effects of brand communication and service quality in building brand loyalty through brand trust; the empirical research on global brands. Procedia-Soc. Behav. Sci. **24**, 1218–1231 (2011)

Bandura, A., Walters, R.: Social Learning Theory. Prentice-Hall, Englewood Cliffs (1977)

van Hooijdonk, C., Liebrecht, C.: "Wat vervelend dat de fiets niet is opgeruimd! Heb je een zaaknummer voor mij? ^EK". Conversational human voice in webcare van Nederlandse gemeenten. Tijdschrift voor Taalbeheersing **40**(1), 45–82 (2018)

Kelleher, T., Miller, B.: Organizational blogs and the human voice: relational strategies and relational outcomes. J. Comput.-Mediated Commun. **11**, 395–414 (2006)

User Perception of Text-Based Chatbot Personality

Elayne Ruane[1,2](✉), Sinead Farrell[1], and Anthony Ventresque[1,2]

[1] School of Computer Science, University College Dublin, Dublin, Ireland
{`elayne.ruane,sinead.farrell1`}`@ucdconnect.ie`
[2] LERO - The Irish Software Research Centre, Limerick, Ireland

Abstract. This work explores the effect of chatbot personality on user experience and investigates how users perceive agent personality when conveyed through text. Building on previous work in the field of human-computer interaction on designing chatbot personality, we investigate whether users in a low-stakes conversation have a preference for a specific personality type when the agent does not use voice, is not visually represented, and does not provide identity cues such as gender. We developed two chatbots that interact with users in a multi-turn conversation and designed them to have distinct personalities along two axes of the Five Factor Model (extraversion and agreeableness). We conducted a user study to evaluate user engagement, user perception of the agents, and the effect of user personality on user experience.

Keywords: Conversational agent · Chatbot · Personality · User experience · HCI

1 Introduction

Chatbots are designed to mimic a uniquely human activity: conversation. Human-human communication is full of complexity and nuance. When we interact with one another, our personalities inform how we build connections and form relationships [16]. Our behaviours, and how we interpret the behaviour of others, is heavily influenced by our personality [1,17]. It follows that when a human user is interacting with, and forming their perception of, a chatbot that is imitating human behaviour, they may infer personality traits from its language and response style, as well as from other anthropomorphic cues such as visual representations of the chatbot, including non-verbal behaviours like animated facial expressions and gestures. Additionally, agents with voice capabilities have other features including tone, pitch, and cadence that may influence user perception by cuing gender, age, and other perceived identity markers.

A person's personality has the power to sway the direction of a conversation [16]. Correspondingly, in commercial contexts such as customer service, a human representative's personality can be the key to ensuring a satisfying user experience [27]. The literature, as described in Sect. 2, suggests the same is true

© Springer Nature Switzerland AG 2021
A. Følstad et al. (Eds.): CONVERSATIONS 2020, LNCS 12604, pp. 32–47, 2021.
https://doi.org/10.1007/978-3-030-68288-0_3

for chatbots, in both commercial and other scenarios. However, designing chatbot personality that maximises user satisfaction and provides an engaging user experience and, thus, a better service, is a non-trivial task. Many interesting questions remain around how to choose an appropriate personality for a chatbot and how to design dialogue that reliably conveys this simulated personality.

While much of the literature focuses on multi-modal agents that have several avenues to leverage in expressing personality, we are interested in text-based agents that do not have a visual or audio representation. Text-based agents are pervasive. For example, the popular entertainment chatbot and five-time winner of the Loebner Prize Turing Test, Mitsuku[1], is a text-based chatbot (albeit with an avatar but without voice capabilities), as are many recommendation agents[2], information retrieval chatbots (e.g. news[3] and weather[4]), therapy chatbots[5], and customer service and FAQ chatbots embedded in company websites. As such, personality design and user perception of personality in text-based agents warrants investigation. To this end, we have defined two research questions; RQ1) Can personality be reliably simulated by a chatbot via text such that the user perceives personality or personality traits as intended? and RQ2) Does the perceived personality of a text-based chatbot affect user experience?

To address these questions, we have developed two text-based chatbots (i.e. without voice capabilities and not represented with a visual avatar) with distinct personalities and conducted a user study to evaluate whether users perceive the personality traits expressed through dialogue design as intended and whether they exhibit a preference for one personality over another. The rest of this paper is structured as follows: in Sect. 2 we discuss related work, in Sect. 3 we outline the design of the chatbots used in this study, in Sect. 4 we detail our methodology and experiment design, we provide the results and a discussion of those results in Sect. 5 and 6 respectively, in Sect. 7 we discuss the limitations of this study, and lastly we conclude the work in Sect. 8.

2   Related Work

In this section, we discuss previous work that aims to understand how users perceive and interact with chatbots, specifically studies that investigate how chatbot personality design affects user experience, how users perceive agent personality, and how agent personality can be conveyed through text.

2.1   Five Factor Model Studies

Many studies of chatbot personality use the well-established Five Factor Model (FFM), also referred to as the Big Five Trait Taxonomy [9], to model both

---

[1] Mitsuku: https://www.pandorabots.com/mitsuku/.

[2] Beauty recommendation chatbots: https://beauty.bot/directory/makeup/.

[3] CNN Chatbot: https://marutitech.com/news-made-personal-with-chatbots/.

[4] Weather chatbots: https://chatbottle.co/bots/messenger/weather.

[5] Woebot: https://woebothealth.com/.

agent and user personality. The model consists of five characteristics: openness to experience, conscientiousness, extraversion, agreeableness, and neuroticism. Each trait is a continuum describing a dimension of the most common traits perceived in individuals. Trait-based models of personality such as FFM are widely used in both Psychology and in Affective Computing. Such models are useful in evaluating individual differences [4] and thus lend themselves to design of agent personality and investigations of personality effects on user experience.

Hanna and Richards (2015) [6] investigated the effect of agent personality on team work, specifically the development of a shared mental model between human users and a virtual agent, while completing a collaborative game task. Two dimensions of FFM, extraversion and agreeableness, were expressed by the agent using both verbal and non-verbal cues. The authors found participants were able to identify the personality traits as intended and that an agent designed with explicit personality traits is likely to improve team performance.

Kang et al. (2008) [10] found participant personality traits (modelled by FFM) affect their sense of rapport with, and their perception of, a virtual agent, regardless of the agent's personality design. This is supported by later work in which Von der Pütten et al. (2010) [22] investigated how participant personality, gender, and age affect both their behaviour when interacting with a virtual agent and also their evaluation of that agent. They found gender and age did not affect the evaluation but some personality traits were predictive, including agreeableness and extraversion where agreeableness had a positive impact on how participants perceived the interaction and extraversion impacted participant's verbal behaviour, in particular, the number of words they used. The agent in this study uses both verbal and non-verbal cues but only the non-verbal cues were varied. It should be noted that while gender was found not to be a predictive factor, the agent was coded female, including using a female voice, and research has shown users treat female- and male-coded systems differently [25].

Other studies have investigated whether a "match" in user-agent personality improves user experience. Isbister and Nass (2000) [8] studied how perceived extraversion/introversion of an agent affected user experience in a low-stakes discussion task. They found users prefer consistency across both verbal and non-verbal personality cues and prefer a personality complementary to theirs, rather than entirely similar. Similarly, Liew and Tan (2016) [12] developed two pedagogical virtual agents, one introverted and the other extroverted, also expressed using both verbal and non-verbal cues. The results of the study support the complementary-attraction principle such that learners' experience was improved when the agent's personality complemented their own. These studies that include visual non-verbal cues draw conclusions that support the complementary-attraction principle, unlike previous work [11,18] that shows users prefer agents that exhibit similar personality traits (similarity-attraction principle) when communicated through voice and text only.

Smestad and Volden (2018) [26] investigated the effect of a match in personality between a chatbot and the user where the chatbot is representing a brand. The authors used the FFM model and created two chatbots, one with an "agreeable" personality and the other with a "conscientious" personality. The chatbots were varied to different degrees across the five dichotomies; the neuroticism trait was excluded for one chatbot and both chatbots appear to have high conscientiousness. The main difference between the two chatbots is one is high in agreeableness and extraversion and the other is low on those traits. This study did not use non-verbal cues but varied across lexical features and also used voice, leveraging *tone* of voice specifically. The authors acknowledge previous work [25] that has shown female-coded agents are more likely to be stereotyped and receive abusive messages and although gender was not included as a factor in the study, both chatbots were represented with a human avatar and coded as female. The authors found the agreeable personality had a more positive effect on user experience with the particular brand and user group involved in this study.

2.2 Expressing Personality Through Text

Many studies in this area, including those discussed above, focus on voice-based agents and leverage visual cues such as animated facial expressions or body language to express personality. However, many chatbots in the wild do not use these cues, instead relying largely or solely on text to convey personality. Neff et al. (2010) [20] identified verbal and non-verbal cues that can be used to demonstrate extraversion in a chatbot. Drawing on the Psychology literature, the authors detail the linguistic parameters of their language generation model used to display extraversion. These include high verbosity, content polarity, and acknowledgements, along with low negation, filled pauses, and softener hedges.

Roffo et al. (2014) [23] explored identification of personality in textual human-human conversation via three stylometric features. We apply these features to human-agent conversation in both the expression of personality on the part of the agent, and as features in our analysis of user behaviour. *Lexical* features such as the number of words or characters used per turn may be a sign of user engagement but from the user's perspective, these features may convey personality traits of the chatbot and may also be linked to how informative or effective the agent is. *Syntactic* features such as the use of emoticons or expressive punctuation can be used to convey emotion or sentiment. Lastly, *turn-taking* features include turn duration and answer time, which will vary markedly for the user and the chatbot. In this study, we use these features to inform the dialogue design and to analyse the conversation logs from the study.

2.3 Interaction Questionnaire Design

Liu et al. (2015) [13] compared two types of questionnaires for measuring user perception of agent personality; open-ended questions and Likert-scale personality inventories (such as the Big Five Inventory). The personality traits examined in this study were extraversion/introversion and neuroticism. The authors found both question styles yield different yet complementary results. The open-ended questions do not prime participants and thus give insight into aspects of personality or agent design that resonated most with the participant. Personality inventories can be useful for eliciting opinion on traits that may have been observed but subsequently forgotten or were not otherwise verbalized. However, such inventories can also prompt the participant to think of the agent in a way they had not previously. Based on this work, and as we are conducting a within-subject study, we elected to use open-ended questions and did not ask users to fill out an agent personality inventory.

Luger et al. (2016) [14] interviewed conversational agent users to understand their experience with agents like Siri, Google Now, Cortana, and Alexa. The authors found higher user expectations of agent capabilities can lead to lower user satisfaction. They discuss why expectations may go unmet such as a gap in the user's understanding of agent capabilities due to a lack of technical knowledge or experience. Based on these findings, we include two questions in our pre-interaction demographic questionnaire that ask users to (i) describe their understanding of a chatbot and (ii) describe their frequency of use. This allows us to understand their mental model and evaluate if their previous experience affects their perception of the interaction.

3   Design and Development of Chatbots with Personality

We designed and implemented our chatbots using the Microsoft Bot Framework[6] and its NLP service, LUIS[7]. We carefully considered the impact of the application domain when selecting the topic of conversation for this study. We did not want the conversation to be high-stakes, commercially driven, or to focus on a strategic task. We wanted participants to have a truly conversational experience (as opposed to conversational search or a button-based interaction). It was not feasible for us to build an open-domain agent, thus we designed the bots to have a multi-turn conversation about a specific topic familiar to the participants; third-level education, or, more specifically, computer science courses and university campus experiences.

As we are investigating the effect of personality on user experience, we endeavoured to mitigate any other persona-related effect. Previous work [27] has shown the use of an avatar can both positively or negatively impact how users perceive a chatbot, even before they interact with it. Silvervarg et al. (2012) [25] have shown how female-coded agents are treated more poorly than male-coded agents. As a result, we have not provided visual representation of the agents, have not used identity-specific language, and have given the chatbots androgynous names[8].

---

[6] Microsoft Bot Framework: https://dev.botframework.com.

[7] https://www.luis.ai/.

[8] The bots were called Makoto and Nasoto. Makoto is an ungendered Japanese name, and Nasoto is a non-word. These names are culturally distant from the cultural background of our sample and thus unlikely to be readily associated with a specific gender, age-group, or other identity.

In chatbot personality design, there are limits to the expression of some personality traits through text dialogue [7], even more so when designing dialogue for a domain not usually associated with emotive language. As such, some traits in the FMM may be more difficult to express than others and some more appropriate than others. For example, high neuroticism may be inappropriate for an agent designed to assist the user with a routine task. With this in mind, and in context of the related work discussed in Sect. 2.1, we focus on two dimensions of the FFM; extraversion and agreeableness.

Extraversion can be broken down into five distinct components: activity level, dominance, sociability, expressiveness, and positive emotionality [9]. Agreeableness includes traits relating to trust, altruism, compliance, modesty, and tender mindedness [9]. Tables 1 and 2 show language cues that distinguish extroverts from introverts, and highly agreeable people from those who are less agreeable. These cues were compiled from work in the Linguistics and Psychology literature [2,3,5,19,21]. Although a 2 × 2 factorial design such that participants interact with agent personalities that vary across all combinations of extraversion and agreeableness may be of interest, we decided to create two chatbots with personalities that combine high extraversion with high agreeableness (and vice versa) due to their complementary linguistic presentations and previous work [14,15] that suggests users respond to *distinct* agent personalities.

The applicable speech patterns and response styles were applied to the conversation flow for each chatbot to generate responses that demonstrate a consistent, distinct personality. Chatbot A was designed to exhibit high extraversion by demonstrating (i) high energy through punctuation including exclamation points, (ii) a talkative nature through verbosity of phrasing, and (iii) sharing information by asking questions of the user. High agreeableness is shown through complementary language and positive reinforcement. Chatbot B was designed to exhibit a contrasting personality with low extraversion and low agreeableness. As such, the dialogue is designed to demonstrate low energy, passiveness, and overall show less interest in participating in chitchat than chatbot A. Chatbot B uses a direct style of communication with less interest in the user as an individual; the questions posed are more factual in nature, rather than personal to the user.

By way of example, when the user tells the chatbot how many courses they are taking in the current semester, Chatbot A may respond "Wow <num> modules! Which one would you say is your favourite?" (See Fig. 1 for other response examples). This response is (i) relatively informal (ii) uses an exclamation mark (iii) contains no negations and (iv) uses cheerful, positive language. In comparison, Chatbot B may respond "Which module is your favourite? Mine would be secure software engineering" (See Fig. 2 for other response examples). This response is (i) self-focused (ii) more direct, and (iii) the language is less positive. While the response text differs, both chatbots follow the same conversation flow and can discuss the same scope of topics about university life including course modules, exams, the campus, and extracurricular activities. In addition, the chatbots can discuss the Covid-19 pandemic and how it has impacted the previously listed topics.

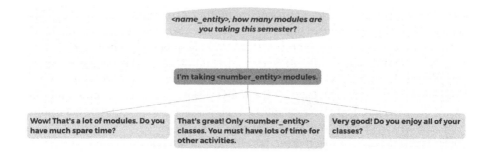

Fig. 1. An example conversation flow snippet for Chatbot A (high extraversion and high agreeableness).

4   Methodology

The experiment was designed to provide insight into user perception of the chatbots including their attitudes towards the agents and their behaviour while interacting with them. The participants were final year undergraduate computer science students in University College Dublin selected using convenience sampling via both email mailing lists and shared forum. A total of 22 people signed up to partake in the study, 5 of whom failed to complete all required components and so were excluded from the analysis (thus n = 17). One participant fell in the 35–39 years age range while the rest were ages 18–24. The sample was comprised of 12 males and 5 females. As the scope of the conversation is the participants' college experience, they already possessed the required domain knowledge to interact with the chatbot and were familiar with the knowledge base of the agent. The study is a within-subject study such that each participant interacts with both chatbots.

Task 1: Pre-interaction Questionnaire. To begin, participants fill out a pre-interaction questionnaire that gathers participant demographic data including age-range and gender. Participants are also asked to detail their previous experience with and understanding of chatbots, including their frequency of use. Lastly, users fill out a personality inventory. We considered several personality questionnaires proposed in the literature including Eysenck's EPQ-R, the NEO-PI-R model, and the Big-Five Inventory (BFI). We decided to use the BFI as it is available freely for use in research, is based on the same model used to design the personalities of the chatbots, and has been used in similar work (see Sect. 2). The BFI uses a Likert-scale questionnaire through which the participants self-report their personality traits. While there are limitations around self-reporting, it is an accepted practice for subjective measures. The data collected from the pre-interaction questionnaire was analyzed to determine whether participant demographics, previous experience, or personality has a modulating effect on participant perception of, or behaviour with, each chatbot.

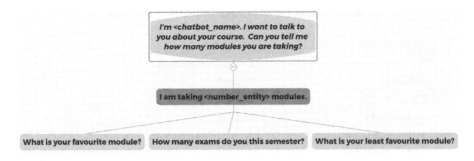

Fig. 2. An example conversation flow snippet for Chatbot B (low extraversion and low agreeableness).

Task 2: Interaction with the Chatbot. For each chatbot the participants were instructed to click on the link associated with the chatbot interface. Once the interface had loaded they were directed to an input box where they began the conversation by typing and sending any message to the chatbot. They were advised that the conversation would be directed primarily by the chatbot asking questions about their university experience. Below are the instructions given to participants:

> *When you click the link below a white screen will appear, on the bottom of this screen there will be an input box that says "Type your message". When you are ready to begin your conversation type anything into the input box and click enter to send the message. Converse with the chatbot by answering its questions about your university experience. When you are finished conversing with the chatbot close the window.*

Task 3: Post-Interaction Questionnaire. After the chatbot interaction, participants complete a post-interaction questionnaire about their experience that asks them (i) to describe the chatbot in an open-text field, (ii) whether they enjoyed the interaction, and (iii) to rate the chatbot across three dimensions (knowledge, quality of conversation, and attitude/personality) on a Likert scale. The participants also have the option to qualitatively expand on each rating in open-text fields. The results from the post-interaction surveys were analysed to determine participant attitudes to each chatbot and the descriptions were analysed for language describing demographic features such as age, gender, and cultural background that users may have ascribed to the chatbot(s).

After completing tasks 2 and 3 for the first chatbot, the participants repeat these steps for the second chatbot. To mitigate the order effect half of the participants are randomly selected to interact with Chatbot A first, while the other half will interact with Chatbot B and then Chatbot A. The questions in both post-interaction questionnaires are the exact same.

Table 1. Extraversion vs introversion language cues

Extraversion	Introversion
Self-references	Few self-references
Informal	Formal
Pleasure talk	Problem talk
Agreement	Listens
Few tentative words	Many tentative words
Talks more about social topics	Self-focused
Many verbs, adverbs, pronouns	Many nouns, adjectives, prepositions
Few words per sentence	Many words
Few negations, articles	Many negations, article
Many social words	Few social words
Many positive emotion words	Many negative emotion words

Table 2. Agreeableness vs disagreeableness language cues

Agreeableness	Disagreeableness
Prompting	Negations
Listens more	Swearing
Longer words	Words relating to anger
Shorter sentences	
Positive emotion words	
Social words	
Self-references	
Cheerful language	

Task 4: Comparison Questionnaire. Lastly, participants complete a final post-interaction questionnaire. The objective of this questionnaire is to understand participants' chatbot preference and to identify the differences they perceived between the chatbots. Participants were asked to describe any differences they noticed in their interactions with the chatbots in an open-text field. This was followed by a multiple choice question where participants chose their preferred chatbot. Finally, the participants explained this choice in an open-text field.

The questionnaires were carried out using Google Forms and the chatbots were connected to a web channel that would allow them to be accessed via link and used remotely while an online database container was used to store the experiment data.

A pilot study with four participants from the same population as the main study was conducted to evaluate comprehensibility of the questionnaire design, the conversation flow, and the experiment design. After this pilot, minor changes were made to the LUIS model including the addition of colloquial variations of 'yes' and 'no'. Additionally, some questions posed by the chatbots were ambiguous due to the Covid-19 pandemic so these questions were edited and the virus was added as a topic of conversation. Participants reported confusion around the meaning of some words used in the pre-interaction personality questionnaire, such as 'aloof' and 'reserved'. To prevent this confusion a list of definitions was supplied within the questionnaire for reference. The pilot study validated that the data collection was sufficient for addressing the research questions and the participants were excluded from the main study.

5   Results

Participant BFI personality scores for extraversion and agreeableness were calculated with a mean extraversion score of 3.06 ($\sigma = 0.63$) and a mean agreeableness score of 3.97 ($\sigma = 0.43$). We defined thresholds and grouped these scores to label participant personality traits: 5 participants were high in extraversion (score $>= 3.5$), 10 participants were moderately extroverted ($2.5 >$ score < 3.5), and two were low in extraversion (score < 2.5). Overall, the participants are high in agreeableness with 11 participants scoring $>= 3.5$ (high) and the remaining 6 participants scoring between 2.5 and 3.5 (moderate). All participants stated they knew what a chatbot was, 6 of whom described their understanding with technical detail. Their frequency of use was varied with 6 participants having never used a virtual assistant, 7 using them somewhat frequently, and 4 using them daily. So while all participants have a clear, and in some cases technical, mental model of chatbots, their experience using such agents is mixed.

To understand how participant behaviour varied between the agents, we analysed stylometric features in the interaction conversation logs. We calculated (i) the *duration* of the conversation in minutes using the timestamp from the first participant utterance until the timestamp of their last message, (ii) the number of participant *conversation turns*, (iii) the participant's *total word count* which is the sum of the count of words in each utterance the participant submits to the bot, and (iv) the participant's *mean utterance length* in words. See Table 3 for descriptive statistics of these features for each agent. Overall, participants conversed more with Chatbot B than Chatbot A, across these engagement metrics. We ran a paired sample t-test for each measure and found the difference in behaviour captured by conversation duration ($p < 0.02$) and turn count ($p < 0.05$) were significant. Thus we can reject the null hypothesis that participants behaviour was the same across both agent interactions.

Participants were asked to rate the interaction with each agent on a Likert scale across 3 measures: knowledge, quality of conversation, and attitude/personality. Our null hypothesis states there is no difference in how participants perceive the personality of the two agents. Our alternative hypothesis

Table 3. Descriptive statistics for stylometric features ($N = 17$)

Measure	Chatbot	Minimum	Maximum	Mean	Variance
Duration (Minutes)	A	1	6	3.18	3.28
	B	2	21	6.35	18.37
Number of turns	A	9	24	15.59	28.36
	B	10	34	20.29	35.38
Total word count	A	14	149	65.47	1951.66
	B	24	281	91.65	3263.64
Mean utterance length (Words)	A	7	36	18	86.67
	B	7	38	19	51.12

states the participant discerns a difference in personality between the agents. We ran a paired sample t-test on each measure and found no statistically significant difference in user perception of agent knowledge (p = 0.886) or conversation quality (p = 0.575). However, we found a statistically significant difference in how users viewed personality (p < 0.02). Given this evidence, we can reject the null hypothesis and determine that participants perceive a difference in personality of the agents. Participants were asked which agent they preferred interacting with; 12 chose Chatbot A and 5 chose Chatbot B. Interestingly, we did not find a statistically significant strong correlation between agent preference and participant personality trait scores. It is likely our sample is too small to capture any matching phenomenon that may exist.

We analysed the language used by participants in their descriptions of each chatbot for syntactic stylometric features (e.g. emoticons or expressive punctuation and language) to understand how they perceived the chatbots. NLTK[9], the NLP library for Python, was used to extract adjectives from the descriptions. The data was also manually analysed for adjectives not picked up by NLTK. Results are shown in Fig. 3. Participants whose chatbot preference was Chatbot B described their experience with it as 'engaging', 'personalised', and 'natural'. However, those who preferred Chatbot A described Chatbot B as 'formal', 'robotic', and the conversation as 'unnatural'. These participants also described the experience as similar to *"being interviewed for RTÉ News"* (the national news service) or *"taking an oral exam when studying a language module"*. Similarly, those who preferred Chatbot B perceived Chatbot A as being 'bland', and 'automated' and felt the conversation was 'not personalised'. Whereas participants who preferred Chatbot A cited its 'cheery', 'bright', 'fun', and 'relaxed' personality, with one participant saying Chatbot A had a *"better personality"* and another comparing the interaction to *"chatting with a friend"*. One participant perceived Chatbot A to be 'nice' but felt overall it was 'bland' and perceived Chatbot B as being more 'engaged' and thus preferred the interaction with Chatbot B. That same participant scored lower in both extraversion

---

[9] Natural Language Toolkit: https://www.nltk.org/.

(2.57) and agreeableness (3) than the average participant, scores which match the personality traits of Chatbot B.

Lastly, the participants open-text responses across all post-interaction questionnaires were analysed for gendered language. A single participant used gender pronouns, specifically 'he' and 'his', but used these pronouns to describe both Chatbot A and Chatbot B. Interestingly, these pronouns were contrary to their own gender. Participants usually referred to the chatbots as 'it', by name, or as 'chatbot' or 'bot'. This contrasts previous research that found users may still gender agents [24] without explicit visual cues. Our results may be due to limited relationship building with the agents or may be due to the participants well-developed mental model of chatbots.

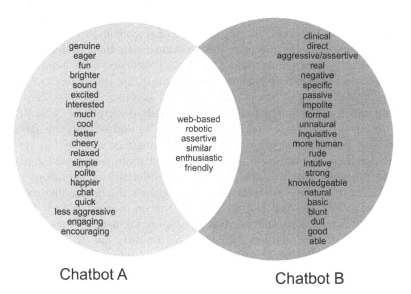

Fig. 3. Venn Diagram of adjectives used to describe Chatbot A and Chatbot B

6   Discussion

This section provides discussion of participant behaviour with, and attitudes towards, the chatbots based on the results presented in Sect. 5. We organize this discussion according to the two research questions outlined in Sect. 1.

6.1   RQ1: Can Personality Be Reliably Simulated by a Chatbot via Text Such that the User Perceives Personality or Personality Traits as Intended?

Our results support previous work (see Sect. 2) that suggest personality can be reliably simulated by a chatbot such that personality traits are perceived by users as intended. Participant descriptions of both chatbots are in line with the personality design; chatbot A was described as 'friendly' and 'cheery', reflecting high agreeableness and extraversion, while Chatbot B was described as 'formal' and 'passive', consistent with low agreeableness and low extraversion. Additionally, the agents were designed to vary on the axis of personality but not on their knowledge base or on the quality of conversation. When rating the chatbots along these three axes participants only perceived a difference in personality.

6.2   RQ2: Does the Perceived Personality of a Text-Based Chatbot Affect User Experience?

The results suggest the personalities of both chatbots had an effect on user experience. Participants showed higher engagement with Chatbot B than Chatbot A in terms of lexical and turn-taking features of conversation. We had hypothesised users would engage in longer conversations with their preferred chatbot but while overall participants spent more time conversing with Chatbot B the majority (70.6%) preferred Chatbot A. One reason for this behaviour may be a reaction to the direct nature and formality of language used by Chatbot B, something which many participants noted in their descriptions of it; *"Nasoto was pretty formal"*, *"very formal, not as friendly as makoto"*. In this case, participants may be mirroring the formality of the language used by the agent. In contrast, participants may have used shorter and more colloquial language to match the language style of Chatbot A. Such difference in behaviour of participants when interacting with the chatbots suggests the personality expressed through text of each chatbot had an overall effect on user experience. However, the effect itself is surprising and suggests (i) user engagement metrics may not be a good indicator of user preference for agent personality, and (ii) the application domain and goals of the agent should be considered when designing agent personality as the users' generally preferred personality may not be the personality that leads to a productive user experience.

7   Limitations

To design two distinct personalities, we simultaneously varied extraversion and agreeableness. This is sufficient to answer our research questions. However, a 2×2 factorial design would allow for the measurement of the effect of each personality trait on user perception. Although our sample size of 17 is consistent with previous work in the literature, a larger sample size would increase the robustness and generalizability of the findings. Additionally, a larger sample size may contain more variance in personality traits among the user group, providing an opportunity to investigate how user personality affects user preference of agent personality in the context of a text-based conversational task (not strategic, collaborative, or commercial task).

8   Conclusion and Future Work

We have found that personality traits can be reliably simulated through text and can be perceived as intended by users without additional audio or visual cues. We have added to the body of evidence that agent personality impacts user experience and thus is an important design consideration. There is a lot of scope for future work that builds on this work and the outlined literature, including the use of more robust models of personality (rather than two dimensions of a five dimension model). Additionally, it would be of interest to investigate the effect of domain on the perception of, and preference for, agent personality. A more emotional subject matter such as those covered by therapy chatbots may see very different user behaviour and attitudes than a chatbot that serves an information need, for example. Lastly, we analysed user perception of agent personality along the two dimensions we manipulated. It would be interesting to observe whether user perceptions of other personality traits differ even when those personality traits have not been explicitly varied. For example, do users perceive an increase in openness to experience (imaginative, spontaneous) when an agent is designed with high extraversion (sociable, fun-loving)?

Acknowledgements. This work was supported, in part, by Science Foundation Ireland grant 13/RC/2094. Thank you to Dr. Brendan Rooney and Dr. Nicola Fox Hamilton for their very helpful advice. Thank you to Thomas Laurent and Glynda Ruane for their useful feedback on an earlier version of this manuscript.

References

1. Allbeck, J., Badler, N.: Toward representing agent behaviors modified by personality and emotion. Embod. Convers. Agents AAMAS **2**, 15–19 (2002)
2. Berry, D.S., Pennebaker, J.W., Mueller, J.S., Hiller, W.S.: Linguistic bases of social perception. Pers. Soc. Psychol. Bull. **23**(5), 526–537 (1997)
3. Dewaele, J.M., Furnham, A.: Extraversion: the unloved variable in applied linguistic research. Lang. Learn. **49**(3), 509–544 (1999)
4. Faur, C., Clavel, C., Pesty, S., Martin, J.C.: PERSEED: a self-based model of personality for virtual agents inspired by socio-cognitive theories. In: 2013 Humaine Association Conference on Affective Computing and Intelligent Interaction, pp. 467–472. IEEE (2013)
5. Gill, A.J., Oberlander, J.: Taking care of the linguistic features of extraversion. In: Proceedings of the Annual Meeting of the Cognitive Science Society, vol. 24 (2002)
6. Hanna, N., Richards, D., et al.: Do birds of a feather work better together? the impact of virtual agent personality on a shared mental model with humans during collaboration. In: COOS@ AAMAS, pp. 28–37 (2015)
7. Holtgraves, T.: Text messaging, personality, and the social context. J. Res. Pers. **45**(1), 92–99 (2011)
8. Isbister, K., Nass, C.: Consistency of personality in interactive characters: verbal cues, non-verbal cues, and user characteristics. Int. J. Hum. Comput. Stud. **53**(2), 251–267 (2000)
9. John, O.P., Srivastava, S., et al.: The big five trait taxonomy: history, measurement, and theoretical perspectives. Handb. Pers. Theor. Res. **2**(1999), 102–138 (1999)

10. Kang, S.-H., Gratch, J., Wang, N., Watt, J.H.: Agreeable people like agreeable virtual humans. In: Prendinger, H., Lester, J., Ishizuka, M. (eds.) IVA 2008. LNCS (LNAI), vol. 5208, pp. 253–261. Springer, Heidelberg (2008). https://doi.org/10.1007/978-3-540-85483-8_26

11. Lee, K.M., Nass, C.: Social-psychological origins of feelings of presence: Creating social presence with machine-generated voices. Med. Psychol. **7**(1), 31–45 (2005)

12. Liew, T.W., Tan, S.M.: Virtual agents with personality: adaptation of learner-agent personality in a virtual learning environment. In: 2016 Eleventh International Conference on Digital Information Management, pp. 157–162. IEEE (2016)

13. Liu, K., Tolins, J., Tree, J.E.F., Neff, M., Walker, M.A.: Two techniques for assessing virtual agent personality. IEEE Trans. Affect. Comput. **7**(1), 94–105 (2015)

14. Luger, E., Sellen, A.: Like having a really bad pa: the gulf between user expectation and experience of conversational agents. In: Proceedings of the 2016 CHI Conference on Human Factors in Computing Systems, pp. 5286–5297. ACM (2016)

15. Ma, X., Yang, E., Fung, P.: Exploring perceived emotional intelligence of personality-driven virtual agents in handling user challenges. In: The World Wide Web Conference, pp. 1222–1233 (2019)

16. Mairesse, F., Walker, M.A., Mehl, M.R., Moore, R.K.: Using linguistic cues for the automatic recognition of personality in conversation and text. J. Artif. Intell. Res. **30**, 457–500 (2007)

17. McRorie, M., Sneddon, I., de Sevin, E., Bevacqua, E., Pelachaud, C.: A model of personality and emotional traits. In: Ruttkay, Z., Kipp, M., Nijholt, A., Vilhjálmsson, H.H. (eds.) IVA 2009. LNCS (LNAI), vol. 5773, pp. 27–33. Springer, Heidelberg (2009). https://doi.org/10.1007/978-3-642-04380-2_6

18. Moon, Y., Nass, C.I.: Adaptive agents and personality change: complementary versus similarity as forms of adaptation. In: Conference Companion on Human Factors in Computing Systems, pp. 287–288 (1996)

19. Nass, C., Moon, Y., Fogg, B.J., Reeves, B., Dryer, C.: Can computer personalities be human personalities? In: Conference Companion on Human Factors in Computing Systems, pp. 228–229. ACM (1995)

20. Neff, M., Wang, Y., Abbott, R., Walker, M.: Evaluating the effect of gesture and language on personality perception in conversational agents. In: Allbeck, J., Badler, N., Bickmore, T., Pelachaud, C., Safonova, A. (eds.) IVA 2010. LNCS (LNAI), vol. 6356, pp. 222–235. Springer, Heidelberg (2010). https://doi.org/10.1007/978-3-642-15892-6_24

21. Pennebaker, J.W., King, L.A.: Linguistic styles: language use as an individual difference. J. Pers. Soc. Psychol. **77**(6), 1296 (1999)

22. von der Pütten, A.M., Krämer, N.C., Gratch, J.: How our personality shapes our interactions with virtual characters - implications for research and development. In: Allbeck, J., Badler, N., Bickmore, T., Pelachaud, C., Safonova, A. (eds.) IVA 2010. LNCS (LNAI), vol. 6356, pp. 208–221. Springer, Heidelberg (2010). https://doi.org/10.1007/978-3-642-15892-6_23

23. Roffo, G., Giorgetta, C., Ferrario, R., Cristani, M.: Just the way you chat: linking personality, style and recognizability in chats. In: Park, H.S., Salah, A.A., Lee, Y.J., Morency, L.-P., Sheikh, Y., Cucchiara, R. (eds.) HBU 2014. LNCS, vol. 8749, pp. 30–41. Springer, Cham (2014). https://doi.org/10.1007/978-3-319-11839-0_3

24. Silvervarg, A., Haake, M., Gulz, A.: Educational potentials in visually androgynous pedagogical agents. In: Lane, H.C., Yacef, K., Mostow, J., Pavlik, P. (eds.) AIED 2013. LNCS (LNAI), vol. 7926, pp. 599–602. Springer, Heidelberg (2013). https://doi.org/10.1007/978-3-642-39112-5_68

25. Silvervarg, A., Raukola, K., Haake, M., Gulz, A.: The effect of visual gender on abuse in conversation with ECAs. In: Nakano, Y., Neff, M., Paiva, A., Walker, M. (eds.) IVA 2012. LNCS (LNAI), vol. 7502, pp. 153–160. Springer, Heidelberg (2012). https://doi.org/10.1007/978-3-642-33197-8_16

26. Smestad, T.L.: Personality Matters! Improving The User Experience of Chatbot Interfaces-Personality provides a stable pattern to guide the design and behaviour of conversational agents. Master's thesis, NTNU (2018)

27. Verhagen, T., Van Nes, J., Feldberg, F., Van Dolen, W.: Virtual customer service agents: using social presence and personalization to shape online service encounters. J. Comput. Med. Commun. **19**(3), 529–545 (2014)

The Ontological Classification of Conversational Agents

An Adaptation of Piaget's Equilibration Theory

Katrin Etzrodt[(✉)] [ID]

Technical University Dresden, 01062 Dresden, Germany
katrin.etzrodt@tu-dresden.de

Abstract. This paper focuses on the attributed nature of the voice-based agents Alexa and Google Assistant in conversational contexts. Using Piaget's equilibration theory, enhanced by Hubbard's concept of personhood the paper considers how people categorize voice-based agents along a thing–person spectrum and whether this categorization reflects assimilation or accommodation of these technologies. The results of two studies (a hypothetical conversation with the agent via an online-survey, N = 1288, and a real conversation with the agent, N = 105) are indicating a modified classification towards *personified things,* which is reinforced by younger age and a higher quality of interaction. Implications, limitations, and further research regarding a more detailed classification of conversational agents are discussed.

Keywords: Classification · Subjectivity · Personhood · Equilibration · Assimilation · Accommodation

1 Introduction

With artificial voice-based agents (VBA) like Alexa or Google Assistant, we can interact in spoken, human natural language. In particular, voices are notably powerful predictors of social presence [29], and being able to talk can be an indicator of being alive [33, p. 48], triggering manifold social reactions towards machines. People build relationships with VBA, personalize them [18,22,28], react with emotional outbursts [25] or behave socially problematic [6]. Nonetheless, social reactions vary profoundly, depending on attributes of the technology [5,19,21], the individual [10,23], or the social setting [14,22,28].

Recent scholars argue that the belief in an artificial agent's mental, moral, psychological, and practical abilities [13] – its subjectivity is related to fundamental social reactions, manifesting in a range of everyday interactions [1]. In this paper, I argue that these beliefs are challenged if not initially triggered by people getting confused [16] with "whom" or "what" [17, p. 54] they are interacting. I, furthermore, argue that the concept of personhood covers the above mentioned subjectivity. However, the respondents' limited ability to express their classification [33] complicates the measurement of this phenomenon, which is

© Springer Nature Switzerland AG 2021
A. Følstad et al. (Eds.): CONVERSATIONS 2020, LNCS 12604, pp. 48–63, 2021.
https://doi.org/10.1007/978-3-030-68288-0_4

further reduced by a lack of a precise vocabulary for hybridity and the agents' disembodiment. Hence, common tests (e.g., on theory of mind) or qualitative approaches that rely on the users' ability to express themselves – that might work for embodied agents may fail to grasp the phenomenon in its complexity and dynamics for VBAs.

The present paper examines how commercialized voice-based agents are classified by applying the equilibration approach of Piaget [26] to suggest an empirical measurement of the being in "betwixt and between" [33, p. 29]. It will be argued that thing and person represent the diametrical poles "object" and "subject" of the same classification, whose irritation is re-balanced by assimilation and accommodation. With Hubbard [20] it will be reasoned that the pole "subject" refers rather to personhood than humanness and that the classification could be understood as gradual. Based on two studies – a hypothetical conversation (N = 1288) with Alexa and the Google Assistant and a real conversation (N = 105) with the Google Assistant – this instrument is tested and its results will be discussed.

2   Theoretical Background

2.1   Voice-Based Agents as Conversational Partner

In this paper, VBAs are defined as a subtype of artificial social agents, with an operating system based on artificial intelligence and natural language processing, using a disembodied voice emanating from a device (e.g., smart phone, loudspeaker box) to communicate with the users and execute their tasks. Commercialized examples are Apple's Siri, the Google Assistant, Microsoft's Cortana, and Amazon's Alexa. These VBAs do not just aim at voice control, e.g., for smart TVs, lights or heatings, but increasingly at conversation. Projects like "Alexa Challenge" from Amazon aim to extend the communication between users and Alexa – transforming it into more fluent conversations. Google Duplex aims at handling appointments and conversations without the other necessarily noticing their artificiality.

Voice-Based Agents as Conversational Subjects. Spoken conversation is based on social interaction's fundamental structures. In this respect conversational partners can be assumed to be 'alter egos' that inhibit at least some kind of subjectivity, regardless whether this alter ego is a real or an assumed one [16]. Since it is not possible to verify the counterpart's subjectivity [17,32], mental states are imputed to them [27]. People describe Siri as an entity [18] and refer to Alexa [28] or other conversational agents [4] by using the personifying pronoun "she".

Voice-Based Agents as Artificial Objects. However, the artificiality of these speaking agents is clearly perceived [4,18,22,28]. Although as smart objects they possess a certain capacity for awareness and agency [12], they lack a body and become only visible through their voice [18]. Moreover, their synthetic voice is at the current stage of development almost but not entirely human-like (e.g., due to a lack of empathy or pronounced communication skills), emphasizing their artificial nature. A similar pattern was found for social robots [11], regarding non-liveness, being man-made or relying on programmed algorithms.

Voice-Based Agents as Irritating and Evocative Objects. Studies found that people are torn between the two poles what and who. Sometimes VBAs appeared as things, sometimes as entities, never entirely as one or the other. Guzman's [18] respondents continually shifted between the pronouns "she" and "it" when they talked about Siri. User comments about Alexa, depicted a mixed-use of these pronouns in the same comment [28], which was confirmed for other VBAs, too [4]. People simultaneously demonstrated social and anti-social behavior by directing bullying and sexual harassment towards Alexa [6]. Thus, it is assumed that this intermediate role between thing and subject irritates [16] the object-subject classification [26], evoking reflections about former boundaries [33, p. 2].

2.2   The Imbalanced Classification and its Equilibration

The Object–Subject Classification. According to Piaget's studies on genetic epistemology, the most fundamental way of classifying an object is figuring out if it is part of the "physicomorph" or the "psychomorph" scheme, which are diametrical poles of the same ontological classification. Turkle [33, p. 34] built on this understanding by suggesting a dichotomy of "physical and psychological properties [that] stand opposed to one another in two great systems." Gunkel [17] drew a similar conclusion by referring to Derrida's distinction of "who" and "what."

The *physicomorph scheme* refers to inorganic, non-living objects, which are sufficiently comprehensible in terms of precise, logical-mathematical categories, and deterministic causal laws [16, p. 233]. It results from empirical experience of physical perception or movement [26, pp. 29–30]. This scheme is "used to understand things" [33, p. 34], which are "mere instruments or tools" [17, p. 54]. A suiting question for an object classified into the physicomorph scheme would be: *What* do I converse with?

In contrast, the *psychomorph scheme* refers to subjects, which are living beings, equipped with capacities like thinking or feeling, and the potential of agency [26, p. 30], originating in the introspective experience of a conscious subjectivity. This scheme is "used to understand people and animals" [33, p. 34], and most of the time concerns "other persons" [17, p. 54]. The suiting question for this scheme would be: *Who* do I converse with?

Thus the classification of an object depends very much on whether the origin of certain phenomena can be explained entirely physically and logically or not. If a phenomenon cannot be explained as extrinsic, people assume intrinsic origins. Yet the intrinsic origins are situated in the object itself and remain unverifiable [17,32]. According to Piaget the differentiation between subject and object evolves in the process of biological development and engagement with the environment. That is, knowledge about an object "arises from interactions that take place mid-way between the two [object and subject, a. o. a.] and thus involve both at the same time" [26, p. 19]. However, the capability to distinguish between subject and object evolves over time [26, p. 21] and an object that was formerly assigned to the psychomorph scheme (i.e., subjects) may drop out of this scheme if the person "discovers an outside force that accounts for its motion" [33, p. 45].[1] Thus, equilibration is understood as an ongoing process, which continues over the whole lifespan. Hence, three conclusions can be made about the object–subject classification in the context of conversation: First, if an object is an alter ego can only be inferenced and mental states are imputed to objects that behave like subjects. Second, people are only assured of their own subjectivity and impute their own experienced origins of actions (e.g., thoughts, needs, desires, goals) to the object. Third, physicomorph and psychomorph schemes as well as assigned objects may change in time.

The Imbalanced Object–Subject Classification. If a new object does not fit into the existent classification, this classification is in conflict, provoking self-reflection about its boundaries [33, p. 2]. This concerns, the realization of what is possible in the existing schemes [2, p. 336] and the distinction between and organization of the classification's schemes. Transferred to artificial agents "new questions about the machine's 'life' and 'mind' [arise] and then ... wondering what was special about their [humans', a.o.a.] own" [33, p. 2]. Once a new object challenges the former well working classification, this irritation has to be eliquibrated.

Equilibration of Schemes and External Objects. Equilibration refers according to Cohen and Kim [8] to a balancing, self-regulating process resulting from an individual's response to (even the simplest) environmental objects or events. Inconsistencies or conflicts in schemes or subsystems[2] would trigger structural changes by placing the individual in a state of imbalance (which Piaget calls "disequilibrium"). The individual must physically or mentally engage with these objects and return to the state of balance (which Piaget calls "equilibrium") through assimilation and accommodation, but at a higher level. While assimilation refers to the acquisition of "new knowledge," accommodation indicates a real "progress of knowledge" [15, pos. 713] by changing people's understanding of the world.

In "The Equilibration of Cognitive Structures" – the final reformulation of his theory – Piaget describes three forms of equilibration: (1) equilibration between schemes and external objects concerning the functions of assimilation and accommodation, (2) equilibration among various schemes through the reciprocal assimilation and accommodation of schemes to each other, and (3) equilibration between individual schemes and the total structures of which they are a part of [7, pos. 1004]. I will subsequently focus on the first form, concerning the function of assimilation and accommodation.

---

[1] Although Piaget and Turkle refer to children, similar patterns could also occur in adults who are confronted with a new object, such as artificial agents.

[2] Complex levels of knowledge organizations in which schemes are combined.

Assimilation is the assignment of a new object to an existing scheme [26, p. 23]: In this paper the thing scheme or the person scheme. Although, the collection of objects in a scheme is expanded [15, pos. 714], the scheme itself is not [2, pos. 334]. Consequently, a VBA, assimilated into the thing scheme would be another example of a mere tool, such as a hammer or a chair, with emphasized features like non-liveliness or artificiality [11], and would be treated as such.

Accommodation refers either to the modification of a pre-existing scheme or the creation of a new one. Hence, possibilities in existing schemes are extended by applying them to new situations and objects [2, pos. 334]. Consequently, the existence of VBAs would expand the features of objects subsumed in the thing scheme or cause the creation of a unique VBA-scheme. In the first case, VBAs would differ from things as mere tools since they were, e.g., tools with a personality. In the second case, VBAs would differ from things *and* from persons due to a unique combination of characteristics (e.g., neither be non-living nor alive). In both cases, a new mix of social and non-social behaviors towards them would be developed.

2.3   Intermezzo: Human or Person Like Conversational Subjects?

While there is consensus about what the classification pole "object" refers to, it is more difficult for "subject." Since I cannot reproduce the full discussion on subjectivity in this paper, I will focus on the concepts of humanness and personhood, addressed in the above-presented theoretical and empirical work.

Conversational Subjects. If Piaget talks about subjectivity, he refers to human beings solely. However, if a conversational Other has to be a real human [16] or even human-like [20] is debatable. Within the framework of social interaction theory, 'conversation' refers to the abilities of interdependence and mutual orientation and an assumption about the Other's behavior as meaningful. That is, if Alexa is saying something in response to my question, I assume Alexa is not randomly making noise, but the sound are words with a meaning, oriented towards answering my question. Thus, conversational subjectivity transcends the ability to interact just effectively by interacting *meaningfully*. Meaningful behavior, however, is culturally determined [31] and closely linked to consciousness [30] and a theory of mind [27]. According to the concept of 'alter ego' in social interaction theory, its subjectivity can solely be inferred from observed behaving and implied advanced capabilities, primarily assigned to human beings. But is inferred subjectivity bound to humanness or human likeness? Or are there alternative concepts that cover the inference of subjectivity better?

In this paper, I argue based on Hubbard [20] that subjectivity refers to approved personhood rather than humanness or human likeness. I will explicate that being a "human" is a biological assignment to a species, whereas being a "person" is the approval of personhood, and thus culturally determined. While humanness cannot be applied to artificial agents – regardless how alike they are to humans – personhood can.

Humanness. Being a human derives from a *biological* systematic, referring to the genus Homo, a species from the family of great apes, which belongs to the order of primates and thus to the group of more sophisticated mammals. Therefore, whether one is a human being or not is a matter of heredity. Although the human species is associated with fundamental advanced capabilities, humans do not have to have the full range of these capabilities to be valid humans [20]. On the contrary, no matter if machines and other biological species have similar or identical advanced capabilities, they can, by definition, never be human.

Personhood. Being a person derives from a *cultural* definition and refers to the entitlement of personhood. According to Hubbard [20, p. 417], all human beings are, in the normative sense, entitled to at least some personhood, with granted rights like life, liberty, emotional well-being, and material prosperity, and for now only humans are entitled to any meaningful degree of personhood. Hence, persons are prevented from being owned by others and, on the contrary, allowed to own property, their destruction is outlawed as murder, and further moral norms are projected onto them. However, the author further argues that other objects such as animals and machines could be granted some degree of personhood [20, p. 440–441]. To be entitled to personhood, an object needs to exhibit behavior demonstrating "(1) the ability to interact with its environment and to engage in complex thought and communication, (2) a sense of being a self with a concern for achieving its plan of or purpose in life, and (3) the ability to live in a community based on mutual self-interest with other persons" [20, p. 419]. But, (human) personhood is gradual, resulting from humans (e.g., children, mentally or psychologically dysfunctional adults) who lack some of the crucial abilities and therefore are not entitled to the entirety of personhood [20, p. 413]. Transferred to Piaget's psychomorph scheme, this would suggest (1) that its pole refers to the advanced degree of personhood, (2) that the scheme may be conceptualized as gradual, and (3) machines could be granted personhood if they exhibit appropriate behavior and, therefore, could be included in the psychomorph scheme.

If conversational subjectivity refers to personhood rather than to humanness, Siri's assigned status as an entity [18] could refer to its status as a person of some degree. Because the respondent, as Guzman explicates, was well aware that Siri was not human. If it was not a person may not have been that obvious to the respondent. It could explain why people react socially towards computers or artificial agents, although they know they are not human [29]. Some degree of personhood, not humanness, would be the trigger for these reactions. Consequently, the paper follows the assumption that conversational VBAs are irritating the object-subject classification in terms of being "betwixt and between" [33, p. 29] the *thing scheme* and the *person scheme.*

3 Research Questions and Hypotheses

The paper aims at the classification of VBAs. Thus, I ask *how people classify voice-based agents in regard to the thing and the person scheme (RQ1).*

Previous research, concerned with the ontological classification of artificial social and conversational agents, found assimilation tendencies in the "spectrum from fully human to fully machine" [18, p. 227], visible, e.g., through the used personal pronoun "she" – emphasizing the classification as an entity – or "it" – emphasizing the classification as a device [18,28]. However, "it" was used by the majority of people, whereas only some favored "she" [28]. This preference for objectification was confirmed for social robots [11]. Therefore, I formulate the hypotheses: *VBAs are assimilated into the thing and the person scheme (H1). If they are assimilated, they are more often assimilated to the thing than to the person scheme (H2).*

Nonetheless, research on VBAs implies accommodation, too. In addition to the spectrum of Siri's classification, an "overlap in the middle" was identified, caused by the reconfigured "understanding of humans and machines to the degree that we now share characteristics" [18, pp. 227, 257]. The mixed-use of the pronouns "she" and "it" by the same person to refer to Alexa [28] confirms this observation. More implicitly some user reactions suggest accommodation through the simultaneous activation of social and non-social scripts, such as inappropriate, rude, or insensitive behavior toward artificial agents: People abuse social robots [3], and direct bullying or sexual harassment toward VBAs [6]. *Hence, it can be assumed that the thing–person classification is accommodated (H3).* However, the extent to which schemes are modified or unique combinations are created and the proportion of accommodation compared to assimilation are not yet documented by research. Consequently, two questions are added: *To what extent are schemes modified or merged (RQ2)? What is the proportion from assimilation and accommodation of the thing-person classification (RQ3)?*

Several moderating effects have to be considered. First, equilibration processes take place continuously [8] and may change during aging [26]. Second, some studies indicate that gender may powerfully affect perceptions and attitudes concerning technology [9,24]. Third, real interactions bear the risk of malfunctions and misunderstandings. Thus, positive expectation violations are less likely to occur, although only these may lead to greater subjectification [11]. Therefore, I ask: *How do previous experience, age, gender, and interaction quality affect the classification (RQ4)?*

4   Measurement

Ontological Classification. The measurement of the object–subject classification draws on the above-described diametrical relation of the thing scheme and the person scheme by asking: "What would you say, is Alexa [or the Google Assistant] rather like a thing (object) or rather like a person (subject) to you?" The continuum between the schemes was addressed by a 100-point scale[3], consisting of the two poles "thing (object)" and "person (subject)." The broad scale allowed

---

[3] Although the scale was continuously selectable, the first study offered orientation marks on the scale for every ten points. As this resulted in a slight distortion towards these orientation marks, they were no longer offered in the second study.

an intuitive answer – independent of the participant's (in)ability to verbalize the classification [33, p. 48], the detection of minor forms of accommodated schemes, and the differentiation of modification and hybridization (Fig. 1).

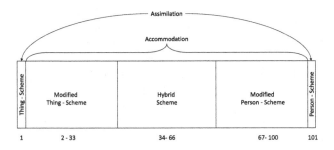

Fig. 1. The classification scale in relation to the thing scheme and the person scheme

Classification as result of *assimilation* into the thing or the person scheme, refers to the absence of any previous accommodation. That is, objects are added to the existing scheme (thing or person), but the scheme itself does neither get in conflict with the other nor does it change. The absence of accommodation and the unchanged scheme is indicated on the scale by the ratings of 1 or 101.

Classification as result of *accommodation* depends – even when new schemes or structures are established – on prior existing structures: "Absolute beginnings are never observed during the course of development and what is new is the result either of progressive differentiations or of gradual co-ordinations" [26, p. 34]. Hence it refers to the reaffirmation of "lines between categories" [33, p. 34]. Consequently, classification resulting from accommodation can be measured as (weak or strong) merging of the thing and the person scheme, implied by the distancing from the poles on the scale.

A weak merging is represented by ratings in the vicinity of the poles (2–33 and 67–100), indicating the *modification* of a dominant scheme by implementing elements of the other. Concerning the thing–person classification attributes of the person scheme may be added to the thing scheme. Hence, VBAs may be considered things that can think like a person but still inhabit dominant thing features. Consequently, VBAs and hammers belong to the same scheme (e.g., due to their artificiality) but differ in their ability to think.

A strong merging refers to a non-existent relevant dominance of either scheme, resulting in a genuine unification. Consequently, it is impossible to distinguish which of the two schemes has been modified to a greater extent. The word 'relevant' is crucial in this context because it implies a potential margin. The orientation towards one or the other scheme is much weaker than in the case of modification; thus, it is more a bias than a dominance. To distinguish this form of merging from modification, it is called *hybridization* implying the almost balanced mixture of formerly two diametrical schemes. Thus, a strong merging is represented by ratings located near the scale's center (34–66), indicating a hybrid scheme with a more or less balanced reunion of both schemes.

Sophistication of the Ontological Classification. To determine how sophisticated the equilibration process was, participants were asked how confident they were in their classification on a 5-point scale from "not sure at all" to "very sure".

Moderating Influences. To distinguish between people who may have had a couple of equilibration processes through prior regular interactions with the VBA from those who interacted for the first time, previous experience with the VBA was assessed. An *initial interaction* is indicated if people stated they have never had contact with the VBA before or solely knew the VBA from secondary sources like fiction or non-fiction media, advertising, or only had seen others using it. Previous *regular interactions* are indicated if people stated they had regular interactions before or owned the VBA[4]. Thus, three conditions can be distinguished: initial interactions without previous knowledge about the VBA, initial interactions with secondary knowledge about the VBA, and regular previous interactions. The *interaction's quality* was measured by two items (satisfaction with the overall interaction, and success in completing the task with the help of the Google Assistant), combined into one component ($\chi^2(1) = 58.936$, p < .001, both factor loadings = .92, KMO = .50, Cronbach's alpha = .79, Spearman-Brown coefficient = .80). *Gender* was measured by the options male, female, diverse and the possibility to not tell the gender.

5   Study 1: The Hypothetical Interaction

Sample. In late 2018, 1288 members of a large German university, recruited via the university's student and staff mailing lists, interacted in an imitated conversation with one of the commercial VBAs Alexa (Amazon Echo) or the Google Assistant (Google Home) in an online survey. The voice of both VBAs was female[5]. Participants had a mean age of 27 (ranging from 17 to 65 years), 52% were male, 47% female and 1% did not tell their gender. The majority (59%) had a Bachelor's degree, 38% had a Master's degree and 1% had a doctoral degree. Most participants already knew the name of their VBA (82%). However, only 18% have had previous interactions, whereas 63% had secondary and 19% none experience.

Procedure. Interactions were simulated to obtain impressions approximating a real conversation with the VBA. During this simulation participants received pre-recorded videos of the original answers of the Google Assistant or Alexa to predefined questions in the German language (Table A1). Before the interaction, participants reported on their experiences with various VBAs (including the assigned VBA). The interaction itself involved clicking on the question to be 'asked' to the VBA, followed by the corresponding video response. Afterwards the next question could be 'asked'. The final simulated interaction included

---

[4] Since none of the participants in both studies had regularly interacted with the VBA without owning it, too, regular interactions are referring to ownership in this paper.

[5] In 2018 the German voices of Alexa and Google Assistant were invariably female.

four video sequences (each between 7 and 17 s) for the assigned VBA, focusing on interaction features, previously promoted by Amazon or Google[6]. After the whole sequence, among other assessments, participants classified the VBA.

6   Study 2: The Real Interaction

Sample. In May 2019, 105 German participants interacted with Google Home – the voice-based speaker using the Google Assistant with a female voice. Participants had a mean age of 25 (ranging from 16 to 46 years), 44% were male, 42% female and 14% did not tell their gender. Most of the participants (70%) had completed a vocational training or were in the process of completing it, 18% had a Bachelor's degree, 5% had a Master's or a doctoral degree. Most participants knew the name Google Assistant (78%). However, 35% had have regular previous interactions, whereas 38% did have secondary experience, and 27% did not know the VBA or could not remember where they knew it from.

Procedure. During the interaction, participants cooperated with the VBA to solve an easy decision task. In the first phase (about five minutes), participants could get familiar with the device and the way the Google Assistant worked in the researcher's presence. They were given the activation key ("Hey, Google" or "OK, Google") and a shortlist of potential questions associated with the task. If problems or questions occurred, the researcher could be asked at any time during this phase. However, the researchers responded only with short phrases, avoided classifying terms (e.g., the adjectives 'using' or 'talking'), and referred to the Google Assistant solely by its name. The second phase covered a ten-minute interaction, which involved solving the task with the Google Assistant's help in the researcher's absence. Although this interaction was, basically, unobserved and unrestricted, the task ensured that the experiment sessions were approximately similar in content between the participants. After the whole interaction, among other assessments, participants classified the VBA.

7   Results

RQ 1. To assess the extent to which participants classified VBAs, the average classification and the distribution of ratings on the classification scale were used (Fig. 2). In the hypothetical interaction (HI) (M = 17.11, SD = 17.87, N = 1280) as well as in the real interaction (RI)(M = 15.22, SD = 20.13, N = 105), the VBA was classified in the vicinity of the modified thing scheme. Participants were very confident about their assessment, both in the HI (M = 4.38, SD = 0.88, N = 1279) and the RI (M = 4.59, SD = 0.74, N = 105).

However, the LOESS graphs (Fig. 2) indicate that as the distance from the poles (i.e., from the existing schemes) increased, participants became less confident, questioning their hybrid classification the most. The HI depicts a significant

---

[6] If a VBA provided multiple answers to the same question, one of them was randomly selected.

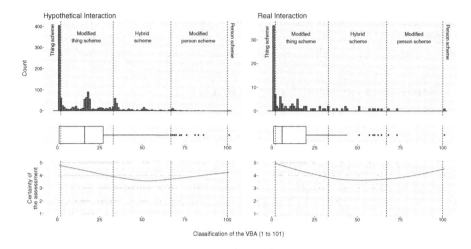

Fig. 2. Classification of the voice-based agent(s) and certainty in this assessment

decline in confidence as the classification moves from the pole "thing" towards the hybrid scheme ($r_{pb} = -0.51$, $T_{pb} = -20.28$, $p < .001$, $N = 1183$) and an ascent tendency as it converges to the pole "person" ($r_{pb} = 0.20$, $T_{pb} = 1.93$, $p = .056$, $N = 88$)[7]. The RI confirmed the decreasing confidence from the pole "thing" to the hybrid scheme ($r_{pb} = -0.52$, $T_{pb} = -5.87$, $p < .001$, $N = 95$) and (a not significant) increasing confidence with respect to the pole "person" ($r_{pb} = 0.41$, $T_{pb} = 1.27$, $p = .24$, $N = 10$).

Hypotheses. As predicted, participants depicted an assimilated (H1) as well as an accommodated classification (H3). In the HI ($N = 1288$) 32% had assimilated the VBA into the thing or the person scheme, whereas 68% depicted accommodation. Similarly, in the RI ($N = 105$) 35% had assimilated and 65% had accommodated. As predicted (H2), if the VBA was assimilated, it was more often assimilated into the thing scheme than to the person scheme. Of those who assimilated, 99.5% in the HI ($N = 406$) and 97.3% in the RI ($N = 37$) chose the thing scheme.

RQ 2. The degree of modification or hybridization is examined in the accommodated classifications ($N = 874$ of HI, $N = 68$ of RI). A majority of 71.7% (HI) and 77.9% (RI) modified their thing scheme. At least 24.6% (HI) and 19.1% (RI) hybridized and 3.7% (HI) respective 2.9% (RI) depicted a modified person scheme. Although modification and hybridization were similar in both studies, a detailed examination uncovered differences in the degree of the thing scheme's modification and the hybridization (Fig. 3). Whereas HI participants primarily modified the thing scheme moderately (50.2%), RI participants modified it only slightly (54.7%). However, if the classification was hybridized, 71.6% in HI had a

---

[7] The scale was divided in the middle (50), robust correlation tests using $\beta = .2$ and the measure of scale $W_{(m)}$ were conducted [34, p. 493].

thing-bias, in contrast to only 46.2% in RI. They hybridized more often (38.5%) than those of HI (17.2%) with a person-bias.

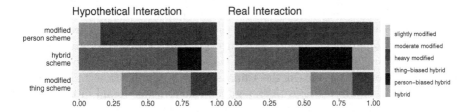

Fig. 3. Degree of modification and bias of hybridization of those who accommodated. To analyze slight, moderate and heavy modifications the areas consisting of 32 points each were divorced by three.

RQ 3. Regardless of hypothetical or real interaction, assimilation and accommodation were thing-dominant (Table 1). One third assimilated the VBA into the thing scheme, and almost half modified this scheme, while hybridization or a (modified) person scheme rarely occurred.

Table 1. Assimilation and accommodation of the VBA's classification

		Hypothetical interaction		Real interaction	
		n	%	n	%
Assimilation	Thing scheme	404	31.56	36	34.29
	Modified thing scheme	627	48.98	53	50.48
Accommodation	Hybrid scheme	215	16.80	13	12.38
	Modified person scheme	32	2.50	2	1.90
Assimilation	Person scheme	2	0.16	1	0.95

RQ 4. Gender had no impact on the classification (Table A4). *Age* and *previous experience* with the Google Assistant affected the classification solely in HI. In contrast, the *interaction quality* was influential in HI and RI. The younger the participants were, the heavier they modified, particularly those *aged* under 40 (Figure A1). Participants who did not *know* the VBA at all were more likely to classify it towards the thing scheme than those who knew the VBA from secondary sources or were regular users (Table A3). The better the *quality* was in RI or the more conversational it was in HI, the heavier people modified (Table A5). However, RI and HI differed in this point: While a too conversation-like sensation in HI weakened the modification, a particularly good quality in RI increased the modification tremendously (Figure A1).

8   Discussion

This paper has analyzed how people classify voice-based agents during conversations. By referring to Piaget [26] and Hubbard [20], an empirically measurable ontological thing–person classification, based on a gradual 100-point scale, was introduced. Using VBA as an example, the extent to which a more detailed understanding of artificial agents' classification can be achieved was demonstrated. It was uncovered that although VBAs were assimilated into being mere things, they more often caused the thing scheme's modification and revealed themselves as *personified things*. Although this pattern was found in hypothetical and real interactions, hypothetical interaction exhibited a stronger tendency of modifying the thing scheme, while real interaction had a more substantial effect on hybridization, was less thing dominant, but resulted as well in more extreme classifications.

Theoretical Contribution. Tests to verify the attribution of subjectivity rely on binary attributions, require the user's verbal skills [1], or include excessive scales [13], which might lead to an artifact of dynamics. The differentiation of assimilation and accommodation in the framework of equilibration allows to distinguish between the acquisition of new knowledge and a real progress in people's understanding of conversational agents. The results of this study indicate that the enforced assimilation into one of the extreme poles (yes/no, thing/person) is only meaningful for one-third of the respondents, while it may result in an over- or underestimation in two-thirds of the cases and may be the cause for oscillating allocations [18,28]. The gradual classification allows an intuitive measurement relieved of verbal skills and a forced binary. The origin of supposedly contradictory and weakly developed social behaviors can be better understood and predicted: Ritual social behaviors (due to a weak personhood in the modified thing scheme) can be distinguished from conscious social (in case of hybridization) or antisocial behavior (due to strong thinghood).

Practical Contribution. The acceptance of artificial voice-based agents depends on their classification as conversational partners. Depending on the area of application, however, the extent of this classification can vary, and in some cases, excessive subjectivity may be counterproductive. In this regard, a 'mere' assistant might differ from a companion. Therefore, it is necessary to understand its classified subjectivity. The presented scale can be easily integrated into surveys of hypothetical and real interactions to assess the amount of attributed thinghood or personhood, monitor the dynamic, and detect subtle shifts of the classification. The different equilibration levels reproduce for VBA and other social robots [11], indicating specific target groups that need to – and with the scale – can be addressed. It was shown that the classification of the (female) VBA was independent of gender, whereas age and experience may be essential predictors. Thus, the presented scale enables a more systematic target group approach, which can be associated with moral and normative values – independent of capabilities of verbalizing.

Limitations and Future Research. The empirical measurement has three limitations. First, the fine-granulated measurement of subtle modifications in a scheme works best with a high number of cases. Second, the scale's testing was limited to VBA. It remains to be clarified whether the discovered classification is specific to this technology or applies to artificial agents in general. Third, the choice of the diametric poles "thing" and "person" is, of course, debatable. The paper justified this choice. However, with Piaget, one can argue that "thing" and "person" represent not only schemes but also subsystems in which various other schemes (alive-not alive, animate-inanimate) are organized. It is conceivable that significant differences in both the included schemes and their organization can be identified within these subsystems.

Conclusion

With the equilibration theory of the late Piaget (1970) occurring modification and hybridization dynamics in human-machine communication can be observed. The present paper has focused on these processes' results and uncovered that VBAs are classified as *personified things*. However, the uncertainty of this classification indicates a still ongoing equilibration process. Due to its demonstrated applicability to a large number of participants, its independence from verbal capabilities, its potential to monitor dynamics, and understand differentiated social reactions, the object–subject classification scale contributes to the reinforcement of human-machine communication, and the expansion of the paradigm "Computers are Social Actors" (CASA).

Acknowledgments. I gratefully acknowledge the support and generosity of the Scholarship Program for the Promotion of Early-Career Female Scientists of TU Dresden, without which the present paper would not have been attainable. Furthermore, supplement material (Tables A1 to A5 and Figure A1) can be accessed via the study's repository on OSF, https://doi.org/10.17605/OSF.IO/GC3Z4.

References

1. Banks, J.: Theory of mind in social robots: replication of five established human tests. Int. J. Soc. Robot. **12**, 403–414 (2019). https://doi.org/10.1007/s12369-019-00588-x
2. Beilin, H.: Piaget's new theory. In: Beiling, H., Pufall, P.B. (eds.) Piaget's Theory (Jean Piaget Symposia Series). Taylor and Francis (Kindle edition ed.), Abingdon (1992)
3. Broadbent, E.: Interactions with robots: the truths we reveal about ourselves. Ann. Rev. Psychol. **68**, 627–652 (2017). https://doi.org/10.1146/annurev-psych-010416-043958
4. Catania, F., Beccaluva, E., Garzotto, F.: The conversational agent "Emoty" perceived by people with neurodevelopmental disorders. Is it a human or a machine? In: Følstad, A., Araujo, T., Papadopoulos, S., Law, E. L.-C., Granmo, O.-C., Luger, E., Brandtzaeg, P.B. (eds.) Chatbot Research and Design. Conversations 2019, vol. 11970 (2020). https://doi.org/10.1007/978-3-030-39540-7_5

5. Creed, C., Beale, R., Cowan, B.: The Impact of an embodied agent's emotional expressions over multiple interactions. Interact. Comp. **27**(2), 172–188 (2015). https://doi.org/10.1093/iwc/iwt064

6. Cercas Curry, A., Rieser, V.: #MeToo Alexa: how conversational systems respond to sexual harassment. In: Proceedings of the Second ACL Workshop on Ethics in Natural Language Processing, ACL, pp. 7–14 (2018). https://doi.org/10.18653/v1/W18-0802

7. Chapman, M.: Equilibration and the dialectics of organization. In: Beiling, H., Pufall, P.B. (eds.) Piaget's Theory (Jean Piaget Symposia Series). Taylor and Francis (Kindle edition ed.) (1992)

8. Cohen, L.M., Kim, Y.M.: Piaget's equilibration theory and the young gifted child: a balancing act. Roeper Rev. **21**, 201–206 (1999). https://doi.org/10.1080/02783199909553962

9. Crowelly, C.R., Villanoy, M., Scheutzz, M., Schermerhornz, P.: Gendered voice and robot entities: perceptions and reactions of male and female subjects. In: 2009 IEEE/RSJ International Conference on Intelligent Robots and Systems, St. Louis, MO, pp. 3735–3741. IEEE (2009). https://doi.org/10.1109/IROS.2009.5354204

10. Druga, S., Breazeal, C., Williams, R., Resnick, M.: "Hey Google is it OK if I eat you?" Initial explorations in child-agent interaction. In: Proceedings of the 2017 Conference on Interaction Design and Children (IDC 2017), New York, NY, USA, pp. 595–600. Association for Computing Machiner (2017). https://doi.org/10.1145/3078072.3084330

11. Edwards, A.: Animals, humans, and machines: interactive implications of ontological classification. In: Guzman, A.L. (ed.). Human-Machine Communication: Rethinking Communication, Technology, and Ourselves, pp. 29–49. Peter Lang (2018). https://doi.org/10.3726/b14414

12. Etzrodt, K., Engesser, S.: Ubiquitous tools, connected things and intelligent agents: disentangling the terminology and revealing underlying theoretical dimensions. First Monday **24** (2019). https://doi.org/10.5210/fm.v24i9.9700

13. Flensborg Damholdt, M., Vestergaard, C., Nørskov, M., Hakli, R., Larsen, S., Seibt, J.: Towards a new scale for assessing attitudes towards social robots: the attitudes towards social robots scale (ASOR). Interact. Stud. **21**(1), 24–56 (2020). https://doi.org/10.1075/is.18055.fle

14. Fortunati, L., Cavallo, F., Sarrica, M.: Multiple communication roles in human-robot interactions in public space. Int. J. Soc. Robot. **12**, 931–944 (2020). https://doi.org/10.1007/s12369-018-0509-0

15. Garcia, R.: The structure of knowledge and the knowledge of structure. In: Beiling, H., Pufall, P.B. (eds.). Piaget's Theory (Jean Piaget Symposia Series). Taylor and Francis (Kindle edition ed.) (1992)

16. Geser, H.: Der PC als Interaktionspartner. Zeitschrift für Soziologie, **18**, 230–243 (1989). https://doi.org/10.1515/zfsoz-1989-0305

17. Gunkel, D.J.: An Introduction to Communication and Artificial Intelligence. Wiley, New York (2020)

18. Guzman, A.L.: Imagining the voice in the machine: the ontology of digital social agents. Ph.D. thesis University of Illinois at Chicago (2015)

19. Horstmann, A.C., Bock, N., Linhuber, E., Szczuka, J.M., Straßmann, C., Krämer, N.C.: Do a robot's social skills and its objection discourage interactants from switching the robot off? PLoS ONE **13**(7) (2018). https://doi.org/10.1371/journal.pone.0201581

20. Hubbard, F.P.: "Do androids dream?": personhood and intelligent artifacts. Temple Law Rev. **83**, 405–474 (2011). https://pdfs.semanticscholar.org/5455/6cf31369a0885066d1ef8e52060906bd6c1c.pdf

21. Lee, K.M., Nass, C.: Social-psychological origins of feelings of presence: creating social presence with machine-generated voices. Media Psychol. **7**(1), 31–45 (2005). https://doi.org/10.1207/S1532785XMEP0701_2

22. Lopatovska, I., Williams, H.: Personification of the Amazon Alexa: BFF or a mindless companion? In: Proceedings of ACM CHIIR conference, New Brunswick, NJ USA, pp. 265–268 (2018). https://doi.org/10.1145/3176349.3176868

23. Moon, Y., Kim, K.J., Shin, D.-H.: Voices of the internet of things: an exploration of multiple voice effects in smart homes. In: Streitz, N., Markopoulus, P. (eds.) Proceedings of DAPI conference held as Part of HCI International, pp. 270–278 (2016). https://doi.org/10.1007/978-3-319-39862-4

24. Nass, C., Moon, Y., Green, N.: Are machines gender neutral? Gender-stereotypic responses to computers with voices. J. Appl. Soc. Psychol. **27**(10), 864–876 (1997). https://doi.org/10.1111/j.1559-1816.1997.tb00275.x

25. Newman, N.: Digital News Project. The future of the voice and the implications of news. Reuters Institute for the Study of Journalism & University of Oxford (2018). https://reutersinstitute.politics.ox.ac.uk/our-research/future-voice-and-implications-news

26. Piaget, J.: The Principles of Genetic Epistemology. Jean Piaget: Selected Works Volume VII. (Original 1970). Routledge (1997)

27. Premack, D., Woodruff, G.: Does the Chimpanzee have a theory of mind? Behav. Brain Sci. **1**, 515–526 (1978). https://doi.org/10.1017/S0140525X00076512

28. Purington, A., Taft, J.G., Sannon, S., Bazarova, N.N., Taylor, S.H.: "Alexa is my new BFF": social roles, user satisfaction, and personification of the Amazon Echo. In: CHI 2017 Extended Abstracts, Denver, CO, USA. ACM (2017). https://doi.org/10.1145/3027063.3053246

29. Reeves, B., Nass, C.I.: The Media Equation: How People Treat Computers, Television, and New Media Like Real People and Places. Cambridge University Press, Cambridge (1996)

30. Reichertz, J.: Von Menschen und Dingen. Wer handelt hier eigentlich? In: Poferl, A., Schröer, N. (eds.) Wer oder was handelt? Zum Subjektverständnis der hermeneutischen Wissenssoziologie, pp. 95–120. Springer Fachmedien, Wiesbaden (2014).https://doi.org/10.1007/978-3-658-02521-2_6

31. Schütz, A.: Der sinnhafte Aufbau der sozialen Welt. Suhrkamp, Frankfurt (1974)

32. Turing, A.M.: Computing machinery and intelligence. Mind **59**, 433–460 (1950). https://www.jstor.org/stable/2251299

33. Turkle, S.: The Second Self: Computers and the Human Spirit (Original 1984). (Twentieth anniversary edition). The MIT Press, Cambridge, Massachusetts London, England (2005). https://doi.org/10.7551/mitpress/6115.001.0001

34. Wilcox, R.R.: Introduction to Robust Estimation & Hypothesis Testing, 4th edn. Elsevier, Amsterdam (2017). https://doi.org/10.1002/jae.1194

Show, Don't Tell.
Reflections on the Design of Multi-modal Conversational Interfaces

Pietro Crovari$^{(\boxtimes)}$, Sara Pidó , Franca Garzotto , and Stefano Ceri

Department of Electronics, Information and Bioengineering, Politecnico di Milano, via Ponzio 34/5, 20133 Milan, Italy
{pietro.crovari,sara.pido,franca.garzotto,stefano.ceri}@polimi.it

Abstract. Conversational Agents are the future of Human-Computer Interaction. Technological advancements in Artificial Intelligence and Natural Language Processing allow the development of Conversational Agents that support increasingly complex tasks. When the complexity increases, the conversation alone is no more sufficient to support the interaction effectively, but other modalities must be integrated to relieve the cognitive burden for the final user. To this aim, we define and discuss a set of design principles to create effective multi-modal Conversational Agents. We start from the best practices in literature for multi-modal interaction and uni-modal Conversational Interfaces to see how they apply in our context. Then, we validate our results with an empirical evaluation. Our work sheds light on a largely unexplored field and inspires the future design of such interfaces.

Keywords: Conversational agent · Chatbot · Multi-modal interaction · Design principles · Interaction design

1 Motivations and Context

A chatbot is a user interface that communicates with the human being through the mean of Natural Language [6]. From the user perspective, chatbots are perceived as intuitive and efficient, since they can remove the friction of the interaction with the Graphical User Interface (GUI), and let the users focus on the task, rather than on the way they have to translate their intention into actions on the interface [35].

For this reason, chatbots are becoming ubiquitous in society. According to Radziwill and Benton, in the last decade more than one-third of online conversations involved a chatbot [31]. This trend is continuously growing; the authors in [14] predicted that soon people will prefer to interact with a chatbot to accomplish their tasks instead of using a "traditional" web application.

In recent years, the power of this technology has been combined with the latest technological advancements in subjects such as machine learning and

© Springer Nature Switzerland AG 2021
A. Følstad et al. (Eds.): CONVERSATIONS 2020, LNCS 12604, pp. 64–77, 2021.
https://doi.org/10.1007/978-3-030-68288-0_5

deep learning to develop chatbots for tasks with increasing complexity. Education, data science, data retrieval, and visualization are examples of application domains in which chatbots were successfully implemented to support the user [13,19,24,30]. When the task's complexity increases, both in terms of quantity of information treated and the number of operations to concatenate to accomplish the task, the conversation alone is no more sufficient in supporting the user. When the information that must be shown to the user starts to be consistent and heterogeneous, empirical evidence shows that the conversation is no longer sufficient for most users [18]. In the same way, when the design of the conversation is not linear but is constituted by several possible branches, the users must be given a hint of what they can do.

As a consequence, the urge for the introduction of new modalities arises. When dealing with written conversational agents (i.e., chatbots), the most natural integration is the visual modality through the addition of visual content aside from the natural language interface. In this way, the conversation is supported by a whole new channel that can be exploited to support the users and provide visual feedback. Even if multi-modal conversational interfaces are increasingly adopted, to the best of our knowledge, very little work has been carried out to understand how to design these interfaces optimally.

In this context, our research takes place. Starting from the design principles present in literature to create optimal conversational interfaces, we want to see how they adapt or must be modified in a multi-modal setting, in particular where the conversation co-exists with visual interaction. We ran a literature review to understand how the problem of integrating a conversation with other modalities was faced. The main contribution of this work is a set of design principles resulting from the performed literature review applicable to multi-modal conversational interfaces, particularly to the ones where the conversation is integrated with a GUI. Then, we provide a concrete example of how the principles can be used to design such an interface. Finally, the interface is preliminarily evaluated to assess the result's quality and gather precious insights into the design process.

These principles have an "heuristic" nature and have been elicited on the basis of both a literature review and by distilling the authors' experience on the design, development, and evaluation of several conversational applications [2–4,9–11,33,36,37]. Different authors have proposed or used different guidelines for chatbot design, but - to the best of our knowledge – a catalogue (and a validation) of the most relevant ones is still missing in the current state of the art. Our principles can be regarded as design guidelines that complement other, more generic heuristics proposed in HCI (e.g., Nielsen's 10 heuristics for inspection-based usability evaluation [26]) since they address chatbot-specific design principles and can be helpful for two main reasons: during the design stage, to use them as a checklist to enhance the usability of chatbot specific product features from early in development; during usability evaluation - at the prototyping or deployment stage, to support expert's inspection[1] of chatbot usability.

---

[1] Usability inspection is the generic name for a set of methods that are all based on having evaluators inspect a user interface [25], without involving user in the testing.

2   Design Principles

In this section, the design principles will be described carefully, to understand the underlying motivations and the consequences they imply.

To elicit these principles, we started from the best practices and the results in the literature for uni-modal conversational agents and multi-modal interfaces, to see if and how they apply for multi-modal conversational agents.

To accomplish our review, we proceeded as follows. We searched for relevant paper Google Scholar and Scopus engines, using the following query: *"(design principles OR guidelines) AND (conversational agent OR multi-modal interface)"*, filtering for paper published in the last 25 years (date > 1995). The resulting list was scanned to filter eligible papers according the following criterion: *from the title and/or the abstract it must be intended that the paper addresses the problem (also) from a design perspective.* 19 papers passed the selection process. To evict the principles, we read the documents integrally and we grouped them according to the design principles exploited in the described interfaces. This process originated seven recurrent themes that reflects the design principles for the design of multi-modal conversational interfaces reported in the paper.

Table 1. Design principles for the design of multi-modal conversational agents

	Design principles
P1	Show, don't tell
P2	Separate feedback from support
P3	Show information only when necessary
P4	Design a light interface—emphasize content
P5	Show one modality at a time
P6	Don't overload multiple modalities beyond user preferences and capabilities
P7	Use multi-modality to resolve ambiguities

Show, Don't Tell. The availability of more communication channels is the most immediate consequence of introducing new modalities in the interaction. Thus, the information can be conveyed to the user in multiple ways.

When dealing with a uni-modal conversational interface, the agent must be designed to be self-explainable. The conversation must contain all the information necessary to continue the interaction, such as the results of the previous operations and some hints on the possible next actions the user can choose. When the choices are many, and the results complex, the conversation becomes verbose, going to increase the length of the messages, or even the number of the interaction required to select the desired operation, consequently reducing the usability of the chatbot [39].

To overcome this problem, we take inspiration from the well-known literature principle *Show, don't tell*. This idea has been formulated over a quote said by the Russian playwright Anton Chekhov, who said that in narration things should not be described but shown through concrete examples [7]. In the same way, in a multi-modal Conversational Agent, information can be shown over multiple modalities, rather than being only textually described in the conversation itself. For instance, visual hints can orient the user through the conversation, giving a clear overview of the performed operations and removing the necessity of written summaries. Graphics can summarize the data retrieved through the conversations [41], and a table can summarize the choices with the previous utterances.

This technique brings a double advantage. In the design of the conversation, all the information reported through another modality can be omitted, creating shorter and more effective messages [18]. The number of messages can be reduced, reducing the cost of the conversations [39]. Second, the risk of loss of information in the conversation is minimized, since the meaningful one is conveyed exploiting the other modalities [41].

Separate Feedback from Support. A conversational agent typically provides two types of information to the user: feedback and support. The first comprises the results of the operations performed, whereas the latter illustrates what the user can or should do in the next interactions.

In a multi-modal interface, these kinds of information can be conveyed through different channels. For example, the results can be shown as graphs in a GUI, the completion of the operation can be represented through the change of the color of a button in the interface, the information on the operations the user can do can be embedded in the conversation or written in a dedicated pane.

According to the structure principle for GUIs introduced by Constantine and Lockwood [8], the users should have clear where to find the results they are seeking and where to look for support. Contrarily to the original principle, though, the division must be consistent not only between the modules of the interface but also between the different modalities.

Geranium [15] is an excellent example of a multi-modal conversational agent that exploits different channels for feedback and support. The application consists of an embodied multi-modal conversational agent for increasing the awareness of the urban ecosystem in children. The agent asks questions on the topic and comments on the answers. Children can choose the correct answer using a set of buttons that appears when the question is asked. When an answer is selected, the agent's avatar plays an animation that is happy or sad according to the given answer's correctness.

Show Information only When Necessary. The presence of multiple channels to communicate with the users can cause a cognitive overload with a loss of usability, if not used properly [34].

To prevent this problem, the modalities should be complementary in their content, without being redundant in their information [28]. We need to think of the conversation as a part of the multi-modal interface, and not as a stand-alone channel. In this way, the information can be distributed over the various channels, conveying the right information at the right moment and through the right channel. Otherwise, the repetitions created between the chatbot utterances and what is on the other channels create ambiguities in the interface, decreasing the usability of the system.

A good multi-modal chatbot design also deals with the removal of the information from the interface. When some data is no more necessary, it should be hidden to free space and lightening the cognitive burden.

This principle is widely adopted in Embodied Conversational Agents (ECA), where often the agents' utterances are transcribed in balloons that disappear when the interaction continues [5].

Design a Light Interface—Emphasize Content. Hearst and Tory [28] highlight how, when the user is engaged in the dialogue with a multi-modal conversational agent, the interface disappears to the user's eye since the only focus is on the provided data. A good design for such a chatbot is hence a design that minimizes the overall impact of the interface on the interaction. Only in this way users can fully concentrate on the focus of the conversation, which is the action they want to perform.

To satisfy this principle, the interfaces must be designed to have the main focus on the channel exploited to convey the information or the data. For example, if the chatbot is integrated into a dashboard for data visualization, considerable space has to be given to the graphs, instead of the conversation itself.

In the same study, the researchers noticed how the interface suddenly became the user's focus when it did not work correctly, or when the system gave unexpected (or undesirable) responses, as in the case of the interruption of the conversation flow. One example is when the dialogue reaches a dead end, leaving the task unaccomplished and the user unsatisfied [28]. This effect can be mitigated by a careful analysis of the dialogue tree, to ensure that each utterance can bring to a proper conclusion of the dialogue.

A good example is provided by Ava [20], a conversational agent that exploits this principle by presenting just two columns, one for the conversation and one for the generated Python notebook, where the interface almost disappears.

Show One Modality at a Time. Studies reveal that users, even if they like multi-modal interaction [28], in most occasions tend to interact with one mode at a time [27,29].

Multi-modal interaction with a chatbot should follow the same principle. The user should be requested to use only a modality at a time. The final task can be multi-modal, but the multi-modality should originate in alternating different uni-modal actions, and not vice versa. For example, a conversational agent for education can be embedded in a visual interface where the tasks are described.

After reading the assignment, students can dialogue with the chatbot to get to the solution, and then report the results in a separate dialogue box [21,38].

Even if the channels are not exploited simultaneously, the information conveyed through the others will influence the conversation. In many cases, the sentences will be simplified since complementary information will be exchanged through the other modalities. This consideration can support the design of the conversation; if a step is too critical or error-prone to be described with words, other modalities can be used instead.

Don't Overload Multiple Modalities Beyond User Preferences and Capabilities. If exploited properly, the multi-modality can facilitate the interaction for the user, but if the combination of channels does not result as natural and intuitive, it will only obstacle the accomplishment of the users' goals [12].

Thus, once the modalities have been established in the design phase of the conversational agent, it is fundamental to carefully decide the best channel over which the user can interact with the platform and the ones the system uses for providing the feedback. Additionally, similar interactions should involve similar modalities. For example, all the visualizations should be conveyed through the same pane, all the search results should be described in the conversation, and the possible action should be suggested through a dedicated list. This consistency will be appreciated by the user, that otherwise will remain unsatisfied from the interaction [16].

Every time the user or the chatbot sends a new message, this is added to the interface's conversation history. As a consequence, as the interaction continues, the amount of text in the dialogue grows, making the retrieval of information written in the messages always harder. For this reason, key information should be stored in other places than in the conversation to allow users to retrieve it at a glance.

AdApt [17] is an agent designed to support the retail sector, specifically the search for available apartments in Stockholm. Users can exploit two channels for the interaction: they can communicate vocally with the agent or interact with a map shown on the screen. Their Wizard-of-Oz study showed how users used different channels for different purposes, coherently with the system design.

Use Multi-modality to Resolve Ambiguities. Natural Language is ambiguous for its nature [32]. When the operations to perform become complex, these ambiguities can compromise the overall result of the interaction. New modalities can be introduced in the interface to eliminate this problem: when an ambiguity generates, the new modality can solve the ambiguity.

For example, in a music chatbot, the agent can make users listen to a short preview of the song to ensure the one the user is referring to [3]; in an e-commerce website the virtual assistant can show pictures of the product to understand the user's tastes and recommends items accordingly [23]; in end-user development, the conversation can ask to point out items on the screen to understand precisely what the user is talking about [22].

3 Exemplifying Our Principles

3.1 Case Study in the Bioinformatics Domain

We designed a multi-modal interface for an bioinformatics application in which the chatbot supports data retrieval and exploration. These are intrinsically complex tasks, for the complexity of the domain and because they require competence in search and analysis techniques, a common skill among computer scientists which often biologists and clinicians lack. This is a complex task since it requires a good understanding of Computer Science, skill that often biologists and clinicians lack [10]. For this reason, Bolchini et al. [1] highlighted the importance of a new family of tools that these users can use in autonomy. The proposed conversational agent is shown in Fig. 1.

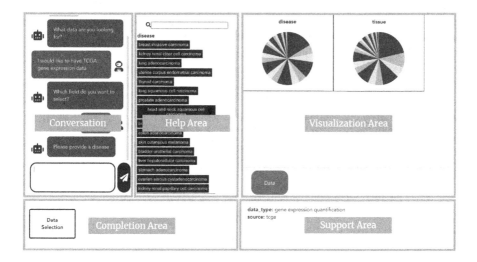

Fig. 1. The interface of the multi-modal chatbot we designed for the study. In the upper row the conversation takes place, next to the support and the visualization area. In the lower section, the completion and the support area helped the user during the interaction. Table 2 illustrates how the principles have been followed in the interface design.

The multi-modality is given by the conversational channel used as the mean tool for the communication and the visual channel used for user support, orientation, and feedback. The interfaces were designed carefully, following the described principles, as described in Table 2. The GUI was divided into five sections, divided into two rows, each one dedicated to a specific function. In the upper part, the conversation occupied the leftmost part, followed by the help and visualization area. In the second row, the completion and the support area took place.

The user could communicate with the system through the chatbot. At every step of the conversation, the help pane is populated with a set of information useful to support the user. For example, at the beginning of the conversation, the users are shown the possible operations, whereas when data are filtered all the possible values to filter are displayed. The user can click on the terms in this area to automatically copy them inside the chat area. When data are selected, descriptive summarizations are shown in the visualization area in the form of pie-charts. When the mouse pointer passes over the graphs, the name of the category and the count of its samples appear. The support area is populated with the query parameters selected by the user, such that the status of the query is comprehensible at a glance. Finally, when the operation has completed, the box in the completion area changes color to represent the end of the task. At the same time, a download button appears in the same box to export the retrieved data.

Table 2. Application of the principles in the define of the interface shown in Fig. 1

	Application of each principle in the design of Fig. 1's interface
P1	Different visualizations are used as feedback and orientation in the process workflow
P2	Help and visualizations are in different section of the GUI
P3	Information in the GUI is dynamically changed according the state of the conversation
P4	Interface is designed around the essential elements – no superfluous information
P5	Relevant information is showed only through one modality at a time
P6	Actions and functionalities are defined for every modality
P7	Hints in Help Area support users in the setting of parameters

3.2   Exploratory Study

We performed an exploratory study to verify that the close adherence to our principles results into multi-modal conversational applications that users perceive as usable and effective. To this aim, we developed a multi-modal interface that integrates a conversational agent in a GUI and was designed according to our design principles; then we ran a small (n = 16) empirical study, devoted to investigate the perceived aspects related both to usability (such as errors performed or task difficulty) and to conversation specific quality issues (such as understandability of the dialogue).

Subjects. We recruited 16 participants on a volunteer base (6 Female, 10 Male, avg. age: 28.61) through a mailing list of our research group's collaborators. These people have a heterogeneous background – mainly Computer Science and Engineering, Biomedical Engineering, and Biology – but with a shared research interest for computational genomics.

Procedure. Due to the current pandemic emergency, we ran an online survey. Participants had a link to the online platform, and one to the research survey. The survey was divided into sections. In the introductory one, participants were introduced to the procedure. They were then invited to use the platform to answer five tasks, described in Appendix A, and report the result in the questionnaire. Since no tutorial was given, users had to understand how to use the platform in autonomy. After completing the tasks, we invited participants to continue exploring the platform in autonomy as long as they believed to have discovered all the functionalities. In the last part, ten questions investigated the perception of the platform from the volunteers' perspective (Appendix B). Some of them asked the users to express their opinion in a grade from 1 (very low) to 5 (very high). In others, they could freely express their thoughts as text. All the conversations were anonymously logged in the backend.

Results. 13 participants were able to complete the study procedure. The other three had issues in the connection that could not support such a data-intensive process. Accounting all the tasks for all the participants, 85% of the tasks were accomplished. In general, users found the system easy to use (3.63/5) and intuitive (4.09/5), despite the difficulty of the tasks proposed. The modalities resulted well integrated into the system (4/5). All participants that completed the evaluation were able to find out all the ways to interact with the interface. From the analysis of the conversations, we see that the users preferred to communicate with the chatbot through keywords rather than with full sentences. Two participants did not even use a single sentence in the whole interaction, limiting themselves to a few nouns or adjectives per utterance. The most liked features of the system were the multi-modal interface (6/13), the ease-of-use (4/13), and the freedom of expression left to the user (2/13). The least liked ones were some bugs found in the conversation and in the Natural Language Understanding (4/13), and the fact that people felt a little constrained by the system's actual capabilities (3/13).

Discussion. The analysis of the above results allow us to comment on how adherence to design principles can enhance the power of chatbots. We are aware that the sample population does not fully reflect the target population of the final platform, as it includes several people with computer science training; prior work shows that people with higher levels of computer science training (or more advanced technical knowledge) results in them being more forgiving of failure [40]. However, modern biologists using bioinformatics analysis tools such as the ones accessed through our platform must also have a computational background, so we expect our results to be confirmed when we will be able to recruit a wider and more balanced set of evaluators.

Multi-modal channels of communication can provide new information that is hardly conveyed through the conversation alone [P1]. We provided the user with support information and visualizations, making the interaction with the conversation easier. Even if the subjects had background expertise in computer science, we don't believe this fact affects our findings, as the interaction with the platform does not require or expect any strong computer science skill, but only basic ability in file retrieval, which is well known to most biologists.

The introduction of the new interactions paradigm did not burden the users, who find our platform intuitive and easy-to-use. In fact, it enhanced the estimation of the "intelligence" of the platform making users disappointed when the conversational agent did not wholly match their expectations in terms of computational capabilities [P4].

The division of the interface in functional areas has been particularly appreciated, since it gave the possibility of understanding at a glance what had already been done and which were the possible next steps [P2]. The help area revealed particularly useful at the beginning when users were not confident with the possibilities offered by the system and played a pivotal role in making participants discover all the functionalities of the system. The users appreciated a lot the dynamically changing content of this area, capable of providing the right information at the right time [P3]. Visualization area acted at the decision-making level, informing the users on the selected data and therefore letting them make the best choices on how to continue the data exploration process. Participants liked the interplay of the conversation with two Help and Visualization Areas since, at every step of the conversation, they were able to find most relevant information on the visual interface, while they relied on the conversation only as a guide throughout the process [P5]. In addition, the support area was appreciated in the short-term strategy, since it allowed users to understand whether the users' utterances were interpreted correctly and the desired operations were executed successfully. As expected, the side effect of introducing a new modality was to make the users' sentences shorter, thereby easing the task of the Natural Language Understanding unit in the backend, which had simpler utterances to parse [P7].

On the other hand, new interaction modalities imply greater attention in the design of the interface. To guarantee the consistency of the information on the various channels implies a careful analysis of each moment of the interaction. At design time, it is necessary to have the complete description of every state of the system, what is shown to the user, and probably even more importantly, what is removed from the interaction. In fact, in an initial prototype of the system, we noticed how much the content not removed at the right time from the interface could induce confusion in the user, even if experienced ones like the chatbot's designer themselves [P6].

4   Conclusions

Chatbots are more and more exploited to accomplish tasks that are increasingly complex, e.g., in terms of process and amount of data involved. Still, conversation alone might not be sufficient and would benefit from the integration of other interaction modes. The introduction of additional modalities facilitates users who need to be supported continuously through the interaction, and can enrich structured assistance and feedback. Even if multi-modal conversational interfaces are increasingly adopted, in literature very little has been done to tackle the optimization of their design.

With this paper, we provided a set of guidelines on the design of effective multi-modal chatbots, which are summarized in Table 1. We started from multi-modal and conversational literature to elicit our principles and then verify them with a preliminary empirical evaluation.

We are aware that our work presents some limitations. First, our principles should not be seen as a guide, but be considered as a starting point on which the interface designer can reflect to produce the interface. Even if result of a comprehensive analysis, we tackled only the surface of this problem. Our work should be considered the starting point for a broader discussion that includes experts from different domains that can contribute to their point of view. Finally, even if promising, the exploratory study should be considered a preliminary step in evaluating the principles, given the small number of participants we were able to get involved in due to the pandemic emergency. For this reason, we will proceed with a complete usability evaluation with a wider sample including more biologists with limited technical skills.

Our contribution is a first attempt to shed light on a largely unexplored field. Within the bioinformatics domain, we will apply our principles to more complex tasks. We will then challenge our design principles by putting them at work in other domains, going beyond bioinformatics data retrieval. Finally we will continue our investigation on design principles, by broadening our approach and adding to the problem a multidisciplinary perspective, including in the discussion experts in related subjects such as cognitive sciences, linguistics, and psychology.

Appendix A: Tasks of the User Study

1. Can you extract the samples from TCGA with assembly GRCh38?
2. Try to download the URLs list regarding transcription factors for cervical adenocarcinoma.
3. Download the URLs list regarding h3k4me3 target extracted with chip seq.
4. Find and download the URLs for extracting the data regarding the simple nucleotide variation.
5. Explore the functionalities of the system in autonomy. List the functionalities you discovered.

Appendix B: Evaluation Questions

Open Questions:

1. What have you liked of the system?
2. What have you NOT liked about GeCo Agent?
3. Which were the main error you and/or the platform did?

Likert-scale Questions (scale 1 Totally Disagree – 5 Totally Agree)

1. Assigned tasks were difficult to accomplish
2. I found the platform easy to use
3. I found that the various functions in the platform were well integrated.

Yes/No Questions

1. Did you understand that you could click on the suggestion in the upper-central column to paste the text in the chat box?
2. Did you understand that you could answer just with the keywords (e.g.. "which data do you want?" - "Annotations")?
3. Did you understand that you could use sentences instead of keywords (e.g.. "which data do you want?" - "I would like Annotations")?
4. Did you understand that going with the mouse pointer over the pie charts you could see their details?
5. Did you understand that clicking on the download button that appears inside the box in the lower left panel you could download the URLs list file?

References

1. Bolchini, D., Finkelstein, A., Perrone, V., Nagl, S.: Better bioinformatics through usability analysis. Bioinformatics **25**(3), 406–412 (2009)
2. Catania, F., Di Nardo, N., Garzotto, F., Occhiuto, D.: Emoty: an emotionally sensitive conversational agent for people with neurodevelopmental disorders. In: Proceedings of the 52nd Hawaii International Conference on System Sciences (2019)
3. Catania, F., et al.: Musical and conversational artificial intelligence. In: Proceedings of the 25th International Conference on Intelligent User Interfaces Companion, pp. 51–52 (2020)
4. Catania, F., Spitale, M., Fisicaro, D., Garzotto, F.: Cork: a conversational agent framework exploiting both rational and emotional intelligence. In: IUI Workshops (2019)
5. Cauell, J., Bickmore, T., Campbell, L., Vilhjálmsson, H.: Designing embodied conversational agents. Embodied Conversational Agents **29** (2000)
6. Chandel, S., Yuying, Y., Yujie, G., Razaque, A., Yang, G.: Chatbot: efficient and utility-based platform. In: Arai, K., Kapoor, S., Bhatia, R. (eds.) SAI 2018. AISC, vol. 858, pp. 109–122. Springer, Cham (2019). https://doi.org/10.1007/978-3-030-01174-1_9
7. Chekhov, A.: The Unknown Chekhov: Stories & Other Writings Hitherto Untranslated. Macmillan, New York (1999)

8. Constantine, L.L., Lockwood, L.A.: Software for Use: A Practical Guide to the Models and Methods of Usage-Centered Design. Pearson Education, London (1999)

9. Crovari, P., Catania, F., Garzotto, F.: Crime story as a tool for scientific and technological outreach. In: Extended Abstracts of the 2020 CHI Conference on Human Factors in Computing Systems, pp. 1–10 (2020)

10. Crovari, P., et al.: Ok, DNA! a conversational interface to explore genomic data. In: Proceedings of the 2nd Conference on Conversational User Interfaces, pp. 1–3 (2020)

11. Cutrupi, C.M., et al.: Smemo: a multi-modal interface promoting children's creation of personal conversational agents. In: Proceedings of the 2nd Conference on Conversational User Interfaces, pp. 1–3 (2020)

12. Dumas, B., Lalanne, D., Oviatt, S.: Multimodal interfaces: a survey of principles, models and frameworks. In: Lalanne, D., Kohlas, J. (eds.) Human Machine Interaction. LNCS, vol. 5440, pp. 3–26. Springer, Heidelberg (2009). https://doi.org/10.1007/978-3-642-00437-7_1

13. Fast, E., Chen, B., Mendelsohn, J., Bassen, J., Bernstein, M.S.: Iris: a conversational agent for complex tasks. In: Proceedings of the 2018 CHI Conference on Human Factors in Computing Systems, pp. 1–12 (2018)

14. Følstad, A., Brandtzæg, P.B.: Chatbots and the new world of HCI. Interactions **24**(4), 38–42 (2017)

15. Griol, D., Callejas, Z.: An architecture to develop multimodal educative applications with chatbots. Int. J. Adv. Rob. Syst. **10**(3), 175 (2013)

16. Grudin, J.: The case against user interface consistency. Commun. ACM **32**(10), 1164–1173 (1989)

17. Gustafson, J., et al.: Adapt–a multimodal conversational dialogue system in an apartment domain. In: The Sixth International Conference on Spoken Language Processing (ICSLP), Beijing, China, pp. 134–137 (2000)

18. Hearst, M., Tory, M.: Would you like a chart with that? Incorporating visualizations into conversational interfaces. In: 2019 IEEE Visualization Conference (VIS), pp. 1–5. IEEE (2019)

19. Hobert, S., Berens, F.: Small talk conversations and the long-term use of chatbots in educational settings – experiences from a field study. In: Følstad, A., Araujo, T., Papadopoulos, S., Law, E.L.-C., Granmo, O.-C., Luger, E., Brandtzaeg, P.B. (eds.) CONVERSATIONS 2019. LNCS, vol. 11970, pp. 260–272. Springer, Cham (2020). https://doi.org/10.1007/978-3-030-39540-7_18

20. John, R.J.L., Potti, N., Patel, J.M.: AVA: from data to insights through conversations. In: CIDR (2017)

21. Kerlyl, A., Hall, P., Bull, S.: Bringing chatbots into education: towards natural language negotiation of open learner models. In: Ellis, R., Allen, T., Tuson, A. (eds.) Applications and Innovations in Intelligent Systems XIV, SGAI 2006. pp. 179–192. Springer, London (2006). https://doi.org/10.1007/978-1-84628-666-7_14

22. Li, T.J.J., Radensky, M., Jia, J., Singarajah, K., Mitchell, T.M., Myers, B.A.: Pumice: a multi-modal agent that learns concepts and conditionals from natural language and demonstrations. In: Proceedings of the 32nd Annual ACM Symposium on User Interface Software and Technology, pp. 577–589 (2019)

23. Liao, L., Zhou, Y., Ma, Y., Hong, R., Chua, T.S.: Knowledge-aware multimodal fashion chatbot. In: Proceedings of the 26th ACM International Conference on Multimedia, pp. 1265–1266 (2018)

24. Messina, A., Augello, A., Pilato, G., Rizzo, R.: BioGraphBot: a conversational assistant for bioinformatics graph databases. In: Barolli, L., Enokido, T. (eds.) IMIS 2017. AISC, vol. 612, pp. 135–146. Springer, Cham (2018). https://doi.org/10.1007/978-3-319-61542-4_12
25. Nielsen, J.: Usability inspection methods. In: Conference Companion on Human Factors in Computing Systems, pp. 413–414 (1994)
26. Nielsen, J.: Ten usability heuristics (2005)
27. Oviatt, S.: Mulitmodal interactive maps: designing for human performance. Hum. Comput. Interact. **12**(1–2), 93–129 (1997)
28. Oviatt, S.: Ten myths of multimodal interaction. Commun. ACM **42**(11), 74–81 (1999)
29. Oviatt, S., DeAngeli, A., Kuhn, K.: Integration and synchronization of input modes during multimodal human-computer interaction. In: Proceedings of the ACM SIGCHI Conference on Human Factors in Computing Systems, pp. 415–422 (1997)
30. Ritzel Paixão-Côrtes, W., Stangherlin Machado Paixão-Côrtes, V., Ellwanger, C., Norberto de Souza, O.: Development and usability evaluation of a prototype conversational interface for biological information retrieval via bioinformatics. In: Yamamoto, S., Mori, H. (eds.) HCII 2019. LNCS, vol. 11569, pp. 575–593. Springer, Cham (2019). https://doi.org/10.1007/978-3-030-22660-2_43
31. Radziwill, N.M., Benton, M.C.: Evaluating quality of chatbots and intelligent conversational agents. arXiv preprint arXiv:1704.04579 (2017)
32. Ratnaparkhi, A.: Maximum entropy models for natural language ambiguity resolution (1998)
33. Rouhi, A., Spitale, M., Catania, F., Cosentino, G., Gelsomini, M., Garzotto, F.: Emotify: emotional game for children with autism spectrum disorder based-on machine learning. In: Proceedings of the 24th International Conference on Intelligent User Interfaces: Companion, pp. 31–32 (2019)
34. Sarter, N.B.: Multimodal information presentation: design guidance and research challenges. Int. J. Ind. Ergon. **36**(5), 439–445 (2006)
35. Shawar, B.A., Atwell, E.: Chatbots: are they really useful? LDV Forum **22**, 29–49 (2007)
36. Spitale, M., Catania, F., Crovari, P., Garzotto, F.: Multicriteria decision analysis and conversational agents for children with autism. In: Proceedings of the 53rd Hawaii International Conference on System Sciences (2020)
37. Spitale, M., Silleresi, S., Cosentino, G., Panzeri, F., Garzotto, F.: "Whom would you like to talk with?" Exploring conversational agents for children's linguistic assessment. In: Proceedings of the Interaction Design and Children Conference, pp. 262–272 (2020)
38. Tegos, S., Demetriadis, S., Psathas, G., Tsiatsos, T.: A configurable agent to advance peers' productive dialogue in MOOCs. In: Følstad, A., et al. (eds.) CONVERSATIONS 2019. LNCS, vol. 11970, pp. 245–259. Springer, Cham (2020). https://doi.org/10.1007/978-3-030-39540-7_17
39. Walker, M.A., Litman, D.J., Kamm, C.A., Abella, A.: Paradise: a framework for evaluating spoken dialogue agents (1997)
40. Webster, J., Martocchio, J.J.: Microcomputer playfulness: development of a measure with workplace implications. MIS Q., 201–226 (1992)
41. Zhi, Q., Metoyer, R.: Gamebot: a visualization-augmented chatbot for sports game. In: Extended Abstracts of the 2020 CHI Conference on Human Factors in Computing Systems, pp. 1–7 (2020)

Social and Relational Chatbots

36 Questions to Loving a Chatbot: Are People Willing to Self-disclose to a Chatbot?

Emmelyn A. J. Croes[(✉)] and Marjolijn L. Antheunis

Tilburg School of Humanities and Digital Sciences, Department of Communication and Cognition, Tilburg University, Tilburg, The Netherlands
E.A.J.Croes@tilburguniversity.edu

Abstract. The aim of the current study was to determine if people are willing to self-disclose to a chatbot to the same extent as to a human interlocutor and to examine the role of four underlying processes, namely trust, social presence, anonymity, and shame. These aims were tested among 150 participants by means of an experiment with three conditions (chatbot, a human via CMC, or a human face-to-face). In all conditions, participants were asked nine questions to stimulate self-disclosure, which varied in terms of intimacy. The results revealed that participants had the most trust in a face-to-face interaction partner and felt the most social presence face-to-face. However, they felt most anonymous in the chatbot condition. Both trust and anonymity significantly mediated the effect of condition on self-disclosure. The findings of this study have important implications for the implementation of social chatbots for psychotherapy to support people with mental health problems.

Keywords: Self-disclosure · Human-chatbot communication · Social chatbots

1 Introduction

In order to give help to an increasing number of people suffering from mental health problems, chatbot applications such as Woebot and Wysa are on the rise. Chatbots are conversational programs designed to show humanlike behavior by mimicking text- or voice-based conversations [1, 2]. These so-called mental health chatbots are designed to be a sort of a virtual companion to its users and monitor the user's mood, by guiding them in disclosing their emotional state [3]. Hence, these chatbots should be able to give some support, are cost-effective, can have many interactions at the same time, are always available, and have infinite patience. The increasing use of these chatbots created to improve people's emotional well-being illustrates the need in society for such a technology. It is, therefore, important to better understand the potential of these chatbots in mental healthcare.

Crucial for the potential success of mental health chatbots is the user giving personal information to the chatbot. Chatbots have several affordances that may stimulate intimate self-disclosure, such as 24/7 accessibility, anonymity, and its non-judgmental nature [4]. However, there are also reasons to believe that these chatbots may hinder self-disclosure

© Springer Nature Switzerland AG 2021
A. Følstad et al. (Eds.): CONVERSATIONS 2020, LNCS 12604, pp. 81–95, 2021.
https://doi.org/10.1007/978-3-030-68288-0_6

of its users. The chatbot has several communication problems (no interaction memory, limited conversational skills) and due to a lack of Theory of Mind [5] and emotional intelligence, the chatbot can be perceived as distant and less reliable, which hampers intimate self-disclosure [6].

There are four important processes that may explain why people self-disclose and that may determine the success of chatbot therapy, namely trust, social presence, shame, and anonymity. The first is a patient's trust in their conversation partner. Only when an individual develops a trusting bond with his/her conversation partner or therapist, will he/she feel comfortable enough to self-disclose and experience the sequential benefits of therapy. Research shows that self-disclosure is closely linked to increased closeness, liking, and trust in text-based chatbot interactions [7]. Furthermore, the more personalized a chatbot is able to communicate, the more people trust the chatbot. Trust is one of the most important factors, along with empathy, in establishing a strong bond with someone [8].

Social presence, defined as the degree of salience of another person in an interaction [9], is also found to enhance self-disclosure. Social presence is believed to be highest in communication environments that allow for the transmission of verbal and nonverbal cues. The social presence theory (SPT) posits that the inability to transmit nonverbal cues in conversation impairs impression formation. Specifically, social presence is believed to enhance involvement in an interaction, which results in more psychological closeness [10]. Although research shows that people are able to experience social presence in reduced-cues environments, it is widely accepted that especially nonverbal, visual cues enhance social presence. It therefore remains unclear whether people are able to experience social presence when conversing with a chatbot, and whether this will enhance self-disclosure.

Another important affordance of chatbot communication, especially text-based chatbots, is anonymity, which may, in turn, stimulate self-disclosure. When communicators feel less identifiable in interactions, they may become less concerned with social evaluation, which may lead to more intimate disclosures [11]. Specifically, feeling anonymous can be important when sharing sensitive issues [12]. In mediated interactions, like chatbot communication, communicators need less social skills to communicate and may feel more in control of the interaction, which enhances a sense of anonymity [13]. Feeling anonymous can make it easier to manage the information one shares about oneself and can lower the threshold to share intimate information. Chatbot communication may evoke the ultimate sense of anonymity, as people are conversing in a mediated environment to a non-human entity [14]. This may stimulate self-disclosure more so than a computer-mediated environment.

Finally, perceived shame may also determine whether people feel comfortable enough to self-disclose. Self-disclosure is a risky process because it can entail an element of secrecy [15]. Certain information people disclose about themselves, especially in psychotherapy, could be embarrassing if shared widely. With every self-disclosure, individuals risk disconfirmation, invalidation and even ridicule. It may be that people experience less shame when interacting with a chatbot, compared to a human interlocutor. After all, the chatbot is non-judgmental which reduces people's fear to self-disclose potentially sensitive information [4]. Chatbots cannot be offended and will never get tired of listening to someone's problems, which allows people to talk freely without being judged [14]. Hence, chatbot communication may reduce perceived shame, which may enhance self-disclosure.

The aim of this study is to experimentally test if people are willing to self-disclose to the same extent as they are willing to disclose to a person either face-to-face (FTF) or via online chat. Furthermore, this study aims to investigate the validity of four potential mediators (i.e., trust, social presence, anonymity, and shame) that may account for the effects of interaction partner (text-based chatbot, human FTF, human online chat) on self-disclosure. In doing so, this study contributes to the existing computer-mediated communication (CMC), interpersonal communication, and chatbot communication literature, by determining whether the processes previously found in CMC that facilitate self-disclosure, also play a role in human-chatbot communication. Previous research has compared either CMC and FTF communication [12], or CMC and human-chatbot communication [4], while the present study compares all three interaction modes to get a more comprehensive picture of what facilitates the self-disclosure process. Potentially, talking to a non-human interaction partner may result in a safer and more anonymous environment, which can enhance self-disclosure. However, chatbots may also decrease a sense of social presence, which can impede self-disclosure. It is therefore important to investigate which processes stimulate people to self-disclose, depending on both the interaction environment and the interaction partner.

2 Theoretical Background

2.1 Social Chatbots

While functional, customer service chatbots work very well in a specific domain, social chatbots are designed to keep people company and build an emotional connection with its users [16]. In doing so, it is crucial that the chatbot is able to detect emotions and respond in an adequate way [17]. Social chatbots attempt to connect with their users by asking questions, gathering information and keeping the conversation going so that people want to keep interacting with the chatbot [16]. A profound advantage of social chatbots over more functional chatbots is that they are able to recognize emotions in social interactions and are able to respond in an empathic way [18].

Social chatbots can thus be employed in therapeutic settings and there is an increasing scientific interest in whether chatbots are capable of offering good quality support [19, 20, for instance]. Research shows that people evaluate chatbot therapy as less valuable and enjoyable compared to regular human-human therapy [19]. In contrast, other research shows that social chatbots are able to offer decent and effective support to individuals in behavioral therapy [20]. Furthermore, research shows that a social chatbot is an accessible and effective tool to support people in psychotherapy [21]. Moreover, research also shows that social chatbots may be effective to help people with depression and to ensure people with psychological problems to not deteriorate [22]

2.2 Self-disclosure in Chatbot Interactions

Self-disclosure, one of the most important conditions of effective therapy, is defined as the act of revealing personal information to others [23]. The act of disclosing personal information involves risk and vulnerability on the part of the discloser, which increases the likelihood of mutual bonding. As people disclose more intimate information, they develop stronger relationships [24]. When one person discloses personal information to another, it is likely that this disclosure is reciprocated which means mutual trust and understanding is enhanced. Furthermore, self-disclosure can create a feeling of relief in the discloser [25]. Technological developments, like chatbots, can lower the threshold for people to engage in self-disclosure, which is found more frequently in computer-mediated interactions [26].

Studies reveal that text-based CMC stimulates intimate self-disclosure [26, 27. for instance]. Additionally, research shows that people share more sensitive information in a depersonalized questionnaire [28] and that people tend to shy away from sharing negative emotions about themselves when their interaction partner is visually visible to them [29]. Thus, people are expected to share more intimate information when interacting with a chatbot, compared to when they are conversing with another human face-to-face. Research supports this contention, as it reveals that people prefer to disclose sensitive or personal information with a chatbot compared to a human interviewer [30]. This is especially the case when the chatbot is involved and shows empathy, as an empathic response ensures someone feels understood, which can enhance the relief they experience [31]. An important advantage of chatbot communication over human communication, is that chatbots are unable to share someone's secrets with other people, which can enhance trust [32]. Chatbot communication can be seen as the ultimate form of anonymity; people are not only visually anonymous, they are unable to see their conversation partner, which can stimulate self-disclosure [28]. Previous research shows that CMC stimulates self-disclosure [26], but for the reasons outlined above, human-chatbot interactions may result in *more* self-disclosure. Thus, we formulate the following hypothesis:

H1: People self-disclose more to a chatbot, compared to a human in CMC and a human FTF.

2.3 Trust in a Social Chatbot

There are a number of social processes that may facilitate self-disclosure and help develop a bond between a person and the therapist. An interpersonal bond is formed through mutual understanding and acceptance and includes elements of honesty, safety and trust [33]. As relationships become deeper and more intimate, communicators become more involved and interpersonal trust develops [34]. Intimacy is strongly related to trust and source credibility. Qualitatively better interactions with a strong sense of comfort are those that promote higher levels of credibility and trust, which enhances the likeability of the interaction partner [35]. Furthermore, greater trust is linked to more self-disclosure [36].

The question is, if individuals are able to trust a chatbot as much as, if not more than, a human interlocutor. Chatbots with unpredictable attitudes can create a strong sense of discomfort in its users. However, chatbots with consistent personalities are seen as more predictable and, thus, more trustworthy [7]. In addition, chatbots that show emotion are generally perceived as more likeable and trustworthy, compared to non-emotional chatbots [8]. Empathic chatbots are also seen as more trustworthy and supportive than non-empathic chatbots [37]. Moreover, importantly, since chatbots are machines and not people, it may be easier for individuals to trust that the information they share with the chatbot will not 'leak' into the real world [14]. Therefore, we expect the following:

H2: People have more trust in a chatbot as an interaction partner, compared to a human in CMC and a human FTF, which, in turn, results in more self-disclosure with the chatbot.

2.4 Social Presence in Chatbot Interactions

Social presence is closely related to interpersonal trust and is defined as "the feeling of being with another in a mediated environment" [37, p. 14]. The more cues, and especially visual cues, a communication environment offers, the more social presence interactants experience [9]. This suggests that text-based chatbot interactions would evoke less social presence than communicating with another human in CMC and FTF communication (the richest form of communication). In fact, research has shown that when people talk to someone whom they believe is another person they experience more social presence, compared to when they believe their interaction partner is a robot [38].

Social presence is believed to have many positive psychological effects and leads to more involved communicators and more intimacy [39]. The more social presence people experience, the closer they feel [40]. Furthermore, social presence is believed to make messages exchanged between people more intimate and emotional. This suggests that social presence enhances intimate self-disclosure. Thus, we expect the following:

H3: People feel less social presence in human-chatbot interactions, compared to human-human interactions via CMC and FTF interactions, which, in turn, results in less self-disclosure in human-chatbot interactions.

2.5 Perceived Anonymity in Chatbot Interactions

Research shows that CMC channels provide controllability and anonymity, which allows individuals to express themselves more freely and honestly compared to FTF communication [41]. Chatbot communication may be even perceived as more anonymous compared to CMC as a chatbot is an artificial interaction partner, will not share any information with other people and will keep your secrets [14]. Self-disclosures will thus never be revealed to the outside world, which can make people feel safe to share intimate information. As a chatbot does not have feelings, people may find it easier to open up, as the chatbot will not judge or condemn its users. Furthermore, this anonymity can lower the threshold for people to share intimate information, which is especially relevant in a mental health setting [42]. Thus, anonymity may enhance self-disclosure, especially in interactions with a chatbot, which is why we expect the following:

H4: People feel more anonymous in human-chatbot interactions, compared to human-human interactions via CMC and FTF interactions, which, in turn, results in more self-disclosure in human-chatbot interactions.

2.6 Perceived Shame in Chatbot Interactions

Finally, when people feel ashamed to self-disclose they may refrain from doing so. Chatbot communication may lower the threshold to self-disclose, which may be due to the fact that people do not experience much shame. A chatbot is a non-judgmental listener, which means people experience less fear of being judged and, hence, less shame when they self-disclose [4]. Furthermore, chatbots cannot be offended, will never get tired of listening to someone's problems, foster a safe environment to vent and will not respond to someone in a negative way. As said, self-disclosure is a risky process, which may involve information people are embarrassed to share. When talking to a chatbot, people may feel safer to disclose and less ashamed, which is why we pose the following hypothesis:

H5: People experience less shame in human-chatbot interactions, compared to human-human interactions via CMC and FTF interactions, which, in turn, results in more self-disclosure in human-chatbot interactions.

3 Method

3.1 Participants

In total, 150 participants participated in this experiment of which 66 male (44%) and 84 female (56%). Participants were, on average, 21.97 years old ($SD = 3.15$). The majority of the participants indicated that their highest level of education was university (76.7%), followed by a university of applied science degree (12%) and a high school degree (7%). Regarding chatbot experience, most of the participants indicated that they communicated with a chatbot several times a year (63.3%), followed by 23.3% who indicated that they have never communicated with a chatbot before. 12% of participants interacted 1–2 times per month with a chatbot and only 1 participant communicated 2–3 times a week with a chatbot. The majority of chatbot interactions were for the purpose of customer service (72.7%), followed by online shopping (19.3%) and fun or entertainment (8.7%). We deliberately chose for a (largely) student sample as students are technology savvy and, therefore, confident and competent in the use of digital devices.

3.2 Design

The experiment consisted of three conditions with a between-subjects design. Participants were randomly assigned to one of the experimental conditions. The conditions were: a human-chatbot condition, a human-human CMC condition, and a human-human FTF condition. In the human-chatbot condition, participants chatted with a chatbot via text. In the CMC condition, participants chatted with another human being via a text-based chat. In the FTF condition, participants sat in a room at a table across from a female confederate with whom they had a conversation.

3.3 Procedure and Materials

After signing informed consent, all participants first filled out a pretest questionnaire with demographic questions along with questions about the participants' personality and their experience with chatbots. Next, participants were randomly asked to have a conversation with either a chatbot, a human via CMC, or a human FTF. In the chatbot condition (1) participants chatted with a chatbot via Facebook. The chatbot that was used in this study was built in Flow.ai, which is a platform to design chatbots. In order to allow unlimited word entry, the chatbot was connected to Facebook, using an application programming interface (API). Two Facebook accounts were created. One to connect the chatbot, and one for the participants to communicate with the chatbot. The screen name of the participants' Facebook was 'Participant'. The screenname of the chatbot was Chatbot TU and the name the chatbot introduced itself with was 'Robin', as this is a gender-neutral name. The chatbot did not have a profile picture; the profile picture was a standard Facebook icon, shown when users do not upload a profile picture. Participants talked to the chatbot via Facebook Messenger. They were instructed beforehand that they would be talking to a chatbot. The interaction took place on a computer in the lab, which was already signed into the account. Participants did not receive any credentials related to the account, nor did they have to sign in to Facebook themselves. In the CMC condition (2), participants communicated via the chat function in Skype. To do so, an anonymous Skype-account was created. The name of the account for the participant was 'Participant' and the person they were chatting to was also called 'Robin', a confederate in the experiment. The procedure of this condition was similar to the chatbot condition; the only difference was that the participants were aware that they were communicating with a real human being instead of a chatbot. In the FTF condition (3) participants sat in a room at a table across from a female confederate who greeted them and started the conversation by asking the first question.

All three conditions were question and answer sessions, in which participants were asked nine questions by the interaction partner, in order to provoke self-disclosure. Participants were instructed to only answer the question, without asking any questions back. They were also told that their interaction partner would not respond to their answers. The questions were derived from previous research [43] which used 36 questions as a means to generate closeness (*36 questions to love*). The 36 questions were divided into three sets of twelve questions. For the current experiment, three questions from each set were used. In all three conditions, the same nine questions were asked. After participants had answered all nine questions, the conversation ended and they were led to a room to fill out a posttest questionnaire with measurements for the variables of interest for this study.

3.4 Self-report Measures

All self-report measures were measured on a 5-point Likert Scale ($1 = $ *totally disagree*, $5 = $ *totally agree*). First, self-disclosure was measured with the following statements [44] (1) 'During the conversation I was able to share personal information about myself', (2) 'During the conversation I felt comfortable sharing personal information' (3) 'During the conversation it was easy to share personal information', (4) 'During the conversation I felt that I could be open' ($M = 3.50$; $SD = .96$; $\alpha = .91$).

Trust was measured by means of four statements [45]: (1) 'My conversation partner was honest', (2) 'My conversation partner was trustworthy', (3) 'My conversation partner was understanding', and (4) 'My conversation partner had good intentions' ($M = 3.16$; $SD = 0.62$; $\alpha = .70$).

Social presence was measured with seven statements [46, 47]: (1) 'During the conversation I was able to respond to the reactions of my conversation partner', (2) 'During the conversation I felt that I was face to face with my conversation partner', (3) 'During the conversation I felt as if I was in the same room as my conversation partner', (4) 'During the conversation my conversation partner came across as "real"', (5) 'During the conversation I felt that I could really get to know my conversation partner', (6) 'During the interview I felt that I was having a conversation with a social being', (7) 'During the conversation I felt that I was having a conversation with an intelligent being' ($M = 2.60$; $SD = 0.93$; $\alpha = .88$.)

The anonymity scale consisted of seven items [48–50] : (1) 'During the conversation I felt like my conversation partner did not know me', (2) 'During the conversation I felt like my conversation partner recognized me' (*reverse-coded*), (3) 'During the conversation I felt like my personal identity was not visible to my conversation partner', (4) 'During the conversation I felt anonymous', (5) 'During the conversation I felt unrecognizable', (6) 'During the conversation I did not feel identifiable', and (7) 'During the conversation I felt like I could share more about myself because my conversation partner did not know me' ($M = 2.99$, $SD = 0.77$; $\alpha = .79$).

Perceived shame was measured by means of four statements [51]: (1) 'I experienced shame during the conversation', (2) 'During the conversation I worried about what my conversation partner thought of me', (3) 'During the conversation I concealed who I truly am', and (4) 'During the conversation I sometimes felt ashamed about what I shared with my conversation partner' ($M = 2.32$, $SD = 0.94$; $\alpha = .66$).

4 Results

To investigate the effect of condition on self-disclosure and whether this can be explained by trust, anonymity, social presence, or shame, a mediation analyses was performed in SPSS using the procedures developed by Preacher and Hayes (PROCESS) [52]. In the analysis, 'condition' was entered as a predictor for self-disclosure and trust, anonymity, social presence and shame were entered as mediators. For the analysis, the categorical 'condition' variable was recoded into two dummy variables, namely for the 'chatbot condition' (1 = chatbot, 0 = CMC and FTF) and the 'CMC condition' (1 = CMC, 0 = chatbot and FTF). The FTF condition served as the reference group.

The first hypothesis proposed that people disclose more information to a chatbot, compared to a human in CMC and a human FTF. The analysis revealed that the effect of both the chatbot condition ($b = -.01$, $SE = 0.22$, $p = .950$) and the CMC condition ($b = .19$, $SE = 0.20$, $p = .349$) on self-disclosure was not significant. Therefore, H1 was not supported.

The means and standard deviations are displayed in Table 1.

H2 proposed that trust would be a mediator in the relationship between condition and self-disclosure. Although we did not find a significant direct effect of condition on self-disclosure, we could still find significant mediating effects. First, we found a direct effect of both the chatbot condition ($b = -.68$, $SE = 0.11$, $p < .001$) and the CMC condition ($b = -.59$, $SE = 0.11$, $p < .001$) on perceived trust. As the means in Table 1 show, people had the most trust in a FTF interaction partner, followed by a

Table 1. Means and standard deviations

	FTF	CMC	Chatbot
Dependent variable	M (SD)	M (SD)	M (SD)
Self-disclosure	3.64 (0.75)	3.50 (1.03)	3.36 (1.07)
Trust	3.58 (0.56)	3.00 (0.52)	2.90 (0.54)
Social presence	3.49 (0.64)	2.32 (0.66)	2.01 (0.73)
Anonymity	2.67 (0.61)	3.03 (0.73)	3.27 (0.86)
Shame	2.31 (0.88)	2.44 (1.07)	2.21 (0.85)

human in CMC, and finally the chatbot. Furthermore, trust was found to significantly impact self-disclosure, $b = .53$, $SE = 0.14$, $p < .001$. As expected, trust explained a significant portion of the effect of condition on self-disclosure. More specifically, the indirect effect for the chatbot condition was $b = -0.36$, $SE = 0.13$, 95% BCa CI [-0.62, -0.13] and the indirect effect for the CMC condition was $b = -0.31$, $SE = 0.12$, 95% BCa CI $[-0.56, -0.11]$. However, contrary to our expectations, both indirect effects were negative. This suggests that trust positively impacted self-disclosure in the FTF condition, but had a negative impact in the chatbot and CMC condition. Therefore, H2 could not be supported.

H3 posed that people feel less social presence in human-chatbot interactions, compared to human-human interactions via CMC and FTF interactions, which, in turn, results in less self-disclosure in human-chatbot interactions. The analysis revealed a direct effect of the chatbot condition ($b = -1.47$, $SE = 0.14$, $p < .001$) and the CMC condition ($b = -1.17$, $SE = 0.14$, $p < .001$) on social presence. As expected, people experienced the most social presence in the FTF condition, followed by the CMC condition and, finally, the chatbot condition (see Table 1 for the means). However, social presence did not significantly impact self-disclosure, $b = 0.12$, $SE = 0.12$, $p = .312$. In addition, the indirect effect of condition on self-disclosure via social presence was not significant either ($b = -.18$, $SE = 0.21$, 95% BCa CI $[-0.61, 0.21]$ for the chatbot condition; $b = -.14$, $SE = 0.16$, 95% BCa CI $[-0.48, 0.17]$ for the CMC condition). So H3 was only partially supported.

H4 predicted that people feel more anonymous in human-chatbot interactions, compared to human-human interactions in CMC and FTF interactions, which, in turn, results in more self-disclosure in human-chatbot interactions. We found a direct effect of the chatbot condition ($b = .60$, $SE = 0.15$, $p < .001$) and the CMC condition ($b = .36$, $SE = 0.15$, $p = .015$) on perceived anonymity (see Table 1 for the means). People felt most anonymous in the chatbot condition, followed by the CMC condition and, finally, the FTF condition. Additionally, anonymity had an effect on self-disclosure, $b = .42$, $SE = 0.10$, $p < .001$. Furthermore, the indirect effect of condition on self-disclosure via anonymity was also significant. The indirect effect for the chatbot condition was $b = .25$, $SE = 0.09$, 95% BCa CI [0.10, 0.46] and for the CMC condition $b = 0.15$, $SE = 0.07$, 95% BCa CI [0.04, 0.31]. This suggests that in both the chatbot and the CMC condition anonymity explained the effect on self-disclosure, and this effect was stronger in the chatbot condition. Thus, H4 was supported.

The final hypothesis proposed that people experience less shame in human-chatbot interactions, compared to human-human interactions via CMC and FTF interactions, which, in turn, results in more self-disclosure in human-chatbot interactions. The analysis showed that the direct effect of the chatbot condition ($b = -.10$, $SE = 0.19$, $p = .595$) and the CMC condition ($b = .13$, $SE = 0.19$, $p = .478$) on perceived shame was not significant. Furthermore, both indirect effects of the chatbot condition ($b = .02$, $SE = 0.04$, 95% BCa CI [-0.06, 0.12]) and the CMC condition ($b = -.03$, $SE = 0.04$, 95% BCa CI [-0.14, 0.06]) on self-disclosure via perceived shame were not significant either. So H5 could not be supported.

5 Discussion

The aim of the current study was to determine (1) if people are willing to self-disclose to a chatbot to the same extent as to a human interlocutor and (2) the role of four underlying processes that may explain this self-disclosure, namely trust, social presence, anonymity, and shame.

Our findings revealed no differences between the three conditions concerning self-disclosure. This suggests that people are equally willing to disclose to a human inter-locutor and a chatbot. Additionally, we found that trust and anonymity both impacted self-disclosure: when people trusted their interaction partner more and when they felt more anonymous, they self-disclosed more. However, trust was found to be highest in the FTF condition, which is contrary to what we expected. We believed that people would trust a chatbot more than a human interaction partner, as a chatbot will never leak the information you share to other people [14]. Previous research, however, also shows the importance of nonverbal cues in establishing trust [53]. It may thus be that nonverbal cues play a more important role in trust, than the artificiality of the interaction partner.

Furthermore, in line with our expectations, we found that people self-disclosed in the chatbot condition because they felt more anonymous. As predicted, chatbot communication creates a sense of ultimate anonymity, more so than communicating with another human using the same modalities. In the literature, anonymity is central to explain why people self-disclose more in reduced-cues environments and our findings show that chatbot communication evokes more anonymity than CMC communication.

We also found that FTF communication leads to the highest feeling of social presence, which is also what we expected. Although social presence was not found to impact self-disclosure in this study, we did find that visible, co-present interaction conditions evoke the strongest sense of social presence, which is in line with SPT [9] and previous research [53, for instance]. People experience less social presence in chatbot interactions, compared to CMC interactions, which is also in line with previous research which showed that an artificial interaction partner leads to lower expectations of social presence, compared to a human interlocutor [38]. Our findings add to this research and show the importance of perceived humanness in establishing social presence.

We did not find a difference between the conditions regarding shame, which is contrary to what we expected. It seems the chatbot does not create a communication environment in which people feel safer and less embarrassed to self-disclose. It may be that participants felt that the information they shared in all three conditions would be treated confidentially; which is generally the case in scientific research. Hence, they may have felt equally safe to disclose in all three conditions.

5.1 Theoretical and Practical Implications

Our findings have implications for research and theory on social chatbots and self-disclosure. First, our findings show that people are willing to self-disclose to a chatbot, just as much as to a human interaction partner. This is an important implication, as it shows potential for social chatbots to support people in psychotherapy. One of the most important conditions of successful therapy is self-disclosure and as our study shows that people disclose personal information to a chatbot, this may suggest that chatbots could potentially play a (supporting) role in psychotherapy.

Second, our findings show the importance of anonymity as an underlying explanation as to why people self-disclose in chatbot interactions. First, it shows the importance of anonymity when disclosing personal information, and second it shows that people feel highly anonymous in chatbot interactions. This anonymity, in turn, has positive effects: it lowers people's perceived risks and ensures that they feel safe to self-disclose. Although previous research has highlighted the negative results of anonymity in human-chatbot interactions, such as an increase in profanity [14], our study adds to this by showing that this sense of anonymity can have positive effects as it allows for a safe environment for intimate self-disclosure.

Finally, our findings have practical implications for chatbot developers. Based on our study, we can conclude that FTF communication is still the golden standard regarding social presence and trust. As trust is an important aspect in psychotherapy, and enhances self-disclosure, it is important for developers to create chatbots that come across as trustworthy interaction partners. In the present research, the chatbot was designed to ask questions, which may have impacted our findings. In fact, research shows that reciprocal self-disclosure can increase trust and liking [54]. Therefore, creating a chatbot with visual aspects, to enhance social presence, which is capable of reciprocating the user's self-disclosure, may enhance trust and, in turn, self-disclosure.

5.2 Limitations and Suggestions for Future Research

First, since this study used a chatbot incorporated into Facebook Messenger, this may have affected our findings. Specifically, data collected on Facebook Messenger are subject to Facebook's own privacy policy and this data may be shared with third parties. Although participants conversed using an anonymous account created for the experiment, they may have been cautious with the information they shared. Facebook outlines that it uses data for the improvement of services, especially advertising services, so the risk to participants was low. Furthermore, the present study opted for a chatbot integrated into Facebook Messenger because of low cost and the fact that people were likely already familiar with the technology. However, future research could attempt to build an independent mobile chatbot application, which means more control over the information collected and less vulnerability for the potential release of confidential information.

A second limitation of the present study lies in its design. In all three conditions participants partook in a question and answer session, where the interaction partners did not respond to their disclosures or disclosed anything themselves. As reciprocal self-disclosure may evoke trust and, as a result, self-disclosure it may be interesting for future studies to examine the impact of self-disclosure on the chatbot's end. Is a chatbot capable of self-disclosing in a way that makes the user trust them more? Furthermore, creating a chatbot with an avatar and/or other visual modalities may enhance social presence, which is also something future research could examine. Finally, it may be interesting to further analyse the effects of self-disclosure on people's overall well-being. Although we know, based on the findings in this study, that people self-disclose equally often to a human interlocutor and a chatbot, we do not know what the impact is of this self-disclosure. Do people experience relief after disclosing personal information to a chatbot? Does self-disclosure to an artificial interaction partner improve wellbeing? These are questions that future studies may attempt to answer.

6 Conclusion

The findings in the present study show potential for social chatbots to support psychotherapy and stand by people with mental health problems. We find that people self-disclose equally often to a chatbot, compared to a human interaction partner and that anonymity plays an important role in why people self-disclose to a chatbot. Furthermore, people do not experience trust and social presence in chatbot interactions, which is where improvements can be made. Finally, more research is needed to determine the potential beneficial effects of self-disclosure in human-chatbot interactions.

References

1. Abdul-Kader, S.A., Woods, J.: Survey on chatbot design techniques in speech conversation systems. Int. J. Adv. Comput. Sci. Appl. **6**, 72–80 (2015)
2. Vassallo, G., Pilato, G., Augello, A., Gaglio, S.: Phase Coherence in Conceptual Spaces for Conversational Agents, pp. 357–371. Wiley, Hoboken (2010)
3. D'Alfonso, S., et al.: Artificial intelligence-assisted online social therapy for youth mental health. Front. Psychol. **8**, 796 (2017)
4. Mou, Y., Xu, K.: The media inequality: comparing the initial human-human and human-AI social interactions. Comput. Hum. Behav. **72**, 432–440 (2017)
5. Heyselaar, E., Bosse, T.: Using theory of mind to assess users' sense of agency in social chatbots. In: Følstad, A., Araujo, T., Papadopoulos, S., Law, E.L.-C., Granmo, O.-C., Luger, E., Brandtzaeg, P.B. (eds.) CONVERSATIONS 2019. LNCS, vol. 11970, pp. 158–169. Springer, Cham (2020). https://doi.org/10.1007/978-3-030-39540-7_11
6. Perlman, D., Fehr, B.: The development of intimate relationships. In: Perlman, D., Duck, S. (eds.) Intimate Relationships: Development, Dynamics, and Deterioration, pp. 13–42. Sage Publications, Inc. (1987)

7. Chaves, A.P., Gerosa, M.A.: Single or multiple conversational agents? an interactional coherence comparison. In: Proceedings of the 2018 CHI Conference on Human Factors in Computing Systems, pp. 1–13 (2018)
8. Creed, C., Beale, R., Cowan, B.: The impact of an embodied agent's emotional expressions over multiple interactions. Interact. Comput. **27**(2), 172–188 (2015)
9. Short, J., Williams, E., Christie, B.: The Social Psychology of Telecommunications. Wiley, London (1976)
10. Biocca, F., Harms, C., Gregg, J.: The networked minds measure of social presence: pilot test of the factor structure and concurrent validity. In: 4th Annual International Workshop on Presence, Philadelphia, PA, pp. 1–9 (2001)
11. Lea, M., Spears, R., de Groot, D.: Knowing me, knowing you: anonymity effects on social identity processes within groups. Pers. Soc. Psychol. Bull. **27**(5), 526–537 (2001)
12. Walther, J.B., Boyd, S.: Attraction to computer-mediated social support. Commun. Technol. Soc. Audience Adopt. Uses **153188**, 50–88 (2002)
13. Philippot, P., Douilliez, C.: Impact of social anxiety on the processing of emotional information in video-mediated interaction. In: Kappas, A., Kramer, N.C. (eds.) Face-to-face Communication Over the Internet: Emotions in a Web of Culture, Language and Technology, pp. 127–143. Cambridge University Press, Cambridge (2011)
14. Skjuve, M., Brandtzæg, P.B.: Chatbots as a new user interface for providing health information to young people. Youth and news in a digital media environment–Nordic-Baltic perspectives (2018)
15. Jourard, S.M.: The Transparent Self. Van Nostrand Reinhold Company, New York (1971)
16. Shum, H.Y., He, X.D., Li, D.: From Eliza to XiaoIce: challenges and opportunities with social chatbots. Front. Inf. Technol. Electron. Eng. **19**(1), 10–26 (2018)
17. Augello, A., Gentile, M., Dignum, F.: An overview of open-source chatbots social skills. In: Diplaris, S., Satsiou, A., Følstad, A., Vafopoulos, M., Vilarinho, T. (eds.) INSCI 2017. LNCS, vol. 10750, pp. 236–248. Springer, Cham (2018). https://doi.org/10.1007/978-3-319-77547-0_18
18. Ho, A., Hancock, J., Miner, A.S.: Psychological, relational, and emotional effects of self-disclosure after conversations with a chatbot. J. Commun. **68**(4), 712–733 (2018)
19. Bell, S., Wood, C., Sarkar, A.: Perceptions of chatbots in therapy. In: Extended Abstracts of the 2019 CHI Conference on Human Factors in Computing Systems, pp. 1–6 (2019)
20. Fitzpatrick, K.K., Darcy, A., Vierhile, M.: Delivering cognitive behavior therapy to young adults with symptoms of depression and anxiety using a fully automated conversational agent (Woebot): a randomized controlled trial. JMIR Mental Health **4**(2), e19 (2017)
21. Fulmer, R., Joerin, A., Gentile, B., Lakerink, L., Rauws, M.: Using psychological artificial intelligence (Tess) to relieve symptoms of depression and anxiety: randomized controlled trial. JMIR Mental Health **5**(4), e64 (2018)
22. Martínez-Miranda, J.: Embodied conversational agents for the detection and prevention of suicidal behaviour: current applications and open challenges. J. Med. Syst. **41**(9), 135 (2017)
23. Archer, R.L., Burleson, J.A.: The effects of timing of self-disclosure on attraction and reciprocity. J. Pers. Soc. Psychol. **38**(1), 120 (1980)
24. Valkenburg, P.M., Peter, J.: Social consequences of the internet for adolescents: a decade of research. Curr. Direct. Psychol. Sci. **18**(1), 1–5 (2009)
25. Choi, Y.H., Bazarova, N.N.: Self-disclosure characteristics and motivations in social media: Extending the functional model to multiple social network sites. Hum. Commun. Res. **41**(4), 480–500 (2015)
26. Joinson, A.N.: Self-disclosure in computer-mediated communication: The role of self-awareness and visual anonymity. Eur. J. Soc. Psychol. **31**(2), 177–192 (2001)

27. Antheunis, M.L., Schouten, A.P., Valkenburg, P.M., Peter, J.: Interactive uncertainty reduction strategies and verbal affection in computer-mediated communication. Commun. Res. **39**(6), 757–780 (2012)
28. Tourangeau, R., Couper, M.P., Steiger, D.M.: Humanizing self-administered surveys: experiments on social presence in web and IVR surveys. Comput. Hum. Behav. **19**(1), 1–24 (2003)
29. Sproull, L., Subramani, M., Kiesler, S., Walker, J.H., Waters, K.: When the interface is a face. Hum. Comput. Interact. **11**(2), 97–124 (1996)
30. Bhakta, R., Savin-Baden, M., Tombs, G.: Sharing secrets with robots? In: EdMedia+ Innovate Learning, pp. 2295–2301. Association for the Advancement of Computing in Education (AACE) (2014)
31. Farber, B.A., Berano, K.C., Capobianco, J.A.: Clients' perceptions of the process and consequences of self-disclosure in psychotherapy. J. Counsel Psychol. **51**(3), 340 (2004)
32. Joinson, A.N., Paine, C.B.: Self-disclosure, privacy and the Internet. In: The Oxford Handbook of Internet Psychology, p. 2374252 (2007)
33. Tillmann-Healy, L.M.: Friendship as method. Qual. Inq. **9**(5), 729–749 (2003)
34. Burgoon, J.K., Hale, J.L.: The fundamental topoi of relational communication. Commun. Monograph. **51**(3), 193–214 (1984)
35. Houser, M.L., Horan, S.M., Furler, L.A.: Dating in the fast lane: how communication predicts speed-dating success. J. Soc. Pers. Relationsh. **25**(5), 749–768 (2008)
36. Gibbs, J.L., Ellison, N.B., Lai, C.H.: First comes love, then comes Google: an investigation of uncertainty reduction strategies and self-disclosure in online dating. Commun. Res. **38**(1), 70–100 (2011)
37. Biocca, F., Harms, C., Burgoon, J.K.: Toward a more robust theory and measure of social presence: review and suggested criteria. Presence Teleoper. Vir. Environ. **12**(5), 456–480 (2003)
38. Lachlan, K.A., Spence, P.R., Edwards, A., Reno, K.M., Edwards, C.: If you are quick enough, I will think about it: Information speed and trust in public health organizations. Comput. Hum. Behav. **33**, 377–380 (2014)
39. Walther, J.B.: Interpersonal effects in computer-mediated interaction: a relational perspective. Commun. Res. **19**(1), 52–90 (1992)
40. Walther, J.B., Loh, T., Granka, L.: Let me count the ways: The interchange of verbal and nonverbal cues in computer-mediated and face-to-face affinity. J. Lang. Soc. Psychol. **24**(1), 36–65 (2005)
41. Valkenburg, P.M., Peter, J.: Online communication among adolescents: an integrated model of its attraction, opportunities, and risks. J. Adolesc. Health **48**(2), 121–127 (2011)
42. Antheunis, M.L.: Friendships and the internet. In: Berger, C.R., Roloff, M.E. The International Encyclopedia of Interpersonal Communication. Wiley-Blackwell, New-York (2015)
43. Aron, A., Melinat, E., Aron, E.N., Vallone, R.D., Bator, R.J.: The experimental generation of interpersonal closeness: a procedure and some preliminary findings. Pers. Soc. Psychol. Bull. **23**(4), 363–377 (1997)
44. Ledbetter, A.M.: Measuring online communication attitude: Instrument development and validation. Commun. Monograph. **76**(4), 463–486 (2009)
45. Chiou, J.S., Droge, C.: Service quality, trust, specific asset investment, and expertise: direct and indirect effects in a satisfaction-loyalty framework. J. Acad. Mark. Sci. **34**(4), 613 (2006)
46. Nowak, K.L., Biocca, F.: The effect of the agency and anthropomorphism on users' sense of telepresence, copresence, and social presence in virtual environments. Presence Teleoper. Virt. Environ. **12**(5), 481–494 (2003)
47. Lee, K.M., Peng, W., Jin, S.A., Yan, C.: Can robots manifest personality? An empirical test of personality recognition, social responses, and social presence in human–robot interaction. J. Commun. **56**(4), 754–772 (2006)

48. Rains, S.A.: The impact of anonymity on perceptions of source credibility and influence in computer-mediated group communication: a test of two competing hypotheses. Commun. Res. **34**, 100–125 (2007)
49. Qian, H., Scott, C.R.: Anonymity and self-disclosure on weblogs. J. Comput. Mediat. Commun. **12**(4), 1428–1451 (2007)
50. Hite, D.M., Voelker, T., Robertson, A.: Measuring perceived anonymity: the development of a context independent instrument. J. Meth. Measur. Soc. Sci. **5**(1), 22–39 (2014)
51. Andrews, B., Qian, M., Valentine, J.D.: Predicting depressive symptoms with a new measure of shame: the experience of shame scale. Br. J. Clin. Psychol. **41**(1), 29–42 (2002)
52. Bohannon, L.S., Herbert, A.M., Pelz, J.B., Rantanen, E.M.: Eye contact and video-mediated communication: a review. Displays **34**(2), 177–185 (2013)
53. Werkhoven, P.J., Schraagen, J.M., Punte, P.A.: Seeing is believing: communication performance under isotropic teleconferencing conditions. Displays **22**(4), 137–149 (2001)
54. Bevacqua, E., Richard, R., De Loor, P.: Believability and co-presence in human-virtual character interaction. IEEE Comput. Graph. Appl. **37**(4), 17–29 (2017)

"I'm Here for You": Can Social Chatbots Truly Support Their Users? A Literature Review

Marloes M. C. van Wezel$^{(\boxtimes)}$, Emmelyn A. J. Croes, and Marjolijn L. Antheunis

Tilburg University, Warandelaan 2, 5037 AB Tilburg, The Netherlands
m.m.c.vanwezel@tilburguniversity.edu

Abstract. Applications of chatbots are becoming more diverse. One application that is specifically interesting is social chatbots, as they are designed to provide its users with social support and improve wellbeing and mental health outcomes. It is questionable to what extent social chatbots are successful support providers, as there are several differences between chatbots and humans. Given the diverse subconcepts of social support, this paper aims to evaluate to what extent relevant subconcepts (structural support, perceived support, received support, and support adequacy) are captivated in extant research on social chatbots, in order to draw conclusions about its potential. Support adequacy turned out to be most under scrutiny in extant research, while measures of structural support and received support received less attention. Surprisingly, directionality of support was another important subconcept of social support in social chatbot literature. Theoretical and practical implications as well as suggestions for future research are discussed.

Keywords: Social chatbots · Social support · Wellbeing

1 Introduction

The number of chatbots is increasing exponentially, and their applications are becoming more diverse. A chatbot is a dialogue-based technology designed to execute simple conversations through text or voice [1]. In extend of functional, rule-based chatbots, there are now also social chatbots aiming to establish an emotional bond with its users and provide companionship and support [2]. Social chatbots are not developed to solve specific problems in predefined situations, but rather to converse freely and socially with their users, about any topic [2]. Applications of this chatbot type can in turn be found in mental health contexts [e.g., 3, 4], physical health contexts [e.g., 5–7], and as social companions [e.g., 8–10].

An important aim that social chatbots share, is providing its users with social support [2]. It is debatable to what extent social chatbots are truly able to support their users due to several differences between chatbots and humans. Given the diversity and richness of social support as a construct, it is necessary to evaluate to what extent important subconcepts are captivated in extant research on social chatbots, in order to draw conclusions about its potential in comparison to human support providers. Hence, the research questions that are central to this paper are:

© Springer Nature Switzerland AG 2021
A. Følstad et al. (Eds.): CONVERSATIONS 2020, LNCS 12604, pp. 96–113, 2021.
https://doi.org/10.1007/978-3-030-68288-0_7

RQ1: Which subconcepts of social support are investigated in social chatbot research?
RQ2: Which subconcepts remain unexplored and deserve more attention in future research?

1.1 Background

Social support has been given many definitions, but in a broad sense indicates any process in social interactions that might positively affect wellbeing [11]. In social support research, the concept is often broken down into several subconcepts, each illuminating a different aspect of social support. Relevant subconcepts for social chatbot research are provided in Table 1 [12].

Table 1. Different concepts of social support and proposed operationalisations in social chatbot research.

Social support concept	Definition	Operationalizations in social chatbot research
Structural support	The number and pattern of (in)direct social ties around an individual	User behavior Frequency of support seeking
Perceived support	Beliefs about the availability of support	Perceived availability of social chatbot
Received support	Reports about received support types	Self-reports about received support types
Support adequacy	Evaluations of quantity/quality of received support	Perceived (mis)understanding Measures of feeling supported Willingness to self-disclose Wellbeing outcomes Improved mental health outcomes

A first subconcept that is important to consider when mapping supportive abilities of social chatbots, is the way in which users address these technologies to seek support (i.e., structural support). After all, what use is a supportive chatbot if users are not seeking support from it? To investigate to what extent social chatbots can support their users, it is therefore crucial to evaluate how users interact with them. Hence, quantitative variables such as usage time, usage frequency, usage period, and number of words are relevant.

Second, an important subconcept of social support is its perceived availability (i.e., perceived support). People are better able to reappraise stressful situations when they experience available social support [13]. Sometimes the lack of 24/7 availability of human-human support can be problematic. To illustrate, in mental health counselling online extensions of offline therapy still lead to limited session times and long virtual queues, increasing depressive symptoms of the help-seekers [14]. Social chatbots could potentially fill this gap, as they are available to its user from any place at any time [15].

A third subconcept is the scope of support types that can be provided by social chatbots. Generally social support is subdivided into instrumental support (i.e., tangible support), informational support, and emotional support [16]. While instrumental support cannot be offered in an online setting, the latter two are easily communicated through text messages, and should in turn be present in social chatbot conversations.

The final subconcept that seems relevant in social chatbot research is support adequacy. Support adequacy is an important measure to evaluate the effectiveness of social support provision, and can be operationalized in several ways. First, effective social support is proposed to make the receiver feel truly understood by the provider [17], where provided support is responsive to and understands one's needs [18]. Therefore, the expressed support should include a component that reflects true understanding, which is enabled by clear communication of the receiver's needs and the ability to understand those needs by the provider. Because of the inequality of language abilities between (social) chatbots and their users, chatbot responses are often characterized as repetitive and impersonal [19], leading to experienced miscommunication and frustration by users [20–22]. Irrelevant or inappropriate responses can be detrimental for user satisfaction and might hinder appropriate social support [23], for example because users feel neglected or misunderstood [24]. Besides these 'informational misunderstandings', there are also concerns that a social chatbot cannot show genuine empathy, as it does not have access to true feelings of emotions [25–27]. The question is whether a social chatbot's lack of emotionality hinders their abilities to accurately mimic empathetic responses. Research suggests that effective social chatbots should entail a sophisticated empathy module to convey understanding [28], without being creepy [27, 29, 30]. Support adequacy of social chatbots may thus be evaluated by measures of perceived (empathetic) understanding.

A second construct that clarifies support adequacy is the level of self-disclosure. Self-disclosure refers to the verbal sharing of one's thoughts, feelings and experiences [31]. Intimate relationships often stimulate self-disclosure between individuals [e.g., 32], which in turn relates to increased social support [e.g., 33, 34]. Hence, a high relational closeness is suggested to result in more empathetic understanding, and in turn in a higher quality of perceived support [35]. In contrast though, Kristiansen, Tjørnhøj-Thomsen and Krasnik [36] found that cancer patients perceived the support provided by – socially distant – health care professionals as valuable, partly because they could understand the situation without causing more distress. Thus, effective support provision might also be possible in less close relationships (e.g., with social chatbots). Indeed, several researchers in the field of online counselling suggest that an online environment – such as a social chatbot – might enhance self-disclosure and in turn adequate social support, due to its lack of physical presence [37], lack of non-verbal cues [14], and perceived anonymity [38]. This combination of characteristics, and the non-judgmental nature of a social chatbot may create a safe space to share embarrassing or sensitive topics that one would not share with another person [15, 39]. Accordingly, several studies have found that people are willing to self-disclose personal things to a (social) chatbot [e.g., 40, 41]. In sum, measures of willingness to self-disclose to social chatbots can contribute to estimating their efficacy to provide support.

As a final notion, perceived social support has been related to wellbeing [e.g., 42–44] and mental health outcomes [e.g., 45–47]. If social chatbots are able to provide adequate social support, this could therefore be visible in wellbeing and mental health outcomes.

1.2 Present Study

Mapping which aspects of social support have been scrutinized and which aspects deserve more attention, will (1) clarify the extent in which social chatbots are known to be (in)supportive up until now and (2) provide directions for future research to deepen this understanding of strengths and weaknesses of social chatbots, as well as settings in which they can be applied adequately. Therefore, the aim of this review is to investigate whether the various subconcepts of social support are accounted for in social chatbot research, focusing on text-based chatbots only (no vocal or embodied conversational agents).

2 Literature Search and Procedures

A literature review was conducted to investigate the status quo of research on social chatbots as support providers. Because research on chatbots exists in several fields, each with their own terminology [48], relevant literature was found by the use of the following search term: ("social chatbot" OR "dialogue system" OR "conversational agent" OR "virtual assistant") AND ("social support" OR "user behavior" OR availability OR perceived support OR perceived understanding OR wellbeing OR therapy) -spoken - vocal -embodied, in the search engines Google Scholar (4,320 hits), ScienceDirect[1] (168 hits), SpringerLink (2,156 hits) and Wiley Online Library (80 hits). If applicable, filters to select only empirical research papers were used.

The original number of hits included many rule-based functional chatbots, hence the selection was narrowed down following this definition of a social chatbot: a dialogue-based program designed to show humanlike behavior with a personality and emotions, in social, relational or therapeutic contexts, in which the main goal is to establish an emotional connection and/or provide social support. The focus is thus mainly on *the emotional aspect of support* rather than informing or educating the user.

In order to be selected for the final review, a paper must have (1) empirically investigated the use of a social chatbot related to subconcepts of social support, following the operationalizations from Table 1 (so no reviews, meta-analyses or design studies), (2) been published in a peer-reviewed journal or conference proceeding and (3) been written in English. This selection criteria led to the selection of 14 articles that were analyzed in more depth (4 conference proceedings and 10 journal articles). An overview of these papers' main findings is given in Table 2.

3 Results

The synthesis of relevant literature revealed that two of the proposed subconcepts of social support are elaborated on in extant social chatbot research: perceived support and

---

1 ScienceDirect only allows 8 Boolean operators so this search excluded "dialogue system" and "virtual assistant".

support adequacy. The subconcepts "received support" and "structural support" received little attention. Surprisingly, an additional subconcept, directionality, was covered in several studies.

3.1 Perceived Support

The all-time availability of social chatbots, and its impact on perceived social support and wellbeing, was investigated. The 24/7 availability of social chatbots was often recognized as beneficial [6, 10, 49, 50], especially when users would have limited access to more traditional sources of support, such as their friends or close kin [49]. Additionally, breast cancer patients felt comforted by the idea that someone could answer their questions at any time, and 88% experienced the conversations with a social chatbot to be supportive [6]. Besides these practicalities, the all-time availability of a social chatbot was also valued by users as the chatbot functioned as a positive, supporting feel-good app on demand [10]. In turn, besides the possible positive effects of actual support provision, users also experienced positive feelings as a result of knowing that they carried a support provider with them at all times [50]. Even when the social chatbot was not actively supporting its user, its mere presence could suffice.

3.2 Support Adequacy

Many papers investigated to what extent social chatbot users feel (mis)understood and how this impacts the adequacy of social support and wellbeing. Miscommunication and annoyance were frequently mentioned in several qualitative analyses of social chatbot interactions [4, 46, 49, 50]. More specifically, the repetitiveness of conversations with a social chatbot were often reported as annoying. Besides, social chatbot users indicated to receive messages that made no sense [49] or that miscommunication occurred [4, 46]. Indications of miscommunication were mostly informational [4, 49]. Woebot users, for example, indicated that they confused the social chatbot when using the free-input option rather than proposed multiple-choice options [4].

Interestingly, despite miscommunications, the social chatbots in these studies were all perceived as successful support providers or they improved (mental) wellbeing. Ly et al. [50] for example found that participants who had interacted with a companionship chatbot experienced improved wellbeing and lower perceived stress as compared to a waitlist control group. Additionally, Fitzpatrick and colleagues [4] found that the use of Woebot significantly reduced depressive symptoms, while an e-book about mental health did not.

Furthermore, special attention was devoted to social chatbots' abilities to emotionally understand their users. To illustrate, Liu and Sundar [27] developed four social chatbot types and measured perceived message supportiveness when (1) reading a hypothetical conversation and (2) when actually conversing with a social chatbot. At first sight, message supportiveness was perceived to be higher from sympathetic or affective empathetic chatbots as compared to advice-only chatbots. However, when participants interacted with a social chatbot themselves, all messages were perceived as equally supportive [27].

The willingness to self-disclose to a social chatbot and its impacts on the adequacy of social support and wellbeing were also covered. While Ly et al. [50] found that social chatbot conversations were perceived as shallow, most studies found that the non-judgmental character of the social chatbot was inviting to discuss intimate topics, such as sexuality problems or hair loss related to cancer treatments [6, 52]. For example, more than 80% of the participants indicated that sensitive questions were more easily discussed with a social chatbot than with another person [53]. Moreover, participants experienced lower thresholds to express affection or gratitude to significant others when a social chatbot functioned as a mediator [10]. Interestingly, while social chatbots lowered thresholds to self-disclose, the impact of self-disclosure as compared to self-disclosure to a human seemed to be similar [54].

3.3 Received Support

Only one of the fourteen papers that were reviewed explicitly distinguished between different types of received social support. Ta and colleagues [49] noted that user reviews of companionship chatbot Replika frequently mentioned companionship support (77.1%) and emotional support provision (44.6%). Informational support (15.6%) and appraisal support (9.3%) were also found, but these support types were clearly outnumbered. Replika users specifically sought informational support regarding mental wellbeing. Emotional support was provided along two dimensions: (1) users felt safe to discuss their true feelings with Replika, and (2) the social chatbot would regularly inquire about their wellbeing. These two dimensions made users feeling loved and being cared for, which might also explain that users reported reduced feelings of loneliness when interacting with Replika. Though this is not made explicit, Chaix et al. [6] also mentioned that users had established an emotional connection with their social chatbot, which suggests the presence of emotional support.

3.4 Structural Support

Structural support measures such as word count or interaction frequency were included in only three of the fourteen studies under review. Lee and colleagues [46] investigated the word count of disclosures towards self-disclosing social chatbots (high vs. low vs. no disclosure) and found that participants used more words to answer sensitive questions when they interacted with a high self-disclosing social chatbot. Chaix et al. [6] were the only ones to consider user behavior of a social chatbot developed to support cancer patients, in their analysis of usage data from one year. Specifically, they investigated usage time, interest in several themes, and level of interactivity. This analysis for example showed that participants were more eager to answer multiple-choice questions rather than open questions asked by the social chatbot. They also found that 31% of the participants still interacted with the social chatbot after 8 months. Finally, Fitzpatrick et al. [4] included a measure of usage frequency and found that participants checked in with their social chatbot 12.14 times in 2 weeks on average.

3.5 Directionality

Unexpectedly, directionality of social support was covered in several studies, even though social chatbots are not capable of feeling distress and hence do not need to be supported.

Table 2. Selected papers and their main findings

Authors	Sample	Country	Method	Chatbot Type	Chatbot Input	IV/moderator/ covariates	DV	Main Findings
Narain et al. (2020)	$N = 24$ students and young professionals M_{age} = unknown	USA	Experiment, survey and interview	Companion	Free input	Chatbot interaction (yes vs no)	Wellbeing, Self-esteem	Qualitative outcomes: more self-reflection, increased relationship depth with friends and SD that would not occur F2F. Quantitative outcomes: increased self-esteem and wellbeing in experimental group, but not significant.
Ta et al. (2020)	Study 1: $N =$ 1,854 reviews Study 2: $N = 66$ adults M_{age} = 32.64	World	Field study (thematic analysis and interview)	Companion	Free input, MC answer options	None	Perceived social support	Companionship support (77.1%) and emotional support (44.6%) most commonly referenced. Chatbot perceived as helpful support provider.

(continued)

Table 2. (*continued*)

Authors	Sample	Country	Method	Chatbot Type	Chatbot Input	IV/moderator/ covariates	DV	Main Findings
Liu & Sundar (2018)	Study 1: $N = 85$ adults $M_{age} = 34.76$ Study 2: $N =$ 88 students and adults $M_{age} = 25.75$	USA	Experiment	Physical health	Free input	Chatbot type (advice-only vs sympathy vs cognitive empathy vs affective empathy)	Perceived understanding, message supportiveness, message effectiveness, perceived social support	Sympathy and affective empathy chatbots more supportive and perceived understanding than advice-only when reading hypothetical interaction (study 1) but no such effects after an actual interaction with a chatbot (study 2).
Inkster et al. (2018)	$N = 129$ young adults $M_{age} =$ unknown	World	Quasi- experiment	Mental health	Free input, MC answer options	Usage intensity (high vs low)	Depressive symptoms	Both groups had improved in terms of depressive symptoms significantly, but high users significantly improved more than low users.

(*continued*)

Table 2. (*continued*)

Authors	Sample	Country	Method	Chatbot Type	Chatbot Input	IV/moderator/ covariates	DV	Main Findings
Oh, Jang, Kim, & Kim (2020)	$N = 41$ adults $M_{age}= 40.97$	South Korea	Randomized Controlled Trial and thematic analysis	Mental health	Free input, MC answer options	Condition (chatbot vs book)	Clinical outcomes such as anxiety, depression and panic disorder	Decreased panic disorder severity and social phobia, no further effects. Only 3 participants reported that received support was the best thing about the chatbot.
Ho, Hancock, & Miner (2018)	$N = 98$ students $M_{age}= 22.00$	USA	Experiment	None	Free input	Partner identity (human vs chatbot) Disclosure type (emotional vs factual)	Emotional experiences, perceived understanding, disclosure intimacy	Regardless of partner identity, participants reported improved emotional experiences and feeling better after the emotional disclosure as compared to the factual disclosure.
Greer et al. (2019)	$N = 45$ adults $M_{age}= 25.00$	USA	Randomized Controlled Trial	Physical health	Free input, MC answer options	Content access chatbot (full vs emotion ratings only)	Anxiety, depression, positive and negative emotions	Chatting sessions were seen as helpful. 4 weeks chatbot access reduced anxiety significantly compared to waitlist control. No effects on depressive symptoms and emotions.

(*continued*)

Table 2. (*continued*)

Authors	Sample	Country	Method	Chatbot Type	Chatbot Input	IV/moderator/ covariates	DV	Main Findings
Chaix et al. (2019)	$N = 958$ breast cancer patients $M_{age} = 48.00$	France	Prospective study and survey	Physical health	Free input, MC answer options	None	Qualitative user experiences, conversation content	88.00% said the chatbot was supporting. Users claimed to have established an emotional connection.
De Gennaro, Krumhuber, & Lucas (2020)	$N = 128$ students $M_{age} = 24.12$	UK	Experiment	Mental health	Free input, MC answer options	Condition (empathetic chatbot *vs* control questionnaire)	Mood	The mood of participants that interacted with the chatbot was significantly more positive compared to the control group after being ostracised. This effect holds when controlled for the feeling of exclusion.

(*continued*)

Table 2. (*continued*)

Authors	Sample	Country	Method	Chatbot Type	Chatbot Input	IV/moderator/ covariates	DV	Main Findings
Lee et al. (2019)	$N = 67$ $M_{age} = 25.10$	Holland	Longitudinal experiment	Mental health	Free input, MC answer options	Condition (CG chatbot vs CR chatbot)	Self-compassion	CG chatbot did not increase self-compassion, CR chatbot did. Effects were stronger for women; they increased in self-compassion for both conditions, where CR had strongest effect.
Lee, Yamashita, & Huang (2020a)	$N = 47$ $M_{age} = 23$	USA	Longitudinal experiment	Mental health/ Companion	Free input, MC answer options	Condition (chatbot no SD vs chatbot low SD vs chatbot high SD)	SD, sharing with MHP; trust	More SD of feelings to the MHP and the chatbot after conversing with high SD chatbot. >80% of the participants found it easier to talk about sensitive questions with a chatbot vs MHP. 90% shared their answers with MHP. Conversing with high SD chatbot related to high MHP trust.

(*continued*)

Table 2. (*continued*)

Authors	Sample	Country	Method	Chatbot Type	Chatbot Input	IV/moderator/ covariates	DV	Main Findings
Lee, Yamashita, Huang, & Fu (2020b)	$N = 47$ $M_{age} = 23$	USA	Longitudinal experiment	Companion	Free input, MC answer options	Condition (chatbot no SD vs chatbot low SD vs chatbot high SD)	Word count SD depth trust intimacy	Answering to sensitive questions: more words and more feelings in high SD condition than in no SD or low SD. Over time increased SD and perceived intimacy in high SD condition when answering sensitive questions. SD decreased when journaling.
Ly, Ly, & Andersson (2017)	$N = 27$ adults $M_{age} = 26.2$	Sweden	Randomized Control Trial and interview	Companion	Free input, MC answer options	Condition (chatbot vs waitlist control)	Wellbeing Perceived stress Life satisfaction App engagement	Chatbot condition showed improved wellbeing and lower perceived stress than the waitlist control group. No effect on life satisfaction.

(*continued*)

Table 2. (*continued*)

Authors	Sample	Country	Method	Chatbot Type	Chatbot Input	IV/moderator/ covariates	DV	Main Findings
Fitzpatrick et al. (2017)	$N = 70$ students $M_{age} = 22.20$	USA	Randomized Controlled Trial	Mental health	Free input, MC answer options	Condition (chatbot vs. self-help e-book)	(Among others) Anxiety Positive and negative affect Depressive symptoms	Woebot reduced signs of depression while the control group that was given an e-book did not show improvement. Completers showed reduced anxiety in both conditions. No effects were found on affect.

Note: IV = Independent Variable, DV = Dependent Variable (only relevant ones included), F2F = Face to Face, MC = Multiple Choice, CG = Care Giving, CR = Care Receiving, SD = Self–Disclosure, MHP = Mental Health Professional

In these studies, the focus was mainly on reciprocal self-disclosure [46, 46, 54]. Conversing with a social chatbot that shared many self-disclosures resulted in more trust in the social chatbot and the mental health professional it later referred to, as compared to a social chatbot that shared no or little information about himself [46]. Also, more feelings were shared with a self-disclosing social chatbot [46].

4 Discussion

The aims of this paper were twofold: (1) to concisely summarize empirical research on social chatbots' social support abilities, and (2) to explore which subconcepts of social support are still missing from this body of literature.

Several researchers question the capability of social chatbots to act as support providers because they are unable to deeply understand their interlocutors [e.g., 20, 21], specifically on an emotional level [25–27]. The present synthesis found that support adequacy received most attention: even though social chatbot users experienced miscommunications, they still gained benefits from the interaction in terms of experienced social support and improved wellbeing. Even when people valued an emotional component when reading human-chatbot interactions, this was not confirmed in actual human-chatbot interactions [27]. It is therefore questionable how important this proposed communication problem really is. Experiences of miscommunication were mainly of informational nature (responses that were off-topic or repetitive) and did not seem to impact the adequacy of social support or users' wellbeing. The reviewed studies also revealed that – mainly due to its non-judgmental character – people were willing to self-disclose about intimate, personal topics to a social chatbot. Mostly in relation to support adequacy, numerous papers considered the subconcept of perceived support when they determined how the all-time availability of social chatbots was perceived by and impacted their users. Measures of structural support and received support were only discussed to a limited extent.

Interestingly, in contrast with our initial expectations, the subconcept of "directionality" [12] was also covered: a few studies suggested that in order to maximize the benefits of a human-chatbot interaction, the social chatbot should self-disclose too. This relates to the norm of reciprocity in natural communication, where people expect that both interaction partners provide input to the conversations [55]. Reciprocal self-disclosure may facilitate the development of a profound relationship, which some participants indicated to desire before they fully self-disclose [e.g., 55].

4.1 Theoretical and Practical Implications

To feel truly understood on a deep and emotional level is often seen as a prerequisite to improve wellbeing through supportive acts [17, see also 26, 27]. However, present findings do not fully corroborate this notion. This questions to what extent profound emotional understanding is necessary to provide adequate support. In turn, developing social chatbots that can mimic empathy perfectly may not only be unnecessary, it may even backfire [29, 30].

Rather, social chatbot developers may benefit from investing in a self-disclosure module, to exploit the benefits of chatbot technologies in sensitive, personal domains such as mental and physical health. The reviewed studies suggest that high self-disclosing social chatbots can provoke more detailed self-disclosure and more trust in both the social chatbot as in possible external sources the technology refers to (such as a mental health professional). These are important practical implications to consider, for example when a client is reluctant to open up to his/her therapist, when a patient does not fully self-disclose to his/her doctor, or when a victim is reluctant to talk to the authorities. To illustrate the latter, Park and Lee [56] discuss the potential of chatbot technologies to lower the burden of sexual assault victims when filing a report. The use of social chatbots may thus be particularly fruitful in delicate circumstances.

4.2 Future Directions for Social Chatbot Research

This overview poses several directions for future research. First of all, more attention should be devoted to structural support (i.e., the number and types of social ties around an individual). While most reviewed studies already applied a repeated-measures design with several weeks of intervention [e.g., 51, 3, 4], little attention was devoted to user behavior. Usage time and frequency are important factors to consider for future research, as these may influence outcomes [see 51] and are important operationalizations of structural support. To illustrate its importance, it is imaginable that annoyance about the repetitiveness of the chatbot's replies increases as users have had more interactions. Future research should therefore consider user behavior rather than the time-frame of the study as relevant quantitative variable.

Secondly, little attention was devoted to explicit measures of the types of social support that are (adequately) provided by social chatbots (i.e., received support). Users' support demands may depend on the context [27, 52] or individual differences [46, 49, 54]. Greer et al. [52] for example propose that different cancer types and stages of illness may require different types of support provision from a social chatbot. More focus is therefore needed on such individual differences related to the subtypes of social support to further explore the boundaries within which social chatbots can be helpful in general, and to what extent personalization is necessary.

5 Conclusion

Despite experienced misunderstandings, social chatbots showed potential in the studies that were reviewed, and particularly their non-judgmental character and availability were valued. Social chatbots showed promising results as they provided companionship support, mental health support, physical health support or acted as a facilitator of real-life companionship. Moreover, social chatbots seemed to be capable of improving its user's wellbeing. Though, follow-up research is needed to include received support types and structural support as informants of social chatbots' abilities to provide adequate social support to their users.

References

1. Vassallo, G., Pilato, G., Augello, A., and Gaglio, S.: Phase coherence in conceptualspaces for conversational agents, pp. 357–371. Wiley, Hoboken (2010).
2. Shum, H.-Y., He, X.-D., Li, D.: From Eliza to XiaoIce: challenges and opportunities with social chatbots. Front. Inf. Technol. Electr. Eng. **19**(1), 10–26 (2018). https://doi.org/10.1631/FITEE.1700826
3. Inkster, B., Sarda, S., Subramanian, V.: An empathy-driven, conversational artificial intelligence agent (Wysa) for digital mental well-being: real-world data evaluation mixed-methods study. JMIR mHealth uHealth **6**(11), e12106 (2018)
4. Fitzpatrick, K.K., Darcy, A., Vierhile, M.: Delivering cognitive behavior therapy to young adults with symptoms of depression and anxiety using a fully automated conversational agent (Woebot): a randomized controlled trial. JMIR Mental Health **4**(2), e19 (2017)
5. Dubosson, F., Schaer, R., Savioz, R., Schumacher, M.: Going beyond the relapse peak on social network smoking cessation programmes: ChatBot opportunities. Swiss Méd. Inf. **33**(00) (2017).
6. Chaix, B., Bibault, J.E., Pienkowski, A., Delamon, G., Guillemassé, A., Nectoux, P., Brouard, B.: When Chatbots meet patients: one-year prospective study of conversations between patients with breast cancer and a Chatbot. JMIR Cancer **5**(1), e12856 (2019)
7. Schulman, D., Bickmore, T.: Persuading users through counseling dialogue with a conversational agent. In: Proceedings of the 4th International Conference on Persuasive Technology, pp. 1–8. Association for Computing Machinery, New York (2009).
8. Replika.ai.: https://replika.ai/about/story (2020).
9. Mitsuku.: https://www.pandorabots.com/mitsuku/ (2002).
10. Narain, J., Quach, T., Davey, M., Park, H.W., Breazeal, C., Picard, R.: Promoting wellbeing with sunny, a chatbot that facilitates positive messages within social groups. In: Extended Abstracts of the 2020 CHI Conference on Human Factors in Computing Systems, pp. 1–8 (2020).
11. Cohen, S., Underwood, L.G., Gottlieb, B.H.: Social support measurement and intervention: a guide for health and social scientists. Oxford University Press, Oxford (2000).
12. Gottlieb, B.H., Bergen, A.E.: Social support concepts and measures. J. Psychosomatic Res. **69**(5), 511–520 (2010)
13. Cohen, S., Hoberman, H.M.: Positive events and social supports as buffers of life change stress. J. of Appl. Soc. psychology **13**(2), 99–125 (1983)
14. King, R., Bambling, M., Lloyd, C., Gomurra, R., Smith, S., Reid, W., Wegner, K.: Online counselling: the motives and experiences of young people who choose the Internet instead of face to face or telephone counselling. Counsel. Psychotherapy Res. **6**(3), 169–174 (2006)
15. Følstad, A., Brandtzaeg, P.B., Feltwell, T., Law, E.L.C., Tscheligi, M., Luger, E.: Chatbots for social good. In: Extended Abstracts of the 2018 CHI Conference on Human Factors in Computing Systems (2018).
16. House, J.S., Kahn, R.L.: Measures and concepts of social support. In: Social Support and Health, edited by S. Cohen and S.L. Syme, pp. 83–108, Academic Press, Orlando (1985).
17. Lun, J., Kesebir, S., Oishi, S.: On feeling understood and feeling well: The role of interdependence. J. Res. Personal. **42**(6), 1623–1628 (2008)
18. Sarason, B., Sarason, I., Gurung, R.: Close personal relationships and health outcomes: a key to the role of social support. Handbook of Personal Relationships: Theory, Research and Interventions (2nd ed), pp. 547–573, Wiley, Chichester (1997).
19. Mou, Y., Xu, K.: The media inequality: comparing the initial human-human and human-AI social interactions. Comput. Hum. Behav. **72**, 432–440 (2017)

20. Chang, Y.K., Morales-Arroyo, M.A., Chavez, M., Jimenez-Guzman, J.: Social interaction with a conversational agent: an exploratory study. J. Inf. Technol. Res. (JITR) **1**(3), 14–26 (2008)

21. Hill, J., Ford, W.R., Farreras, I.G.: Real conversations with artificial intelligence: A comparison between human–human online conversations and human–chatbot conversations. Comput. Hum. Behav. **49**, 245–250 (2015)

22. Callejas, Z., López-Cózar, D., Ábalos, N., Griol, D.: Affective conversational agents: the role of personality and emotion in spoken interactions. In: Pérez-Marín, D., Pascual-Nieto, I. (Eds.) Conversational agents and natural language interaction: techniques and effective practices, IGI Global, pp. 203–222 (2011).

23. Chaves, A.P., Gerosa, M.A.: How should my chatbot interact? Manuscript submitted for publication, A survey on human chatbot interaction design (2019)

24. Jain, M., Kumar, P., Kota, R., Patel, S.N.: Evaluating and informing the design of chatbots. In: Proceedings of the 2018 Designing Interactive Systems Conference, pp. 895–906, Association for Computing Machinery, New York (2018)

25. Beran, O.: An attitude towards an artificial soul? Responses to the "Nazi Chatbot".Philosoph. Investigations, **41**(1), 42–69 (2018)

26. Fung, P., et al.: Towards empathetic human-robot interactions. In: International Conference on Intelligent Text Processing and Computational Linguistics, pp. 173–193. Springer, Cham (2016)

27. Liu, B., Sundar, S.S.: Should machines express sympathy and empathy? Experiments with a health advice chatbot. Cyberpsychol. Behav. Soc. Netw. **21**(10), 625–636 (2018)

28. Smith, K.A. Masthoff, J.: Can a virtual agent provide good emotional support?: exploring whether personality or identity effect the perceived supportiveness of a message. In: Proceedings of the 32nd International BCS Human Computer Interaction Conference, p. 10, BCS Learning and Development Ltd., Swindon (2018).

29. Mori, M.: The Uncanny Valley. Energy **7**(4), 33–35 (1970)

30. Stein, J.P., Ohler, P.: Venturing into the uncanny valley of mind—the influence of mind attribution on the acceptance of human-like characters in a virtual reality setting. Cognit. **160**, 43–50 (2017)

31. Derlega, V.J., Metts, S., Petronio, S., Margulis, S.T.: Self-Disclosure. Sage Publications, Inc. (1993).

32. Perlman, D., Fehr, B.: The development of intimate relationships. In: Perlman, D., Duck, S. (Eds.) Intimate Relationships: Development, Dynamics, and Deterioration, pp. 13–42, Sage Publications, Inc. (1987).

33. Lee, K.T., Noh, M.J., Koo, D.M.: Lonely people are no longer lonely on social networking sites: the mediating role of self-disclosure and social support. Cyberpsychol. Behav. Soc. Netw. **16**(6), 413–418 (2013).

34. Zhang, R.: The stress-buffering effect of self-disclosure on Facebook: An examina-tion of stressful life events, social support, and mental health among college students. Comput. Hum. Behav. **75**, 527–537 (2017)

35. Jackson, P. B.: Specifying the buffering hypothesis: Support, strain, and depression. Social Psychology Quarterly, 363–378 (1992).

36. Kristiansen, M., Tjørnhøj-Thomsen, T., Krasnik, A.: The benefit of meeting a stranger: Experiences with emotional support provided by nurses among Danish-born and migrant cancer patients. Eur. J. of Oncology Nurs. **14**(3), 244–252 (2010)

37. Cook, J.E., Doyle, C.: Working alliance in online therapy as compared to face-to-face therapy: preliminary results. Cyber Psychol. Behav. **5**(2), 95–105 (2002)

38. Glasheen, K.J., Campbell, M.A.: The use of online counselling within an Australian secondary school setting: a practitioner's viewpoint. Counsel. Psychol. Rev. **24**(2), 42–51 (2009)

39. Skjuve, M.B., Brandtzæg, P.B.: Chatbots as a new user interface for providing health information to young people. In: Yvonne, A., Ulf, D., Jonas, O. (Eds.) Youth and news in a digital media environment – Nordic-Baltic perspectives (2018).

40. DeVault, D., et al.: SimSensei Kiosk: a virtual human interviewer for healthcare decision support. In: Proceedings of the 2014 International Conference on Autonomous Agents and Multi-agent Systems, pp. 1061–1068. International Foundation for Autonomous Agents and Multiagent Systems, Richland (2014)

41. Antheunis, M. L., and Croes, E. A. J.: Your Secret is Safe with Me. The Willingness to Disclose Intimate Information to a Chatbot and its Impact on Emotional Well-Being. Extended Abstract presented at ICA 2020 (2020)

42. Cohen, S. E. and Syme, S. L.: Social Support and Health. Academic Press, Cambridge (1985).

43. House, J.S.: Work Stress and Social Support. Addison-Wesley, Reading (1981)

44. Kessler, R.C., McLeod, J.D.: Social support and mental health in community samples. In: Cohen, S., Syme, S.L. (Eds.) Social Support and Health, pp. 219–240. Academic Press, New York (1985).

45. Aneshensel, C.S., Frerichs, R.R.: Stress, support, and depression: a longitudinal causal model. J. Commun. Psychol. **10**, 363–376 (1982)

46. Dour, H.J., et al: Perceived social support mediates anxiety and depressive symptom changes following primary care intervention. Depression Anxiety, **31**(5), 436–442 (2014).

47. Norbeck, J.S., Anderson, N.J.: Life stress, social support, and anxiety in mid-and late-pregnancy among low income women. Res. Nur. Health **12**(5), 281–287 (1989)

48. Dale, R.: The return of the chatbots. Nat. Lang. Eng. **22**(5), 811–817 (2016)

49. Ta, V., et al.: User experiences of social support from companion chatbots in everyday contexts: thematic analysis. J. Méd. Internet Res. **22**(3), e16235 (2020).

50. Ly, K.H., Ly, A.M., Andersson, G.: A fully automated conversational agent for promoting mental well-being: A pilot RCT using mixed methods. Internet Interventions **10**, 39–46 (2017)

51. Oh, J., Jang, S., Kim, H., Kim, J.J.: Efficacy of mobile app-based interactive cognitive behavioral therapy using a chatbot for panic disorder. Int. J. Méd. Inform. **140**, 104–171 (2020)

52. Greer, S., Ramo, D., Chang, Y.J., Fu, M., Moskowitz, J., Haritatos, J.: Use of the chatbot "Vivibot" to deliver positive psychology skills and promote well-being among young people after cancer treatment: randomized controlled feasibility trial. JMIR mHealth uHealth **7**(10), e15018 (2019)

53. Lee, Y. C., Yamashita, N., Huang, Y.: Designing a chatbot as a mediator for promoting deep self-disclosure to a real mental health professional. In: Proceedings of the ACM on Human-Computer Interaction, 4(CSCW1), pp. 1-27. Association for Computing Machinery, New York (2020).

54. Ho, A., Hancock, J., Miner, A.S.: Psychological, relational, and emotional effects of self-disclosure after conversations with a chatbot. J. Commun. **68**(4), 712–733 (2018)

55. Lee, Y. C., Yamashita, N., Huang, Y., Fu, W.: " I Hear You, I Feel You": encouraging deep self-disclosure through a chatbot. In: Proceedings of the 2020 CHI Conference on Human Factors in Computing Systems, pp. 1-12, Association for Computing Machinery, New York (2020)

56. Lee, M., Ackermans, S., van As, N., Chang, H., Lucas, E., IJsselsteijn, W.: Caring for vincent: a chatbot for self-compassion. In: Proceedings of the 2019 CHI Conference on Human Factors in Computing Systems, p. 13. Association for Computing Machinery, New York (2019).

57. Altman, I., Taylor, D.A.: Social Penetration: The Development of Interpersonal Relationships. Holt, Rinehart and Winston (1973)

58. Park, H., Lee, J.: Can a conversational agent lower sexual violence victims' burden of self-disclosure?. In: Extended Abstracts of the 2020 CHI Conference on Human Factors in Computing Systems, pp. 1–8 (2020).

59. De Gennaro, M., Krumhuber, E.G., Lucas, G.: Effectiveness of an empathic chatbot in combating adverse effects of social exclusion on mood. Front. Psychol. **10**, 3061 (2020)

Grätzelbot: Social Companion Technology for Community Building among University Freshmen

Christian Löw[✉], Lukas Moshuber, and Albert Rafetseder

Cooperative Systems Research Group, University of Vienna, Vienna, Austria
{christian.loew,lukas.moshuber,albert.rafetseder}@univie.ac.at

Abstract. Proper onboarding procedures for freshmen (first-semester students) at the university have many positive effects, especially the increase in retention rates. This paper presents Grätzelbot, a chatbot designed to help with onboarding freshmen by means of connecting them in a network-building 12-day scavenger hunt. The onboarding concept that led to Grätzelbot was developed in a participatory design process together with students, and implemented during the start of the semester with more than 100 participants. The evaluation results revealed that the students felt more familiar with the faculty building and the university campus after the scavenger hunt, also met other students, made new friends, and, by participating, their sense of belonging to the student community got stronger. As a social companion fostering relatedness among its users, Grätzelbot serves as an example for the reach and benefits of Social Software.

Keywords: Chatbots · Social software · Companion technology · HCI

1 Introduction

Every semester, a few hundred new computer science students start their academic studies at the University of Vienna. They all face the first difficult task – the transition from high school to university. Many first-year students struggle with this transition, and some even fail [6,23]. The transition from a predetermined, structured school system to the independence of a university system leads to students feeling disoriented and often having difficulties motivating themselves [5,19]. They must also adapt to higher academic demands and different teaching methods [23]. A smooth transition is, therefore, more likely if students have access to the information they need and feel socially connected [5]. Concerning the social aspect of transition, social presence is consistently linked to the motivation of the students and is also supposed to influence motivation [34].

"Grätzel" is a local Viennese colloquial term for one's adjacent neighborhood in the city, and rhymes with "pretzel".

This paper is partially based on material created by the second author in his Master's thesis [28].

© Springer Nature Switzerland AG 2021
A. Følstad et al. (Eds.): CONVERSATIONS 2020, LNCS 12604, pp. 114–128, 2021.
https://doi.org/10.1007/978-3-030-68288-0_8

The right support for freshmen in this transition phase can help the university to achieve a significantly higher persistence rate of first-year students [7], and universities regularly pursue strategies of supporting such transitional phases, especially directed at marginalized groups.

In their transition to university, freshmen rely heavily on ICT-based social networks for communication, building and managing workgroups, and exchanging information or lecture materials [25,27]. At the same time, and prompted by advances in fields of Artificial Intelligence and Natural Language Processing, ICTs have adopted agents such as chatbots as simple, yet powerful interfaces.

This work reports on Grätzelbot, a design case of a chatbot aimed at supporting university freshmen in their transition to university life. The goal of this project is to implement a virtual companion as a Chatbot and evaluate its benefits in a user study conducted with first-semester students. The companion accompanies the students during the first two weeks of the semester and supports them in a gamified way to ease their transition from high school to university.

2   Background

The larger context for the implementation of a Conversational Agent in this work exceeds the mere technical frame of language processing explored in the rich history of the field. Instead, our focus is on the user, and on social benefits for the user in particular.

2.1   Situating Chatbots as Social Companion Technology

Accompaning the progress surrounding their technological capabilities, questions on how chatbots can be understood and situated in relation to their human users have been subject to recent discussion. Følstad et al. [13] proposed the notion of "Chatbots for Social Good" as a democatic endeavour and explore their potential in relation to human psychological needs formulated in Ryan and Deci's self-determination theory (SDT) [36]. In their agent-like quality, chatbots relate well to the notion of companion technology as technological systems that serve as cooperative assistants, also giving a sense of companionship to their users [1]. Niess and Woźniak [30] suggest a framework of understanding companion technology, based on psychological needs (including SDT) and a humanist philosophical fundament, and, in light of the increasing prevalence and popularity of smart technological artifacts, call for future work detailing on this notion.

Their interactional modality triggers natural interpersonal communication in users, thus being inherently social and relational, feasibly making them instances of social software themselves (e.g. referred to as *"relationship interfaces"* by [37]). In this sense, relatedness can be understood as a subject within the scope of chatbot design, represented by the relationship between user and a deliberately crafted chatbot persona, prompting questions on how such offerings and possibilities can satisfy the basic psychological need for (social) relatedness (harness its satisfaction for the design of technology supportive of wellbeing), both in itself as a "parasocial" relationship [21] and as an intermediary to human sociality; as e.g. remarked by [15], who call for research on how the "parasocial" relationship between chatbot and user can foster human social relationships.

2.2 Onboarding and Scavenger Hunts

If done in a right way, newly onboarded people become active and can perform tasks in a self-directed manner in an earlier stage, in any environment [12]. Regarding the academic context, students are more likely to finish their studies, finish them faster, have better grades, and have a more positive mindset about their education in general [7,8,16,22]. Onboarding in the academic context is often realized as a mentoring program or with an additional entering course [10].

Asher [29] implemented a chatbot to support new employees in large organizations in their onboarding process, finding that a chatbot helps to bridge the communication gap between new employees and the organization. Another chatbot-supported onboarding concept was developed by Westberg [39]. In this concept, the chatbot was not only a virtual, passive contact person but also played an active role in the onboarding process and processed tasks previously performed by Human Resources personnel. For example, adding a personal photo to the personnel database. Chandar et al. [9] also created a chatbot-based assistant called "Chip" for the onboarding process. In addition to the tasks described in [29] and [39] (knowledge base, proactive reminders, and small talk) this chatbot was also able to tell the new employee who to contact with a problem, especially with regard to technical questions (expert search). They observed an accuracy of around 60% using both objective (message level annotations) and subjective (questionnaire) evaluations in a field study with 344 new hires.

As a form of gamification, scavenger hunts have been used to onboard new people or bring people closer to a new environment [17,24,35]. In a scavenger hunt, information can be communicated playfully, and teamwork can be strengthened in a new group of people.

2.3 Constructive Approaches to Social Network Design

Apart from a subject of analysis in terms of structure and connectivity, social networks are also understood as something that can be created and fostered towards a deliberate purpose. Plastrik & Taylor developed a framework for network building and further described what types of networks there are, how they work, how they develop, in which ways their members can profit from them, which roles exist within the network, and what you should pay attention to when building a network [31]. Preece designed the guideline of "Community Centered Development". Community Centered Development is a methodology that engages the members of a community in a participatory design process with the developers. It describes an evolutionary process that goes along with the community [32]. Gunawardena et al. [18] developed a theoretical framework as a foundation for building online communities of practice when a social networking application is designed or used for collaborative learning. Väänänen et al. conceptualized and evaluated chatbots for youth civic participation [38].

2.4   Research Interest

In summarizing these references, the research interest of this project lies in exploring the potential of chatbots in a social context, specificically the potential of chatbots as an onboarding mechanism. In a broader understanding of onboarding objectives, this comprises the potential of chatbots to act as an intermediary for a constructive network building approach, facilitating social relatedness among users.

3   Methodology

The work presented here aims to design support technology for a community. The actual implementation as a chatbot-supported scavenger hunt for onboarding new computer science students developed iteratively over the two-year course of research. It was inspired by thorough explorations of the context, communication and networking practice of the students. This yielded cues about the solution space. The implementation and evaluation of the 12-day scavenger hunt embraced important leads from the topical literature. Data obtained from respective qualitative methods was analyzed by means of Thematic Analysis [4].

3.1   Context of Use Analysis and Design Phase

To be able to support new students when they enter university, it is necessary to take a close look at their situation. Therefore, we conducted two user studies to understand the needs, wishes, doubts, and problems freshmen have when they start their academic careers. This approach was inspired by the framework of Gunawardena et al. [18].

Freshmen participants were invited to **Participatory Design Workshops** (see § 4.1) and encouraged throughout different design tasks to communicate their expectations, wishes, and concerns regarding the beginning of their studies and also to design possible solutions for their problems themselves. The methods used in the workshops were based on concepts taken from Design Thinking [11], Participatory Design [3], Contextual Design [20], and Focus Group Interviews [33]. 11 students (4 females, 7 males), who are currently in their first semester of computer science, participated. There were 3 sessions of 120 min each.

To obtain additional quantitative insight from a larger group of people, an in-depth online **Social Networks Survey** (see § 4.2) was conducted on the topic. Two groups of students were surveyed, participants of a class from the first semester, and participants of a class intended for a higher semester.

More informally, we also connected with the student council and mentoring representatives to tap on their experiences with onboarding freshmen.

3.2 Concept and Prototype Evaluation, Follow-Up Inquiry

The findings were integrated into a concept for the **implementation** of a chatbot prototype (see § 5). The chatbot was part of a comprehensive scavenger hunt and tested in a 12-day field study. At the end of the field study, we performed an **evaluation** (see § 6) in the form of a quantitative online survey, and in-depth qualitative Focus Group Interviews [33]. The implementation approach of the chatbot, its integration into an existing student Online Social Network, and the scavenger hunt followed the development frameworks of Preece [32] and Gunawardena et al. [18]. The quests, i.e. puzzles and quizzes to be solved during the scavenger hunt, were designed based on the PLEX framework by Lucero et al. [26] so that the objectives we had set would convey a playful touch.

4   Context of Use Analysis and User Needs

This section documents selected results from initial Design Workshops with students (§ 4.1) and topical surveys (§ 4.2), leading to the final concept for the onboarding support chatbot and scavenger hunt (§ 5).

4.1 Participatory Design Workshops with Freshmen Students

First Experiences, Thoughts, and Feelings of Freshmen. The participants were invited to share positive and negative experiences from their first weeks as students. The topics were the everyday student life, orientation on the university campus, networking with other students, and gathering information. Table 1 overviews the grouped answers. Students were also asked to describe their goals, expectations, wishes, hopes, fears, and anxieties for the current situation as well as for the future.

Table 1. First experiences, thoughts and feelings of freshmen.

Campus	Information
Some courses take place at other locations	More advanced students are happy to help, but you have to find them
No cafeteria	Student council is happy to help with open questions
All food facilities a little further away	Mentoring program is good to have a contact person
Good learning workplaces, often crowded	Online systems are complicated at first use
Well-equipped library with learning spaces	Different online platforms make search for information difficult
	Big WhatsApp group for information exchange

Everyday Student life	Networking
Extreme shift from organized highschool life	More introverted people find it difficult to network despite of the available support
Needs self-discipline to go to classes early in the morning or late in the evening	Mentoring program was a good help to get to know people
High degree of self-organization is expected	You can get to know people well at the events
Many regular submissions and tests	
A lot of bureaucracy	

The Magic Assistant. A "Magic Assistant" was to be developed, i.e., an artifact with no limitations in the real world which supports them in their life as a student, prompting the participants to ideate over what they would perceive as helpful:

The Magic Assistant often acted as a support for everyday activities, made the scheduling on its own and reminded the students to leave in time for the lectures, to start studying for the exams, or to do assignments. It also often acted as a motivator to overcome the inner laziness and go to lectures. An example story developed by workshop participants was this: The student is unhappy with the meeting place suggested by peers. Magic Assistant finds a better-suited one, motivating the student to get out of bed. In some scenarios, the assistant also acted as a study buddy or helped to find learning partners, ideally those who are currently working on the same task. One student drew this storyboard: The student is in despair over a homework assignment. Magic Assistant knows a student that has solved the assignment already and calls them in virtually. In other storyboards, the assistant was often able to answer any questions about everyday student life. More details about the workshops can be found in [28].

4.2   Social Networks Survey with Freshmen

To obtain finer-grained insight from a larger group of people on their social network use, an online survey was conducted. Table 2 overviews selected survey results. Group 1, freshmen from a first semester course, consisted of 35 participants. Group 2 consisted of 58 participants of a course from a higher semester.

Table 2. Results from the survey among freshmen and older students.

	demographics					memberships in WhatsApp groups				time spent on Social Media
	total	female	male	average (median) age in years	Relocated to the city	large (>50)	medium	small (<15)	No Facebook	average (median) in hours per day
Freshmen	35	12	23	21.5 (20)	40 %	2	1	1	50 %	2.37 (1)
Later-semester	58	11	46	27 (25.5)	35 %	0	0	3	38 %	2.29 (1)

WhatsApp is the most popular application in both groups for the private and uinversity use of social networks. The two groups' use of WhatsApp groups differ. Group 2 use WhatsApp primarily for individual communication and are mainly members of smaller WhatsApp groups (with less than 15 people). In contrast, the vast majority of Group 1 stated that they were members of at least one large WhatsApp group (of more than 50 people in size).

Since chatbots can be integrated into Facebook, students were asked whether Facebook is still a relevant medium for freshmen. The survey confirmed the findings from the Design Thinking Workshops that new computer science students at University of Vienna hardly use Facebook (nor the Facebook Messenger) anymore.

Participants were also asked whether they had come to Vienna to study. This was true for 40% and 35% of the students in Groups 1 and 2, respectively. This result supports the presumption that many new students do not have a large local social network at the beginning of their studies.

5 Prototype: Chatbot-Based Onboarding Scavenger Hunt

The foregoing context of use analysis motivated the following overall aims for our technology-mediated onboarding support platform: network building between freshmen, getting to know the university campus and the vicinity, and collecting knowledge and best-practices (from experienced students).

Network building support is an essential point in the onboarding process since networking is essential at the beginning of a study [7]. It should be a network that exists both online and online, with the two worlds complementing each other and including getting to know the faculty building, the university campus and the vicinity [16]. Finally, a basis for the exchange between new and experienced students should be created. The goal is to combine all these aspects in a common concept and integrate it into the existing onboarding structures.

This online-offline bridging, group-integrating means was developed as a digital companion in the form of a chatbot that accompanies freshmen during the first two weeks of the first semester. The chatbot can be classified as *chatbot-driven* with a *long-term* relationship with the user, following the typology of [14]. It has the typical characteristic of Companion technology to respond to the user's situation and needs [2].

The qualities of the network (see Plastrik & Taylor [31]) supported by the chatbot lie in its connection of freshmen students among each other and with older students, structurally forming an easy-to-participate online network that functions to interconnect students in the offline world.

To aid this connecting function, the chatbot was integrated into an university-independent **online social network** based on the "Discord" platform, set up and run by students. The platform was established independently of this project during our context analysis phase. The popularity of Discord among the students made it a logical deployment target, letting us leverage existing communication structures within the body of students.

5.1 Scavenger Hunt

To motivate a large proportion of new students to participate in the onboarding program, the companion chatbot and the network building concept were integrated into a technology-based scavenger hunt.

30 quests were designed to aid the aims stated in the previous section, and include elements of playfulness as described in the PLEX framework by Lucero et al. [26], that is: competition to motivate the participants, completion of many quests, discovery of relevant landmarks and social contacts, exploration of the

surroundings, fellowship with other students, and humor to maintain a colloquial, friendly tone.

The scavenger hunt consisted of a selection of different components, including Quests as basic puzzles and riddles to be solved by visiting the campus and university, Special Quests requiring interaction on the campus with, e.g., attending events, Tips of the Day with additional information, and Impulses like appointment reminders or notifications about (in)activity in the hunt. Through this, students were led to get to know the university buildings and library, meet the student union and council as well as the study service center, find lecture halls (in other buildings), visit nearby restaurants and supermarkets, and get useful information besides study-related topics such as suggestions for enrolling in university sport courses.

5.2   Gamification Elements

A significant focus of the scavenger hunt was to connect people and strengthen existing relationships. For this reason, some quests were designed in such a way that participants had to get in touch with other people, or had an advantage in the scoring system when working together. So, additional points could be earned by solving the quests quickly, and in simple-to-setup teams.

The high score was accessible through the chatbot. The top 10 players were also posted daily with their score in the Online Social Network. There were prizes for the first 11 places, which were selected for the target group of computer science students. The award ceremony took place on the evening of the last day of the scavenger hunt. Afterward, there was a small party/networking event.

5.3   Chatbot Prototype

The chatbot was implemented in Node.js for the messenger platform Discord and was directly integrated into the students' online social network. After creating a Discord account, the students could start chatting with the Grätzelbot via mobile or desktop Discord App. Since Discord was very popular among the students, many participants could start even without registration. The conversation started with a quick tutorial on the scavenger hunt and then the students could start right away with the first quest. The Grätzelbot occasionally contacted the participants proactively with tips and impulses to keep them motivated.

For the intent detection a pattern matching engine was implemented, which could link keywords with *AND*, *OR* and *NOT* conjunctions and considered the last 3 intents triggered by the user. Besides 14 main intents the chatbot was also able to make some small talk and deal with insults. As the target group was students between 19 and 25, the language of the chatbot was chosen rather informal and youthful, the chatbot also used emojis and GIFs. To improve usability, clickable buttons were implemented at chosen points in the conversation. Figure 1 shows two conversations with the chatbot. More details about the implementation of the Grätzelbot can be found in [28].

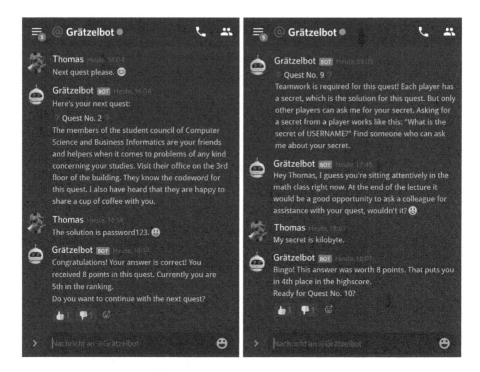

Fig. 1. Screenshots of the Grätzelbot prototype. A user recieves a quest (left). A user solves a quest requiring team-work (right).

6   Concept and Prototype Evaluation

The chatbot-based scavenger hunt was conducted at the beginning of the winter semester 2019 at the University of Vienna with first-semester students from the computer science department. During the hunt, user data was logged anonymously in order to evaluate the user activity afterward. The access logs show that the chatbot reached 122 people, of whom 102 actively participated in the scavenger hunt, and 65 players completed at least one quest. In total, 3,477 messages were sent to the chatbot during the 12 days of the scavenger hunt. Three players managed to have more than 385 out of 400 possible points. 8 players scored over 350 points. In total, 579 quests were solved during the scavenger hunt, and 8,072 points were scored. Over the scavenger hunt period, the Online Social Network grew by 221 new members. To compare: in that semester, 403 new students started studying computer science at the University of Vienna.

6.1   Post-Hunt Survey

At the end of the scavenger hunt, an in-depth online survey was conducted to evaluate the companion chatbot, the network building concept, and the scavenger hunt. Of the 65 active players, 28 took part in the survey.

50% of the participants already had a Discord account before the scavenger hunt. Three-quarters of all participants (75%) said that they use the Online Social Network daily or even several times a day. This shows that using the existing student Online Social Network for Grätzelbot was a prudent approach.

Prototype Evaluation. Participants were asked to rate their experiences with Grätzelbot on a 5-point Likert scales of opposing qualifiers or degree of agreement with given statements. In the following paragraph, descriptive values are given as pairs of respective average and related standard deviation.

The chatbot was perceived as very supportive (avg 1.39, sd 0.50), helpful (1.64, 0.83), motivating (1.75, 0.75), and entertaining (1.68, 0.77). Regarding the choice of technology, the chatbot was described as original (1.61, 0.88) and innovative (1.68, 0.72). Using a chatbot for an onboarding scenario was seen by participants as an exciting and modern approach (1.43, 0.57), and they preferred the chatbot over a smartphone app (4.18, 1.25). The usability was rated highly, with adjectives such as "supportive" and "helpful" finding much agreement. Regarding the natural language processing skills of the chatbot, the participants believed that the chatbot understood everything very well that was relevant for the scavenger hunt (1.25, 0.52 and 4.32, 0.86), the general language understanding was experienced slightly worse but still good with a score of 1.86, 0.80 and 4.07, 0.98, for the opposite question. The small talk skills of the chatbot were rated rather averagely with 3.25, 1.14.

Scavenger Hunt. The participants stated that the scavenger hunt helped them to get to know the faculty building, the university campus, and the vicinity (1.96, 1.26). They enjoyed the experience overall (1.46, 0.88). Network building aspects such as developing a sense of community received medium grades. Almost all participants (92.9%) said that they had talked with fellow students about the scavenger hunt, and 60.7% said that they had collaborated with colleagues to solve at least one quest together. 71.4% said they had helped other colleagues in the scavenger hunt. About one-third of the participants (32.1%) reported that they got to know other people they had not known previously. Self-identified introverts (in free text) still prefered to work on quests by their own.

6.2   Focus Groups Results

Besides the post-hunt survey, focus groups were conducted with a total of 7 scavenger hunt participants (3 female, 4 male), organized in two groups. Freshmen in one group already knew each other, and worked as a team during the hunt. The other group formed anew, and mentioned that the hunt's teamwork bonus motivated them to stay and work together.

Both groups were asked for improvements on the format of a chatbot-supported scavenger hunt for onboarding freshmen. One idea developed was to integrate the start of the scavenger hunt more into the welcome event on the first day and to form teams already there or to assign them randomly. It also seemed reasonable to implement team building as the first quest or to foster it in the first few quests. One way to do this would be to notify two players when they are working on the same quest. Other ideas suggested to integrate the scavenger hunt even more into events like classes at the university, and use professors and their lectures as quests, so as to also support repeating lecture contents. The participants also liked quests that brought several people to one place at the same time. Besides, proposals were made for alternative game modes and conversational interfaces.

Finally, we discussed which role the chatbot could play in the online platform after the scavenger hunt, and what functions it could perform to further support network building between students. Focus group participants developed use cases for the chatbot such as organizing study groups, setting up private channels on the Online Social Network, or schedule leisure activities. The desire for a virtual companion that regularly reminds them of deadlines and also motivates them to meet these deadlines on time was very strong. It would also be conceivable to use the chatbot as a gamified eLearning component, i.e., before a lecture, the topic of the last lecture can be repeated with a short quiz so that points for the finals could be collected.

7   Discussion

This work presents the results of a case study on chatbots as a Companion Technology in the context of freshmen onboarding at a University. Grätzelbot is a chatbot situated in a student-operated Discord environment, aimed at providing contacts and information useful to freshmen in their first semester at university who are transitioning from a more structured middle school routine. Communication of such information together with initial network building support among freshmen is enframed in a scavenger hunt moderated by Grätzelbot, which acts as a carefully crafted entry-point to a chatbot-mediated network-building concept. The chatbot as parasocial relation remains available to students after the scavenger hunt.

The contribution of this work is two fold: In pursuit of the research interest stated in Sect. 2.4, the presented case study explored with encouraging evaluation results the application of a chatbot in facilitating social relatedness among users. Specifically in relation to the case setting, the study developed an original way of using chatbots in onboarding, adding to recent design cases of chatbot application in onboarding settings [9, 29, 39].

Grätzelbot is aimed at fostering feelings of belonging and social relatedness in two ways: The parasocial relationship to the chatbot ideally sustains beyond freshmen onboarding and remains a contact point for students, situated in the student-operated Discord environment. Second, this parasocial relationship acts as a mediary towards the formation of real social relationships, as e.g. argued for by Gennaro et al. [15]. The Grätzelbot concept places a chatbot at an intermediary role among freshmen at a University and furthermore between them and their new "neighborhood", including University contact persons and offices.

The chatbot acts as a facilitator of social network building, following Plastrik and Taylor's concept of constructive network building towards a self-sustaining structure capable of effecting emergent network effects. Towards this, the network needs to be nurtured and undergo stages of development [31]. In the design phase, several platforms were considered, e.g. placing a chatbot in WhatsApp or Telegram. The setting of a student-operated Discord server was chosen to make use of already existing structures, operated by students themselves, feasibly beneficial to the overall cause of network building [40].

Overall, the Grätzelbot prototype and its functionality was well-received by participating freshmen. Responses gathered from the post-hunt focus groups suggest that such a chatbot could be valuable to freshmen also beyond initial onboarding, supporting the understanding of it as a sustained *Social Companion Technology* situated at the intersection of social networking, study-related content and organizational support. This perspective on future work fits well to the presented, original relation of chatbots and social network building theory, which lends itself to further exploration also beyond initial phases of network building and towards more mature network shapes and purposes beyond mere social connection, such as the formation of networks along user similarity or with the goal of realizing collective productivity [31]. As a further dimension of exploration, the application of chatbots as network building companion technology can feasibly be taken to other domains as well, e.g. civic citizen networking and activism or other learning environments.

Notably, the significance of evaluation results might be limited due to the relative small number of participants in the post-hunt survey (28 out of 65 active players, out of 102 players) and a possible positive selection bias in focus group participants, assuming that players disinterested in or unsatisfied with Grätzelbot would not sign up for this evaluation.

7.1   Conclusion

To investigate chatbot potential, this project pursues a conceptual exploration of the chatbot-user relationship, presenting a case study on a chatbot as mediator of social relatedness in a learning community. We suggest that an emphasis on relational properties of chatbot concepts offers an additional dimension of such potential, accompanying research on algorithmic (AI and Natural Language Processing) and interactional (interface design) properties.

Future work on Grätzelbot will be aimed at refining network building properties at the transition between student onboarding and subsequent everyday life. At this point, with the given possibilities, it is difficult to say whether the applied onboarding concept had a significant influence on the retention of the students. However, we believe that such activities can have a significant impact on the education of students. Therefore, we want to inspire and motivate others to experiment with similar kinds of activities as well as applications of the conceptual idea in other areas.

References

1. Biundo, S., Höller, D., Schattenberg, B., Bercher, P.: Companion-technology: an overview. KI - Künstliche Intelligenz **30**(1), 11–20 (2016). https://doi.org/10.1007/s13218-015-0419-3
2. Biundo, S., Wendemuth, A.: Companion Technology. Cognitive Technologies, Springer International Publishing, Cham (2017)
3. Bødker, S., Kyng, M.: Participatory design that matters-facing the big issues. ACM Trans. Comput.-Hum. Interact. **25**(1), 1–31 (2018)
4. Braun, V., Clarke, V.: Using thematic analysis in psychology. Qual. Res. Psychol. **3**(2), 77–101 (2006)
5. Briggs, A.R., Clark, J., Hall, I.: Building bridges: understanding student transition to university. Qual. High. Educ. **18**(1), 3–21 (2012)
6. Budny, D.: The Freshman Seminar: Assisting the Freshman Engineering Student's Transition from High School to College (2001)
7. Budny, D., Paul, C., Newborg, B.B.: Impact of peer mentoring on freshmen engineering students. J. STEM Educ. **11**(5), 9–24 (2010)
8. Budny, D.: Integrating the freshman seminar and freshman problem solving courses. In: 31st ASEE/IEEE Frontiers in Education Conference, pp. F4B–21-6 (2002)
9. Chandar, P., et al.: Leveraging conversational systems to assists new hires during onboarding. In: Bernhaupt, R., Dalvi, G., Joshi, A., Balkrishan, D.K., O'Neill, J., Winckler, M. (eds.) INTERACT 2017. LNCS, vol. 10514, pp. 381–391. Springer, Cham (2017). https://doi.org/10.1007/978-3-319-67684-5_23
10. Courter, S.S., Johnson, G.: Building community and retention among first-year students: Engineering First-Year Interest Groups (eFIGSs). In: Proceedings - Frontiers in Education Conference, FIE, pp. 3–8 (2007)
11. Dorst, K.: The core of 'Design Thinking' and its application. Des. Stud. **32**(6), 521–532 (2011)
12. Fagerholm, F., Johnson, P., Guinea, A.S., Borenstein, J., Munch, J.: Onboarding in open source software projects: a preliminary analysis. In: 2013 IEEE 8th International Conference on Global Software Engineering Workshops, pp. 5–10. IEEE, August 2013
13. Følstad, A., Brandtzaeg, P.B., Feltwell, T., Law, E.L.C., Tscheligi, M., Luger, E.A.: Sig: chatbots for social good. In: Extended Abstracts of the 2018 CHI Conference on Human Factors in Computing Systems, pp. SIG06:1-SIG06:4. CHI EA '2018, ACM, New York, NY, USA (2018)
14. Følstad, A., Skjuve, M., Brandtzaeg, P.B.: Different chatbots for different purposes: towards a typology of chatbots to understand interaction design. In: Bodrunova, S.S., et al. (eds.) INSCI 2018. LNCS, vol. 11551, pp. 145–156. Springer, Cham (2019). https://doi.org/10.1007/978-3-030-17705-8_13
15. de Gennaro, M., Krumhuber, E.G., Lucas, G.: Effectiveness of an empathic chatbot in combating adverse effects of social exclusion on mood. Front. Psychol. **10**, 3061 (2020)
16. Gerdes, H., Mallinckrodt, B.: Emotional, social, and academic adjustment of college students: a longitudinal study of retention. J. Couns. Dev. **72**(3), 281–288 (1994)
17. Goldman, C., Turnbow, D., Roth, A., Friedman, L.: Creating an engaging library orientation: first year experience courses at university of California. San Diego. Comminfolit **10**(1), 81 (2016)

18. Gunawardena, C.N., Hermans, M.B., Sanchez, D., Richmond, C., Bohley, M., Tuttle, R.: A theoretical framework for building online communities of practice with social networking tools. Educ. Media Int. **46**(1), 3–16 (2009)
19. Harley, D., Winn, S., Pemberton, S., Wilcox, P.: Using texting to support students' transition to university. Innov. Educ. Teach. Int. **44**(3), 229–241 (2007)
20. Holtzblatt, K., Wendell, J.B., Wood, S.: Rapid contextual design: a how-to guide to key techniques for user-centered design. In: Rapid Contextual Design, vol. 1, pp. 1–321. Elsevier, San Francisco (2005)
21. Holzwarth, M., Janiszewski, C., Neumann, M.: The influence of avatars on online consumer shopping behavior. J. Market. **70**, 19–36 (2006)
22. Jaijairam, P.: First-Year Seminar (FYS)–the advantages that this course offers. J. Educ. Learn. **5**(2), 15 (2016)
23. Jones, G., Edwards, G., Reid, A.: How can mobile SMS communication support and enhance a first year undergraduate learning environment? ALT-J **17**(3), 201–218 (2009)
24. Kassens, A.L., College, R., Enz, M., College, R.: Chasing economic knowledge: using an economics themed scavenger hunt to learn and build comradery. J. Econ. Econ. Educ. Res. **19**(4), 1–6 (2018)
25. Lim, J., Richardson, J.C.: Exploring the effects of students' social networking experience on social presence and perceptions of using SNSs for educational purposes. Internet High. Educ. **29**, 31–39 (2016)
26. Lucero, A., Karapanos, E., Arrasvuori, J., Korhonen, H.: Playful or gameful? creating delightful user experiences. Interactions **21**(3), 34–39 (2014)
27. Manasijević, D., Živković, D., Arsić, S., Milošević, I.: Exploring students' purposes of usage and educational usage of Facebook. Comput. Hum. Behav. **60**, 441–450 (2016)
28. Moshuber, L.: Grätzelbot: Using a Chatbot-Based Scavenger Hunt to Support Students' Transition to University. Master's thesis, University of Vienna (2020)
29. Asher, N.: A warmer welcome. Master's thesis, Linnaeus University (2017)
30. Niess, J., Wozniak, P.W.: Embracing companion technologies. In: Proceedings of the 11th Nordic Conference on Human-Computer Interaction. NordiCHI '2020 (2020)
31. Plastrik, P., Taylor, M.: A handbook for network builders seeking social change, pp. 1–117 (2006)
32. Preece, J.: Online Communities: Designing Usability and Supporting Socialbilty, 1st edn. John Wiley & Sons Inc, New York, NY, USA (2000)
33. Rabiee, F.: Focus-group interview and data analysis. Proc. Nutr. Soc. **63**(04), 655–660 (2005)
34. Rau, P.L.P., Gao, Q., Wu, L.M.: Using mobile communication technology in high school education: motivation, pressure, and learning performance. Comput. Educ. **50**(1), 1–22 (2008)
35. Renner, B.R., Cahoon, E., Allegri, F.: Low-tech scavenger hunt model for student orientation. Med. Ref. Serv. Q. **35**(4), 372–387 (2016)
36. Ryan, R., Deci, E.: Self-determination theory and the facilitation of intrinsic motivation, social development, and well-being. Am. Psychologist **55**, 68–78 (2000)
37. Shaked, N.: Avatars and virtual agents - relationship interfaces for the elderly. Healthc. Technol. Lett. **4**, 83–87 (2017)
38. Väänänen, K., Hiltunen, A., Varsaluoma, J., Pietilä, I.: Civicbots - chatbots for supporting youth in societal participation. In: Proceeding of Chatbot Research and Design - Third International Workshop, CONVERSATIONS 2019, pp. 143–157. Springer (2019)

39. Westberg, S.: Applying a chatbot for assistance in the onboarding process. Master's thesis, Linköping University (2019)
40. Willis, K.S.: Making a 'place' for ICTS in rural communities: the role of village halls in digital inclusion. In: Proceedings of the 9th International Conference on Communities & Technologies - Transforming Communities, p. 136–142. C&T '2019 (2019)

Chatbot Applications

Heuristic Evaluation of COVID-19 Chatbots

Sviatlana Höhn[(✉)] and Kerstin Bongard-Blanchy

University of Luxembourg, Esch-sur-Alzette, Luxembourg
{sviatlana.hoehn,kerstin.bongard-blanchy}@uni.lu
https://chatbots.uni.lu

Abstract. Chatbots have been adopted in the health domain and their number grew during the current COVID-19 pandemic. As a new kind of interface, chatbots combine visual elements with natural conversation. While conversational capabilities of chatbots improve, little attention has been given to the evaluation of the user experience and chatbot usability. This paper presents the results of a heuristic review of 24 COVID-19 chatbots on different channels (webchat vs messengers), for diverse topics (symptom-checker vs FAQ) and with varying interaction styles (visual-centric vs content-centric vs conversation-centric). It proposes a generic evaluation framework with 12 heuristics based on Nielsen's ten heuristics and adapted to the conversational interface context. The results point at the strengths (immediate feedback, familiar language, consistent wording and visual design) as well as shortcomings (little user control and freedom, missing permanent menu and help options, lack of context understanding and interaction management capabilities) of COVID-19 chatbots. The paper furthermore gives recommendations for chatbot design in similar contexts.

Keywords: Conversational UX Analysis · Chatbots · Healthcare

1 Introduction

Chatbots specialised in COVID-19 matters have been developed to help people cope with the pandemic. Authorities like the WHO, CDC, Ministries of Health of different countries, Red Cross, hospitals and insurance companies provide free of charge chatbots that talk about Coronavirus. Among them are bots for symptom checking [16], for information about emergencies in the region and world, for psychological distress monitoring [5], and artificial business advisors [15]. Tech companies provide the required infrastructure and templates [22].

Although research on dialogue systems, including robots, chatbots and voice assistants, has advanced in many aspects, such conversational interfaces still pose significant challenges to researchers and designers in the human-computer interaction domain [3]. Consideration for chatbot user experience (UX) has gained momentum, starting with effort to adapt classical UX evaluation methods to the

---

Supported by the Luxembourg National Research Fund (FNR), SLANT, 13320890.

A. Følstad et al. (Eds.): CONVERSATIONS 2020, LNCS 12604, pp. 131–144, 2021.
https://doi.org/10.1007/978-3-030-68288-0_9

chatbot context [9, 21], stretching to user interviews to analyse user needs and expectations [12]. However, basic principles of UX design are not yet commonly applied in the chatbot domain. Current appreciations of chatbots range hence from a *poor relative of an intelligent assistant that performs only one well-defined domain-specific task* [4] to a *fully-capable conversational software that maintains long-term interaction with its user via text messages* [6]. Moore and Arar (2019) [14] argue that chatbots today are similar to the Internet in 1997: made by laypeople based on a set of quickly self-acquired skills.

In this regard, deficits in the accuracy of medical symptom checkers have been found, together with strong risk-averse responses [18]. COVID-19 chatbots for symptom-checking show significant differences in their sensitivity and specificity [16]. However, inaccuracy and unsound conversational design in medical applications can be life-threatening [19].

This paper, therefore, seeks to evaluate the usability of 24 COVID-19 chatbots to answer the **research questions**:

1. What types of COVID-19 chatbots exist?
   (a) On which channels are they available?
   (b) Which service, content or topic within the COVID-19 area do they offer?
   (c) Which interaction styles do they use?
2. How *usable* are COVID-19 chatbots?

Following an overview of related work, Sect. 3 presents 39 evaluation aspects grouped under 12 heuristics and explains the evaluation procedure. Section 4 provides insights in content, topics, channels and conversation styles of COVID-19 chatbots and presents the heuristic evaluation results. Section 5 discusses the strengths and weaknesses of the tested bots. Finally, Sect. 6 formulates recommendations for satisfying conversational UX, especially in e-health domain.

The paper contributes conversational UX analysis with a new framework for the evaluation of conversational interfaces that, in contrast with most recent scholar work [21], covers chatbots of *all* interaction styles. The new framework helps to formulate design recommendations for conversational interfaces.

2   Related Work

Multiple objective and subjective metrics for evaluation of conversational interfaces have been developed within the last two decades by major international initiatives; see, for instance, McTear et al. (2016) [13, Chap. 17]. Objective methodologies cover UX aspects in the best case by the notion of "user satisfaction". The most prominent objective methodology for spoken dialogue system evaluation, PARADISE, dates from the late nineties [25]. Messenger APIs and widgets for interaction management by bots in messengers (e.g. carousel) were not existent by that time. The PARADISE framework has also been used for the prediction of user satisfaction. User satisfaction is expected to be high if the task success is maximised while the dialogue costs are minimised. Methods for subjective evaluation include the Subjective Assessment of Speech System Interfaces (SASSI) questionnaire [10]. It builds on 34 criteria such as system response accuracy, likeability, cognitive demand, annoyance, habitability, and speed.

More recent scholar initiatives suggest to study chatbots from the perspective of *conversational UX design*, see for instance contributions at CHI 2017 conversational UX Design Workshop[1]. Researchers seek to formulate principles and guidelines for conversational UX Design as a distinct discipline.

Moore and Arar (2019) recommend using conversation analysis to improve conversational design. They classify natural language interfaces by their *interaction styles*: system-centric (e.g. voice control, web search; require valid, technical input), content-centric (e.g. FAQ; document-like responses), visual-centric (e.g. desktop or mobile interfaces; use buttons and require direct manipulation) and conversation-centric (similar to natural conversation) [14, p. 16]. The styles are not disjoint: a content-centric chatbot for document retrieval that understands free text input can use buttons for short replies. Buttons increase the speed and efficiency of use; and these two factors have been reported to be the most important reasons for using chatbots [2].

While the conversational UX Design community formulated many guidelines on how to design chatbots [8,14,20], only a few researchers have so far undertaken conversational UX evaluation [7,9,21]. Nielsen's (2005) ten heuristics are frequently used to analyse the usability of user interfaces [17] and they have already been employed for chatbot UX analysis [23]. However, the applicability of this UX evaluation approach to conversational interfaces is subject of scientific debate. While Holmes et al. (2019) [9] found the conventional usability evaluation methods not suitable for the evaluation of chatbots, Sugisaki and Bleiker (2020) argue that Nielsen's (2005) approach provides a sound basis for the chatbot domain [21]. Their, most recent, detailed framework for the evaluation of conversational UX contains 53 so-called checkpoints that cover the ten Nielsen heuristics adapted to conversational interfaces.

The framework proposed by Sugisaki and Bleiker (2020) explicitly excludes chatbots that mainly use visual elements for interaction or only accept a precisely defined set of commands. For certain tasks and use cases, natural conversation is indeed the preferable interaction style. However, in other cases, the UX benefits from additional shortcuts, such as buttons and short replies. Many chatbots use both natural conversation and visual elements. That is why an evaluation framework that covers all types of chatbots, as proposed in this paper, is preferable because it allows the comparison of chatbots with different interaction styles (Table 1).

3   Method

3.1   The 12 Heuristics for Conversational UX Analysis

Chatbots can combine visual elements with natural conversation. They hence require an adapted approach to usability evaluation. We defined the following

---

[1] https://researcher.watson.ibm.com/researcher/view_group.php?id=7539.

12 heuristics to assess Conversational UX based on Nielsen's ten heuristics [17], Shevat's chatbot design guidelines [20] and Conversational UX design guidelines formulated by Moore and Arar [14].

3.2   COVID-19 Chatbots

Starting with ten English webchat symptom checkers analysed in [16], we searched on the Internet for "COVID-19 chatbots" and "Coronavirus chatbot". In this way we found 14 chatbots working also in messengers (Whatsapp, Telegram, Viber, Facebook Messenger) and added German, Russian, French and Ukrainian (languages spoken by authors of this paper). The following bots were inspected:

(1) **Ada** https://ada.com/COVID-19-screener/
(2) **Apple** https://www.apple.com/COVID19
(3) **Babylon** https://www.babylonhealth.com/ask-babylon-chat
(4) **Bobbi** https://www.berlin.de/corona/faq/chatbot/artikel.917495.php
(5) **CDC** https://www.cdc.gov/coronavirus/2019-nCoV/index.html
(6) **Cleveland Clinic** http://COVID19chat.clevelandclinic.org/
(7) **Corona Bot** CoronaBot.tn im Facebook Messenger
(8) **HSE Coronavirus Selfchecker** https://www.hse.ie
(9) **Covid-19 Chatbot** https://www.chatbot.com/COVID19-chatbot/
(10) **Docyet** https://corona.docyet.com/client/index.html
(11) **Dubai Department of Health** https://doh.gov.ae/COVID-19
(12) **e-Bot⁷** https://e-bot7.de/coronachatbot/
(13) **German Red Cross** WhatsApp +49(30)85404106
(14) **HealthBuddy** https://www.euro.who.int/en/health-topics/health-emergencies/coronavirus-COVID-19/healthbuddy
(15) **Infermedica** https://symptomate.com/COVID19/checkup/en/
(16) **Ivan Mask** t.me/ivanmaskbot
(17) **Martha** https://COVID19.app.keyreply.com/webchat/
(18) **MTI Singapore Chat for Biz** https://www.mti.gov.sg/Chatbot/chat
(19) **Providence** https://coronavirus.providence.org/
(20) **Russian Ministry of Health** WhatsApp +7(495)6240168
(21) **Suve** https://eebot.ee
(22) **Symptoma** https://www.symptoma.com/COVID-19
(23) **WHO** WhatsApp +41(79)8931892
(24) **Your.MD** https://webapp.your.md/login

3.3   Expert Review Method

Two experts (one with a PhD degree in UX and one with a PhD degree in chatbots) scored each chatbot from Table 1 on all sub-heuristics (Sect. 3.1) as 0 - 'unsupported', $0,5$ - 'partially supported', and 1 - 'fully supported'. If a sub-heuristic did not apply to the particular chatbot in its particular context, the experts marked it with "n/a". The inter-rater agreement was substantial (Kappa

H1

VISIBILITY OF SYSTEM STATUS

a. Presence of information about the chatbot state in the entire process
b. Immediate feedback (did the last user action work?)
c. Compel user action (what does the chatbot think the user will do next?)

H2

MATCH BETWEEN SYSTEM AND THE REAL WORLD

a. Uses language familiar to the users
b. Visual components (emojis, GIFs, icons) are linked to real-world objects
c. If metaphors are used, they are understandable for the user

H3

USER CONTROL AND FREEDOM

a. Supports undo/redo of actions
b. Offers a permanent menu
c. Provides navigation options
d. Understands repair initiations

H4

CONSISTENCY AND STANDARDS

a. Uses the domain model from the user perspective
b. Has a personality, consistency in language and style

H5

ERROR PREVENTION

a. Prevents unconscious slips by meaningful constraints
b. Prevents unconscious slips by spelling error detection
c. Requests confirmation before actions with signicant implications
d. Explains consequences of user actions

H6

RECOGNITION RATHER THAN RECALL

a. Makes the options clear through descriptive visual elements and explicit instructions
b. Shows summary of collected information before transactions
c. Offers a permanent menu and help option

H7

FLEXIBILITY AND ECIENCY OF USE

a. Understands not only special instructions but also synonyms
b. Can deal with different formulations
c. Offers multiple ways to achieve the same goal

H8

AESTHETIC AND MINIMALIST DESIGN

a. Dialogues are concise, only contain relevant information
b. Uses visual information in a personality-consistent manner to support the user, not just random decoration

H9

HELP USERS RECOGNISE, DIAGNOSE, RECOVER FROM ERRORS

a. Clearly indicates that an error has occurred
b. Uses plain language to explain the error
c. Explains the actions needed for recovery
d. Offers shortcuts to fix errors quickly

H10

HELP AND DOCUMENTATION

a. Provides a clear description of its capabilities
b. Offers keyword search
c. Focuses its help on the user task
d. Explains concrete steps to be carried out for a task

H11

CONTEXT UNDERSTANDING

a. Understands the context within one turn
b. Understands the context within a small number of turns (usually 2-3 user-bot turn pairs)
c. Understands the context of a multi-turn conversation

H12

INTERACTION MANAGEMENT CAPABILITIES

a. Understands conversation openings/closings (e.g., 'hi')
b. Understands sequence closings (e.g., 'ok', 'thanks')
c. Understands repair initiations and replies with repairs
d. Initiates repair to handle potential user errors

Fig. 1. 12 heuristics for conversational UX evaluation

Cohen 0.7245). For the final scoring, we picked the more optimistic value of both raters for non-agreement cases.

To establish a usability score for each chatbot, we first summed the values of the sub-heuristics for each heuristic and then divided the sum by the number

Table 1. Chatbots for COVID-19 matters by channels, content, tested language and interaction style.

Name	Channel	Content	Language	Interaction style
Ada	webchat	symptom checker	EN, DE	visual
Apple	webchat	symptom checker	EN	visual
Babylon	webchat	symptom checker	EN	visual
Bobbi	webchat	FAQ	EN, DE	content/ conversation
CDC	webchat	symptom checker	EN	visual
Cleveland Clinic	webchat	symptom checker	EN	visual
Corona Bot	FB Messenger	symptom checker, FAQ	FR	visual/ conversation
Covid-19 Chatbot	webchat	symptom checker	EN	visual
German Red Cross	Whatsapp	FAQ	DE	system/ conversation
Docyet	webchat	symptom checker, FAQ, mental support	DE	visual
Dubai Department of Health	webchat	FAQ	EN	content/ conversation
e-Bot[7]	webchat	FAQ	DE	content
HealthBuddy	webchat	FAQ	EN, DE, FR, RU	conversation/ content
HSE Corona Selfchecker	webchat	symptom checker	EN	visual
Infermedica	webchat	symptom checker	EN, DE	visual
Ivan Mask	Telegram	FAQ	UK	visual/ conversation
Martha	webchat	symptom checker, FAQ	EN	content/ visual
MTI Singapore Chat for Biz	webchat	FAQ	EN	conversation/ visual
Providence	webchat	symptom checker	FR	visual
Russian Ministry of Health	Whatsapp	FAQ	RU	system/ content
Suve	webchat	symptom checker, FAQ	EN	conversation/ visual
Symptoma	webchat	symptom checker	EN	visual
WHO	Whatsapp	FAQ	EN	system
Your.MD	webchat	symptom-checker, FAQ	EN	visual

of applicable items inside the heuristic. Secondly, we summed the scores for the twelve heuristics. An ideal chatbot would score 1 for each heuristic, hence reach a usability score of 12.

To get an impression which heuristics were overall well implemented compared to others, we summed the sub-heuristic and heuristic scores for all tested chatbots and divided them by the number of applicable items. Given that we looked at 24 chatbots, the highest possible sum per heuristic would have been 24 (=100%). We discuss the results per (sub-)heuristic in Sect. 4.2.

4 Results

4.1 COVID-19 Chatbots: Channels, Topics and Conversation Styles

Although increased chatbot popularity is related to the opening of messenger APIs to bot developers in 2015, 19 of 24 tested COVID-19 chatbots work in webchat: they simulate a messenger-like interface on a website. Only five of 24 bots work in messengers: three in WhatsApp, one in Telegram and one in Facebook messenger. We noticed that messenger bots are available in multiple messengers while webchat bots are only available on webchat. For instance, users can reach the WHO bot in WhatsApp and Viber, and Ivan Mask works in Telegram, Viber and Facebook Messenger. We excluded Viber versions from our benchmark but used them for a qualitative cross-channel comparison.

The choice of a particular channel influences interaction. Viber and Telegram messengers offer similar interfaces, but WhatsApp provides a different set of interactional resources. While Viber provides a standard set of widgets for messenger bots (i.e.; permanent menu, buttons, short replies), WhatsApp requires typing text messages. As a consequence, WhatsApp chatbots have to *simulate* a visual-centric interaction style by introducing number codes. To compare, Ivan Mask chatbot working in Telegram and Viber shows a very similar look-and-feel in both messengers.

In contrast to messengers, webchat allows more freedom in the implementation of the graphical user interface (GUI). Some webchat bots offer an attractive GUI (namely Apple, Infermedica, Symptoma, Docyet, Ada), as reflected by the high scores (cf Sect. 4.2) for heuristic 2 Match between system and the real world, 4 Consistency and standards, and 8 Aesthetic and minimalist design. However, webchat bots often only use a small part of the screen for the chat window, while the rest stays unused. Furthermore, the chat window cannot be moved or resized and the information is usually presented as text only.

Two most popular services in COVID-19 chatbots are symptom-checking and frequently asked questions (FAQ). As Table 1 shows, five chatbots offer both services, and one of them also offers mental support. Although COVID-19 pandemic dramatically affected national and international businesses, we found only one chatbot that addresses business-related topics. FAQ bots frequently cover COVID-19 myths. Instead of a list of the topics, the WHO Viber bot offers a quiz asking the user to answer the bot's questions. Such a strategy helps increase user engagement and support learning [24].

Table 2. Expert review scores for 24 COVID-19 chatbots on 12 heuristics: 1 Visibility of system status, 2 Match between the system and the real world, 3 User control and freedom, 4 Consistency and standards, 5 Error prevention, 6 Recognition rather than recall, 7 Flexibility and efficiency of use, 8 Aesthetic and minimalist design, 9 Help users recognise, diagnose, and recover from errors, 10 Help and documentation, 11 Context understanding, 12 Interaction management capabilities; on the scale 0 unsupported, 0,5 partially supported, 1 fully supported, - not applicable

Chatbot	Score	1	2	3	4	5	6	7	8	9	10	11	12
IDEAL BOT	12	1.0	1.0	1.0	1.0	1.0	1.0	1.0	1.0	1.0	1.0	1.0	1.0
Suve	**7.8**	0.5	1.0	0.15	1.0	0.8	0.5	0.8	1.0	0.6	0.6	0.3	0.5
Apple	**7.1**	0.7	1.0	0.3	1.0	1.0	0.5	0.0	1.0	0.8	0.8	–	–
Infermedica	**7.0**	1.0	1.0	0.6	1.0	1.0	0.7	0.0	1.0	–	0.8	–	–
Symptoma	**7.0**	1.0	0.7	0.6	0.8	0.8	0.8	0.5	1.0	0.10	0.8	–	–
HealthBuddy	6.6	0.8	1.0	0.1	0.8	0.0	0.5	0.5	0.8	0.9	0.5	0.3	0.5
Docyet	6.5	0.8	1.0	0.3	1.0	0.5	0.5	0.3	1.0	0.8	0.4	–	–
Ada	6.3	0.7	1.0	0.3	1.0	0.5	0.3	0.0	1.0	0.8	0.7	–	–
Germ. Red Cr	5.9	0.5	1.0	0.4	0.5	0.0	0.5	0.8	0.8	0.3	0.6	0.3	0.3
Dub. Dpt. of H	5.8	0.8	1.0	0.0	0.5	0.5	0.3	0.8	0.5	0.4	0.3	0.3	0.5
Corona Bot	5.4	0.5	0.8	0.0	0.8	0.8	0.0	0.3	1.0	0.4	0.1	0.3	0.5
Ivan Mask	5.3	0.8	0.8	0.3	0.8	0.3	0.5	0.2	0.5	0.5	0.3	0.3	0.3
Martha	5.3	0.7	1.0	0.0	0.8	0.5	0.2	0.2	0.8	0.1	0.5	0.2	0.5
WHO	5.3	0.8	1.0	0.4	0.5	0.0	0.8	0.7	0.8	0.1	0.4	0.0	0.0
Bobbi	5.3	0.8	0.7	0.1	0.3	0.3	0.2	0.5	0.8	0.6	0.6	0.2	0.4
MTI	5.1	0.5	0.5	0.1	0.5	0.5	0.2	0.8	1.0	0.5	0.4	0.0	0.1
Babylon	4.9	0.7	1.0	0.3	0.8	1.0	0.0	0.0	0.8	–	0.5	–	–
Covid-19	4.9	0.5	0.7	0.0	1.0	1.0	0.5	0.0	1.0	0.0	0.3	–	–
CDC	4.4	0.5	1.0	0.0	0.8	1.0	0.2	0.0	0.5	–	0.5	–	–
HSE	4.4	0.3	1.0	0.0	0.8	1.0	0.0	0.0	1.0	–	0.3	–	–
e-bot7	4.1	0.8	0.5	0.1	1.0	0.5	0.5	0.0	0.5	0.0	0.3	–	–
Providence	3.9	0.5	0.5	0.0	0.8	1.0	0.0	0.0	0.8	0.0	0.4	–	–
Your.MD	3.8	0.7	0.7	0.0	0.8	0.3	0.3	0.2	0.3	0.4	0.4	–	–
Clevel. Clinic	3.7	0.5	0.5	0.0	0.8	1.0	0.2	0.0	0.5	–	0.3	–	–
Russ. M. of H	2.3	0.5	0.8	0.2	0.3	0.0	0.3	0.0	0.0	0.3	0.1	0.0	0.0
Score/heuristic		*64%*	*83%*	*17%*	*74%*	*58%*	*34%*	*28%*	*75%*	*40%*	*44%*	*21%*	*32%*

Most of the bots offer visual-centric or content-centric conversation styles. The FAQ bots mostly offer a selection of topics, and the users can only choose among items from a list, without the possibility to type a question. Some bots also accept free text entry (e.g. German Red Cross and Ivan Mask) but very few bots are capable of information extraction from user utterances. The most disappointing experience appeared when a bot offered a text input line, but the function was disabled (e.g., e-Bot[7]).

Some bots offer both, buttons and free text input for interaction, but are in most cases not able to understand free text input. At least, the perceived experience for non-recognised inputs improves when the bot explains that it is still learning (e.g. Ivan Mask) and recommends using buttons, or when bots are capable of performing simple conversation management, such as recognition of openings and closings (e.g. Suve).

4.2   Results by Heuristic

Our second research question concerns the usability of COVID-19 chatbots. Table 2 presents the results of the expert review. The highest score in our sample is 7.8 out of 12. It was achieved by the Suve chatbot. The following top-scoring bots are the symptom checkers of Apple (7.1), Infermedica (7.0), and Symptoma (7.0). Infermedica and Symptoma were also the best two in the accuracy evaluation of COVID-19 symptom checkers [16].

Nearly all tested COVID-19 chatbots **scored well** on heuristics 1 Visibility of system status, 2 Match between system and the real world, 4 Consistency and standards, and 8 Aesthetic and minimalist design. This might be explained by the fact that messengers and webchat interfaces have already well-implemented UX, and the chatbot developers cannot change much on their appearance. **Ambivalent scores** were observed for the heuristics 5 Error prevention, 9 Help users recognise, diagnose, and recover from errors, and 10 Help and documentation. **Unsatisfying scores** were found for the remaining heuristics 3. User control and freedom, 6 Recognition rather than recall, 7 Flexibility and efficiency of use, 11 Context understanding, and 12 Interaction management capabilities (cf. last row Table 2 for the percentage of the main heuristic). Such low scores related to repairs and flexibility of use may occur because messengers, in contrast to websites, do not offer buttons to go back and forth by default, in a conversational interface, users cannot simply click somewhere to go back in the conversation. The only way to handle errors in a conversation-centric interaction would be a proper implementation of repair as we use it in our interaction with people. This is challenging but doable [8].

The best scores were achieved by bots running in webchat and offering a combination of visual-centric interaction and natural conversation. Those bots also showed well-implemented heuristics 1, 2, 4, 6, 8 and 10. The details of each heuristic give a clearer picture of what specific functionalities (here represented by the sub-heuristics) require further design effort.

1. Visibility of system status was rather well implemented throughout all tested chatbots (64%). Sub-heuristic *(b) Immediate feedback* was close to entirely covered (98%), meaning that the user quickly knows that their input has been received and is treated. Nearly all chatbots showed efforts to *Compel user actions (c)* (56%). However, heuristic *(a) Information about the chatbots status in the process* was a weakness (20%) for all except two top-scoring bots.

2. Match between system and the real world has been very well implemented (83%). The good scoring comes from the high scores for sub-heuristic *(a) Chatbot uses the language familiar to the target user group* (90%), meaning that most chatbots employ easily understandable language. Many bots did neither employ visual components nor metaphors to enhance the communication with the users. For this reason, the two other sub-heuristics, namely *(b) Visual components of the messages (emojis, GIFs, icons) are linked to real-world objects* and *(c) If metaphors are used, they are understandable for the user*, were not applicable for more than half of the tested bots.

3. User control and freedom scored very low throughout all tested chatbots (17%). None of the bots *understood repair initiations (d)* and only a few, among the best scoring bots, provided *navigation options (c)*, offered a *permanent menu (b)*, or *partially supported undo/redo of actions (a)*.

4. Consistency and standards scored well for most of the tested chatbots (74%). They *use the domain model from the user perspective (a)*, and have a *personality with a language is consistent throughout all interaction paths (b)*.

5. Error prevention shows an ambivalent scoring (58%). While the *prevention of unconscious slips by meaningful constraints (a)* is implemented to a basic degree (61%), only a few bots prevent these through *recognition of typos and spelling error correction (b)* (37%). The other two sub-heuristics for error prevention *(c) Chatbot requests confirmation before action with significant implications for the user* and *(d) Chatbot explains consequences of the user action* were not applicable for any of the 24 tested bots.

6. Recognition rather than recall is a usability principle that has not sufficiently found its way into the chatbots we tested (34%). About half make the options at least partly clear by adding *descriptive visual elements and clear instructions (a)* (52%). Few provide a *summary of the collected information before transactions (b)* (32%) which, however, in one-third of the tested chatbots was not even an applicable use case. None of the chatbots offered both a *permanent menu and help option (c)*, although about half had either one or the other.

7. Flexibility and efficiency of use was another low scoring heuristic (28%). Only about half of the sampled chatbots partly understands not only special instructions but also *natural synonym phrases (a)* (38%). One third can to some degree deal with *different formulations of the same intent (b)* (25%) and offer *multiple ways to achieve the same goal for more and less proficient users (c)* (21%). However, only six bots reached score 1 for at least one sub-heuristic here, leaving room for improvement.

8. Aesthetic and minimalist design is among the well-implemented heuristics (75%). Most chatbots reach scores of 1 or 0,5 for their *use of visual information in a personality-consistent manner (b)* (87%), as well as for *concise and precise dialogues (a)* (65%).

9. Help users recognise, diagnose, and recover from errors is a heuristic that was not sufficiently established in our chatbot sample (40%). None of the bots scores 1 for clearly *indicating that an error has occurred (a)* (33%). Only some *use plain language to explain the error (b)* (56%) or *explain the actions needed for recovery (c)* (45%). Even less offer a *shortcut to quickly fix the error (d)* (22%).

10. Help and documentation shows an ambivalent scoring (44%). While nearly all chatbots provide a *clear description of their capabilities (a)* (85%), very few offer *keyword search (b)* (34%). Only the high-ranking bots *focus their* *help on the user task (c)* (26%) and *explain concrete steps to be carried out for a task (d)* (25%).

11. Context understanding was a non-applicable heuristic for half of the tested chatbots and not very well implemented in the applicable cases (44%). When applicable, most *understood the context within one turn (a)* to some extent (55%). However, almost none *understood the context within a small number of turns (b)* (9%), let al.one the context of a *multi-turn conversation (c)* (0%).

12. Interaction management capabilities too was a non-applicable heuristic for about half of the tested chatbots and scored low in the applicable cases (32%). If applicable, most of the bots understood *conversation openings and closings (a)* (68%) as well as *sequence closings (b)* (55%) to some extent. However, they neither *understood repair initiations or replied with repairs (c)* (0%), nor did they *initiate repairs to handle potential user errors (d)* (5%).

4.3   Non-applicable Heuristics

Only 11 of 24 chatbots implemented at least one element per heuristic. 13 of 24 chatbots did not implement any conversational functionality, and therefore, heuristics 11 and 12 were not applicable for them. Five of the chatbots are strictly visual-centred (interaction only via buttons), so that heuristic 9 was not applicable, either. We furthermore find sub-heuristics that have not been applicable for any of the 24 chatbots in our sample. Among them are *(5c) Error prevention - Chatbot requests confirmation before action with significant implications for the user* and (5d) *Error prevention - Chatbot explains the consequences of the user action in chat*. However, the experts did not encounter any situation that would have required these features.

5   Discussion and Limitations

The experience a user lives with a product or service materialises from the interplay of various dimensions [1]. Despite the widespread opinion that natural conversation with chatbots is the ultimate goal in chatbot research, this review shows that the right balance of interaction flexibility and pace can be achieved by merging natural conversation with visual-centric interaction. In this way, a satisfying conversational UX can be ensured for users who value efficiency [2].

Channels, content, and interaction style show mutual dependencies. Messengers such as WhatsApp, are potent communication channels because of their extensive number of users. However, the dominance of webchat channels can be explained by two aspects: 1) security and data protection considerations; 2) greater freedom for design - webchats offer more possibilities to personalise the design and to add visual elements as compared to bots running in messengers. The fact that the highest scores in this study have been earned by webchat bots does not mean that webchat as a channel is per default the best one.

The WhatsApp API does not provide any visual elements, and therefore, it is better suitable for conversation-centric style. The three WhatsApp chatbots

(WHO, German Red Cross (GRC) and Russian Ministry of Health (RMoH)) in our sample chose different message-based interactions that *simulate* visual-centric style. RMoH chatbot understands only number codes (scored 2.3). The WHO chatbot understands number codes and keywords presented in bold in the bot messages (scored 5.3). The GRC chatbot understands the first two variants plus it can extract keywords from natural phrases (scored 5.9).

Intent-based natural language understanding (NLU) is the state of the art in current chatbot building platforms (e.g. Watson, DialogFlow and RASA). Surprisingly, less than half of the chatbots in this study made use of NLU methods. Although almost none of the symptom checkers implemented conversation management or context understanding, this is not necessarily negative for symptom-checkers that simulate a form-filling interaction (Apple, Symptomate, Ada).

Indeed, the advantages of using a chatbot for the sake of informing people about COVID-19 are in many cases unclear. Both FAQ and form-filling (symptom checking) tasks can be presented more user-friendly on a "traditional" website. Building a chatbot just for the sake of having a chatbot may harm the service because of the less optimal UX.

Expert reviews based on usability heuristics are only one among the various tools of UX evaluation [11]. An expert usability review usually analyses only one service/product in-depth and explicitly lists all identified issues - including screenshots, description, and proposed solution. This study sought to give an overview of usability problems in Covid-19 chatbots in general. The heuristics were therefore only used to establish a usability score for each bot. The scoring for each heuristic highlights design rules that are not sufficiently taken into account, and serve to trace specific usability issues. Observing real users during their interaction with the bot will reveal the most critical shortcomings of the system, as well as provide an impression of the user satisfaction with the interaction - insights a heuristic review cannot produce.

Finally, this heuristic review, unfortunately, did not yield conclusions specific to channels, topics, and interaction styles because the different types were not evenly represented in our sample - mostly webchat, mainly symptom checkers, principally visual-centric conversation style.

6   Conclusions and Recommendations

This study shows that our conversational UX evaluation framework is applicable to chatbots of different conversation styles [14]. We can conclude that natural conversations with chatbots are in general not mandatory for good conversational UX. Because the analysed COVID-19 chatbots show a large redundancy in topics and types of service, but are diverse in UX scores, we conclude that conversational E-health applications would be more attractive to users if they invest in UX from the beginning. The following concrete steps need to be taken in order to make pragmatically motivated use of chatbots [2] also satisfying in terms of UX:

DO...

☺ Invest in UX from the beginning! Choose chatbot as a channel if the problem can be easily solved in a conversation.

☺ Break down large pieces of information, choose other channels for large documents.

☺ Implement at least basic conversation management capabilities.

☺ Implement repairs.

☺ Use visual elements if possible.

☺ Offer free text input only if bot can deal with it.

DON'T...

☹ Implement a chatbot for the sake of a chatbot.

☹ Post long text in chat. A long sequence of short messages is not a good alternative.

☹ Reply to a "hello" with "I did not understand your question".

☹ Hope that users make no mistakes.

☹ Force users to type everything.

☹ Invite users to perform actions that are deactivated or not working.

Further research questions arose from this study: What sorts of chatbots would be really helpful in the context of pandemics, going beyond accuracy and UX? Which conversational e-health applications offer real added value to their users? Which topics and services beyond FAQ and symptom checkers can be explored within in the context of the COVID-19 crisis?

References

1. Bongard-Blanchy, K., Bouchard, C.: Dimensions of user experience-from the product design perspective (2014)
2. Brandtzaeg, P.B., Følstad, A.: Why people use chatbots. In: Kompatsiaris, I., et al. (eds.) INSCI 2017. LNCS, vol. 10673, pp. 377–392. Springer, Cham (2017). https://doi.org/10.1007/978-3-319-70284-1_30
3. Brandtzaeg, P.B., Følstad, A.: Chatbots: changing user needs and motivations. Interactions **25**(5), 38–43 (2018). https://doi.org/10.1145/3236669
4. Budiu, R.: The user experience of chatbots. Nielsen Norman Group (2018)
5. Chaix, B., Delamon, G., Guillemasse, A., Brouard, B., Bibault, J.E.: Psychological distress during the Covid-19 pandemic in France: a national assessment of at-risk populations. medRxiv (2020)
6. Danilava, S., Busemann, S., Schommer, C., Ziegler, G.: Towards computational models for a long-term interaction with an artificial conversational companion. In: Proceeding of ICAART'2013 (2013)
7. Fadhil, A., Schiavo, G.: Designing for health chatbots. arXiv preprint arXiv:1902.09022 (2019)
8. Artificial Companion for Second Language Conversation. Springer, Cham (2019). https://doi.org/10.1007/978-3-030-15504-9_14
9. Holmes, S., Moorhead, A., Bond, R., Zheng, H., Coates, V., McTear, M.: Usability testing of a healthcare chatbot: can we use conventional methods to assess conversational user interfaces? In: Proceedings of ECCE, pp. 207–214 (2019)
10. Hone, K.S., Graham, R.: Towards a tool for the subjective assessment of speech system interfaces (sassi). Nat. Lang. Eng. **6**, 287–303 (2000)
11. Lallemand, C., Gronier, G.: Méthodes de design UX: 30 méthodes fondamentales pour concevoir des expériences optimales. Eyrolles (2018)

12. Luger, E., Sellen, A.: Like having a really bad PA: the gulf between user expectation and experience of conversational agents. In: Proceedings CHI'2016, pp. 5286–5297. Association for Computing Machinery, New York, NY, USA (2016). https://doi.org/10.1145/2858036.2858288
13. McTear, M., Callejas, Z., Griol, D.: The Conversational Interface: Talking to Smart Devices. Springer (2016)
14. Moore, R.J., Arar, R.: Conversational UX Design: A Practitioner's Guide to the Natural Conversation Framework. ACM Books (2019)
15. MTI-Singapore: Ministry of trade and industry Singapore, MTI Chat for Biz (2020). https://www.mti.gov.sg/Chatbot/chat
16. Munsch, N., et al.: A benchmark of online COVID-19 symptom checkers. medRxiv (2020)
17. Nielsen, J.: Ten usability heuristics (2005). http://www.nngroup.com/articles/ten-usability-heuristics/. Accessed 25 Jun 2020
18. Semigran, H.L., Linder, J.A., Gidengil, C., Mehrotra, A.: Evaluation of symptom checkers for self diagnosis and triage: audit study. bmj 351, h3480 (2015)
19. Shariat, J., Saucier, C.S.: Tragic Design: The Impact of Bad Product Design and How to Fix It. O'Reilly, United States (2017)
20. Shevat, A.: Designing Bots: Creating Conversational Experiences. O'Reilly, United States (2017)
21. Sugisaki, K., Bleiker, A.: Usability guidelines and evaluation criteria for conversational user interfaces: a heuristic and linguistic approach. In: Proceedings of the Conference on Mensch und Computer, pp. 309–319 (2020)
22. TARS: Chatbot templates to fight coronavirus (Covid-19) pandemic, June 2020. https://hellotars.com/chatbot-templates/coronavirus-covid19-fight/
23. Verma, V.: 10 usability heuristics every chatbot company should follow. UX Collective, Medium (2019)
24. Vijayakumar, B., Höhn, S., Schommer, C.: Quizbot: exploring formative feedback with conversational interfaces. In: Draaijer, S., Joosten-ten Brinke, D., Ras, E. (eds.) TEA 2018. CCIS, vol. 1014, pp. 102–120. Springer, Cham (2019). https://doi.org/10.1007/978-3-030-25264-9_8
25. Walker, M.A., Litman, D.J., Kamm, C.A., Abella, A.: Evaluating spoken dialogue agents with PARADISE: two case studies. Comp. Speech Lang. **12**(4), 317–348 (1998)

Go to Chapter X to Explore Interactive Narrative on Smart Assistants

Lorenz Cuno Klopfenstein$^{(\boxtimes)}$ and Matteo Di Lorenzi

Department of Pure and Applied Sciences, University of Urbino, Urbino, Italy
`cuno.klopfenstein@uniurb.it`

Abstract. Interactive fiction, the narration paradigm that allows players or readers to directly affect the branching of a story, has been the focus both of a popular genre of books (so-called *GameBooks* or *Choose Your Own Adventure* books) and of narrative experiences delivered through interactive computer programs, which includes but is not limited to many popular videogames. This paper explores book-based interactive narrative structures and tools, presenting a novel way to explore existing works of narrative fiction through the conversational audio interface of a smart assistant. The proposed solution is implemented in the form of an Amazon Alexa skill that allows users to listen to works of interactive fiction in a similar fashion to an audiobook, while also allowing them to 'choose their own adventure' expressing choices and commands using their voice. Common GameBook interaction paradigms other than basic junctures within the story are also described and presented through the smart assistant program. Results from a small-scale experiment are presented and the potential of this conversational interface for interactive spoken-word literature is discussed.

Keywords: Interactive narrative · Conversational interfaces · Smart assistant · Amazon Alexa

1 Interactive Narrative

Works of narrative are focused on conveying a *story* to an audience. Traditionally these works are expressed by a narrator, who delivers the story either using his or her voice or using the written language, in the form of written stories such as novels.

Story arcs and common features and tropes in narrative have been widely explored in literature. As screenwriter McKee puts it, a story consists mainly of events that turn (i.e., change) values. A value can be a property of any part of the story, either of a character or a relationship between characters, such as trust, love, hope, and so on. The smallest unit of value change within a story is the "beat". A series of beats make up entire "scenes" of value changes, which drive the story from its beginning to the end [9].

While traditional narrative develops through a story arc and thus has one beginning and one ending, *interactive narrative* presents means of engagement

© Springer Nature Switzerland AG 2021
A. Følstad et al. (Eds.): CONVERSATIONS 2020, LNCS 12604, pp. 145–157, 2021.
https://doi.org/10.1007/978-3-030-68288-0_10

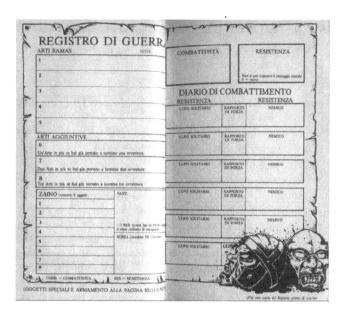

Fig. 1. Sample of extradiegetic elements (inventory, magic arts, combat skills) as seen in the Italian edition of "The Chasm of Doom" in the popular *Lone Wolf* series.

of the audience, which allow the reader (or listener) to exert some kind of agency and control over the narrative itself. Some examples of interactive narrative have multiple ending, allowing the audience to determine the arc of the story and thus the outcome of the narrative experience.

One form of these interactive experiences is the so-called *GameBook* (popularized with the "Choose Your Own Adventure" series in English and the "LibroGame" series in Italian, during the '80s and '90s) [7]. These books present a story, often in the fantasy genre, subdivided into *chapters* or *paragraphs*. Each one of these text units is numbered, starting from 1 (where the reader starts the book). At the end of each text unit, the reader is offered a choice of different destination chapters. GameBooks may depend entirely on the reader's explicit choices or they may implement some game mechanics such as randomness (dice throws, ability checks, etc.), combat simulations (based on dice, data tables to cross check, etc.), or extradiegetic elements (inventory tracking, clue gathering, life point tracking, etc.) as shown in Fig. 1.

Whichever the game mechanics used, the story within a GameBook branches off, chapter per chapter, following a directed graph structure where each node represents a chapter and each arc a choice available to the reader. Each story branch can be seen as an *interaction point*, at which the reader/player may take action and thus influence the narrative, as seen in the "Progression Maps" model developed by Carstensdottir et al. [2], just like "beats" within a story.

Of course interactive narrative has been considered as an effective product for interactive multimedia entertainment systems, such as videogaming platforms. The simulated environment in electronic entertainment is well-suited to provide a realistic and continuous interaction, resulting in a more immersive and compelling experience for players, if compared to simple branching stories of GameBooks [13]. While the basics of branching narrative are preserved, in principle, the freedoms bestowed by the videogame medium and the addition of simulative elements (such as agents and characters with an own agency and effect on the story) introduce complexities that make many interactive electronic entertainment products difficult to understand and model using a graph-based structure [14].

Large contributions to literature in this area have focused on the difficulties of combining the presence of a strong story in the interactive medium, which constrains the narrative, and the inherent strong autonomy provided by videogames in general [6,8], such as in the work by Young and Riedl bringing together free interactions in a 3D world and a tight narration within a given story arc [15]. Based on the recent resurgence of interactive storytelling, on electronic devices and especially in video media (as seen in "Black Mirror: Bandersnatch" released on Netflix), novel interaction modes have also been explored [10].

In this paper, we will focus exclusively on traditional works of interactive narrative, such as GameBooks, and their adaptation to modern conversational interfaces. In particular, we will present a software tool allowing users to play existing textual *Choose Your Own Adventure* books through the voice-based interface of the Amazon Alexa smart assistant. To the extent of our knowledge, this is the first preliminary study on this particular subject in literature. Most previous studies applying conversational voice interfaces to game-like activities focus on trivia or other question-based interactions [1,4]. Few commercial examples of Amazon Alexa interactive storytelling games are more similar to audiobooks, in that they are narrated and have limited interactivity [5].

1.1 Writing Interactive Narrative

While classical textual GameBooks are mainly published and read like traditional printed books, the writing process often relies on computer aids. These tools let authors more easily keep track of the narrative, the branches in the story, and ensuring that the reader's experience is coherent [7].

One of the more popular of these instruments is **LibroGameCreator**, a desktop software suite widely used both by amateur and professional GameBook authors. The software is supported by its author and an active online community of aficionados[1].

The software tool allows authors to write their works as a series of numbered *chapters*, expressing links between story units directly within the text (using numbers between square brackets, for instance writing "[123]" to indicate that the reader may continue at chapter number 123). Other navigation tools (combat, dice throwing, etc.) are generally not handled directly by the software, but all these options can be simply expressed in text [12].

---

[1] The community centers around the *LibroGameLand* web site (http://www.librogame.net), which also collects more than 120 works by amateur authors.

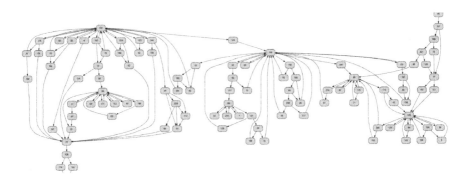

Fig. 2. Sample section of the graph structure in "The Vampire of Havena".

In addition to the basic text-writing functions, LibroGameCreator also allows authors to examine GameBooks as a directed graph. Each node represents a chapter of the story, while an arch between chapters represents a link found in text that the reader may follow. The visual representation of a GameBook can be a very powerful instrument when analyzing the overarching narrative structure and how the book can be navigated during play. In Fig. 2, a partial section of the graph of a GameBook is shown ("The Vampire of Havena", published by *Ulisses Spiele* in 2015).

LibroGameCreator stores all data for a book within a single file, which ensures easy editing and sharing of books.

2   Implementing GameBooks for Smart Assistants

In this paper we present the design and implementation of a prototype software platform that allows users to experience a work of interactive narrative through the voice interface of a smart assistant.

The requirements of the system have been chosen based on an analysis of existing GameBook creation tools seen in Sect. 1.1 and the adaptation of common GameBook file formats to a general purpose voice-based reader. The following main requirements have been identified:

Compatibility with Existing GameBooks. The system should be able to import existing GameBook sources with no or minimal pre-processing. It should also be compatible with most interaction possibilities offered by common GameBooks.

Voice-only Interface. The GameBook should be read back to the user of the system, in a similar fashion to listening to an audiobook. When interaction is required, the user must be able to express commands using voice only.

Multiple Books and Multiple Users. The system must support more than one book and more than one concurrent user.

Context and memory. The system must retain all required context for each user session, allowing users to resume reading, restart from the beginning, and keeping track of extradiegetic elements (such as life points, etc.).

2.1   Book Source Pre-processing

The prototype will make use of standard source files generated by LibroGame-Creator, presented in Sect. 1.1, as they are stored within one single file for easy handling. LibroGameCreator stores books as a single standalone file, encoding it internally as a SQLite 3 database. The database stores all data using a standard entity-attribute-value model, as shown in Fig. 3, where all properties of entity number 1 are stored as 5 different database entries.

	id_entity	id_attributes	attribute_name	attribute_type	attribute_value
	Filtro	Filtro	Filtro	Filtro	Filtro
1	1	1	description	string	For three days you lead ...
2	1	2	flag_final	boolean	false
3	1	3	flag_fixed	boolean	true
4	1	4	flag_death	boolean	false
5	1	5	chapter_title	string	
6	2	1	description	string	You search the bodies o...
7	2	2	flag_final	boolean	false
8	2	3	flag_fixed	boolean	false
9	2	4	flag_death	boolean	false
10	2	5	chapter_title	string	

Fig. 3. Sample entries from the LibroGameCreator database of the "The Chasm of Doom" GameBook from the *Lone Wolf* series.

Most information for each chapter is included directly in its text, such as the list of destination chapters reachable by the user and other book-dependent actions or options. These latter GameBook features and game mechanics (which, depending on the specific book, may include combat, riddles, collecting items, losing or adding points, managing clues, and other operations) are not encoded in any standard way and are usually embedded in the chapter's text as simple natural language phrases.

The pre-processing step is designed to handle differences and idiosyncrasies of different GameBooks. This requires an adaptation process that can change for each book series and, in some cases, even for each book when meaningful differences in text or mechanics exist. In most cases this process can be performed by running the chapter text through filters based on regular expressions that can—for instance—detect a combat event and extract the name and properties of the player's adversaries. In some rare instances, the source text of the book itself can be incoherent in presenting these special options. In this case the source text must be manually fixed and adapted in order to be correctly transformed.

At the end of the pre-processing, an intermediate XML-based representation of the book is generated. The output file is structured into a list of chapters, each containing the text, optional flags if set, and a list of IDs of all chapters that can be reached by the reader. If the chapter includes special game elements, such as combat, this is also encoded in the XML file with all the required data, such as adversaries and their properties. This standardized XML rendition of the book can then easily be handled by the GameBook reader without further processing.

In the context of the presented prototype, all pre-processing was performed using a custom NodeJS script that used regular expressions to detect combat events or dice rolls. The prototype has been tested on a set of published Game-Books provided by the authors. Books based on simple branching mechanics required no further adaptation, while other ones including combat or dice rolls required some tweaking in order to recognize all instances in the source text.

2.2 Alexa Skill Commands

Alexa is a virtual assistant by Amazon that is capable of voice interaction, either through a physical speaker device or through mobile applications on a smartphone, to provide access to services, information, and multimedia for entertainment. The smart assistant also allows developers to provide custom *skills*, that can be programmed and made available to Alexa users in order to provide them with additional functionalities.

Alexa skills are implemented through the *Alexa Skills API*, that allows developers to receive requests and commands through a custom web-based back-end and handle them accordingly. Voice requests are processed by the Automatic Speech Recognition (ASR) and Natural Language Understanding (NLU) systems provided by Amazon Alexa, turning user utterances into easily processable text for the skill developer.

Recognized commands can be defined using a custom syntax, which allows developers to define custom *intents*, as a set of synonymous utterances that express the same specific meaning. The prototype presented in this paper implemented the following intents[2]:

1. *Open GameBook*
   Starts the skill and welcomes the user. Resumes the book if the skill has been started previously.
2. *Read chapter N / Go to chapter N*
   Goes to the chapter (if there is an outgoing connection from the current chapter to the destination or if going to chapter 1 when starting a book) and reads it.
3. *Read again / Read the chapter again*
   Reads the chapter again.
4. *Restart the book / Read from the beginning*
   Forgets the current chapter and starts the book from the beginning.
5. *Throw a die / Generate a random number between X and X*
   Generates a random integer value between two numbers (inclusive). This feature can be used after reading a chapter requiring a die roll to determine the chapter to read.

---

[2] Some training phrases are reported for each intent, but more are provided to the actual skill model. See the source model in the prototype's repository.

6. *Combat/Simulate fight*
   Simulates a full fight against one or more adversaries, if present in the current chapter. Determines whether the player survives the encounter and computes the consequences (e.g., suffered damage). This command is the only one connected to extradiegetic elements that are tracked by the prototype, namely life points and combat strength.
7. *Help/What can I do?/What should I say?*
   Presents a list of commands and describes how the skill works.

2.3   Back-End Processor and Memory

Each continuous user interaction with the skill is assigned a unique session ID, which allows the skill back-end to keep track of the conversation for each user. A database allows the skill's back-end to keep track of which book and specifically which chapter is currently being read by the user.

Other additional properties of the user's read-through can also be stored by the database, such as life points and inventory. A history of visited chapters is also stored for each user.

3   Experiment, Results, and Conclusions

The source code of the implemented skill and its back-end have been released under the MIT license[3].

The GameBook reader prototype has been published as a beta Amazon Alexa skill, in order to be tested and validated in a small-scale trial with a set of experts. Testers were invited to the trial through direct contacts among the community of Italian-speaking GameBook enthusiasts, collectors, and authors.

Participants were given access to the Alexa skill and were then asked to provide their feedback through an anonymous Google Forms questionnaire. The questionnaire was split into 3 sections. The first section focused on anonymous information about the user, such as age group and skill level in reading or writing GameBooks. The second section provided a series of questions about the user experience and user preferences, expressed on a Likert scale (from 1 to 5). The last section asked users for perceived advantages in reading GameBooks through a voice-based interface, general feedback, and suggestions for further improvement.

3.1   Feedback Evaluation and Lessons Learned

Feedback was collected from a total of 8 participants, after filtering out incomplete or duplicate responses. The respondents were clearly split between 2 professional GameBook authors and readers with no publishing experience, as is shown in Fig. 4. As was to be expected from the social channels where the questionnaire

---

[3] Source code on GitHub: https://github.com/m-dilorenzi/librogamereader.git.

was distributed, all respondents had some experience reading GameBooks. The full anonymized responses to the feedback questionnaire are available online[4].

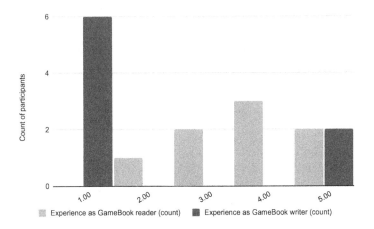

Fig. 4. User expertise as GameBook readers (blue) and writers (red), where 1: no experience and 5: very experienced. (Color figure online)

Evaluation of the prototype was not entirely satisfactory in general, with many users reporting an insufficient experience under some aspects. Figure 5 shows the distribution of user feedback, divided into (1) general experience, (2) quality of command interpretation by Alexa, (3) quality and realism of the smart assistant's voice output, (4) expressivity of narration, (5) clarity of narration, (6) clarity of how the current game state is expressed, (i.e., what is happening, which commands are available?), (7) ease of navigation between chapters and actions.

No user read more than 10 chapters of the book (with a total of almost 300 chapters), while many stopped after 2 or 3 remarking that chapter navigation using the voice-only interface was non-intuitive and difficult to understand.

While, as could be expected, the quality of voice synthesis in terms of expressivity was evaluated negatively, the interface's capability of clearly expressing the contents of the narration and the player's current state have also been reported as less than satisfactory.

In general, the results appear to indicate that the high information density of the source material in GameBooks is a difficult match with the inflexibility of Alexa commands and the short default interaction model assumed by smart assistants.

More specific issues and suggestions are grouped by category and discussed in more detail below.

---

[4] Public Google Sheet (in Italian): https://docs.google.com/spreadsheets/d/1bTfLj-Vg1F2L0NslJnkVvZ7ZX1Gxo2OOoprZ8fzoyLs/edit?usp=sharing.

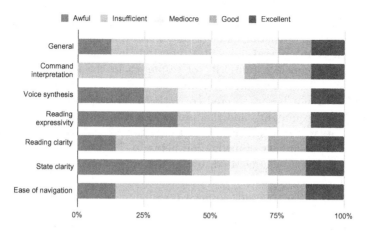

Fig. 5. Evaluation of the reading experience on a 5-value scale, in general and on 6 specific points.

Voice output. Many users reported low (1–2) satisfaction with the default voice synthesis provided by Alexa and the majority of users reported lacking reading expressivity. The raw text, interpreted by the text-to-speech processor in Alexa provides serviceable voice output, which however shows frequent sound artifacts and enunciation imprecisions. Also, the voice output is ill suited to interpret punctuation as intended by the author. This is particularly noticeable in passages that would require dramatic pauses for effect or in dialogues, where quoted phrases are often mixed with the rest of the text.

It is to be considered that providing a professional reading of the GameBook's text would solve this issue and provide a much more satisfying experience to end-users, much alike to published audiobooks. At least 2 users mentioned this as an imperative feature in a commercial product. Likewise, the text could be provided using the Speech Synthesis Markup Language (SSML), which supports tags for controlling reading emphasis, volume, pitch, and rate of speech, allowing GameBook writers to specify *how* the book should be read. Both of these approaches of course require significant effort from the GameBook author, in contrast with the initial design requirement.

Command understanding. In general voice processing has not been reported as problematic by the users, but specific commands have been signaled as difficult or almost impossible to use by some. In particular, for some users, depending on their Alexa configuration and their selected voice language, commands were interpreted differently than intended. For instance, using the Italian skill launch intent (i.e., "apri Libro Game Reader"), Alexa would frequently interpret the first two words ("apri libro" = "open book") and try to open books to read from the integrated Kindle library.

Particular care must be given to providing a sufficient set of synonyms and variations of all commands provided by the skill. Also, for each language supported by the skill, care must be given to checking that commands do not conflict with other existing skills or Alexa features.

Skill termination. Several users also reported that the current status of the skill was often unclear (majority of responses in the low range). There is no clear sign when the skill is terminated (for instance when a sequence of commands cannot be interpreted correctly or an utterance is interpreted as a system-level command) and the user is forced to restart the skill.

Navigation between chapters. An aspect that also received very low satisfaction votes is the quality of navigation between chapters. Possible destination chapters are simply enumerated, by their chapter number, in text, therefore they can be easily overheard. Also, the listener is required to remember which chapter number corresponds to each possible choice, an issue that becomes difficult in chapters with a long selection of options.

This issue could be resolved by adding a command to enumerate the list of possible destination chapters. While reworked versions of GameBook sources could provide more explicit commands (for instance, "open the door to the north" instead of "go to chapter 123"), the relatively inflexible structure of Alexa skill intents (which require a fixed set of training phrases) makes it an unlikely endeavor for a general purpose reader skill.

Game mechanics and extradiegetic elements. All users remarked a high appreciation for the capability of the conversational interface of automating some of the more mechanic aspects of reading a GameBook. In particular handling the generation of random values (usually left to dice throwing or random page opening in traditional GameBooks) and automatically resolving combats.

This aspects indeed connects the aspects of traditional interactive narrative with the ease-of-use and automatisms provided by interactive electronic entertainment, providing a videogame-like experience within a more traditional medium.

The prototype only supported combat simulation with life point tracking, since the existing LibroGameCreator format does not include information about other extradiegetic elements (such as objects, inventory, powers, etc.). Adding more of these elements to the GameBook reader would require reworking how books are encoded and represented, including a fuller representation of the book's mechanics within the exported file.

3.2   Future Work

As discussed previously, while most GameBooks have the same basic branching structure and the LibroGameCreator file format is easy to parse, some amount of work is required to ensure that the book is interpreted correctly and that special game mechanics are extracted as intended from the book's text. Other interactive narrative representation formats that are actively used are *Choice-Script*[5] and *Squiffy*[6]. While none of these fully cover the full wealth of options

---

[5] Web site: https://www.choiceofgames.com/make-your-own-games/.

[6] Web site: http://docs.textadventures.co.uk/squiffy/.

seen in modern GameBooks, we would welcome the development of an encompassing intermediate language for the representation of narrative interactive, possibly with the support of an integrated scripting language allowing authors to directly express how actions and choices are resolved.

Most users have tested the prototype on audio-only devices (such as the Alexa Echo Dot), but several Alexa-integrated devices allow developers to display images or text in addition to speech (for instance, the Alexa Echo Show and the Alexa smartphone app). While this feature was not used in the prototype, it would be possible to provide both spoken-word output and the full text of the chapters that are being read. If the GameBook includes pictures or illustrations, these could also be shown through the devices's screen.

More in general, the spoken-word version of a GameBook certainly lends itself to be used in situations where the users doesn't want or is not able to read written text (cooking, driving, doing sports, or relaxing). However, a text-only prototype delivered through a messaging bot, possibly enhancing the conversation with picture and buttons to handle the user's navigation through chapters, could provide a more efficient experience, closer to the original one of reading a GameBook. An in-depth field-trial will be performed in future, evaluating the perceived performance of the spoken-word GameBook and comparing it to a chatbot text-only version and to an interactive mobile app.

Moreover, while the presented prototype was focused on faithfully reproducing the reading experience of a traditional print GameBook, the flexible nature of the back-end could be further exploited integrating dynamic elements and additional interactive narrative structures, which are impossible to present in a standard book. For instance, at the most basic level, the traditional fixed story arc and the well-defined narrative of conventional GameBooks could be maintained, while the text delivered to the reader could be made dynamic using generative text frameworks such as *Tracery*. This would allow more varied output and make the book more unpredictable [3]. On a more extensive level, additional development in interactive storytelling via electronic media could be incorporated from suggestions in literature. For instance, the generation of narrative variations or adaptive stories that maintain a given 'closeness' to the original source, as seen in the work by Ong and Leggett using genetic algorithms [11], or dynamic narrative generation using an overarching story director, as seen in the work by Riedl and Stern [13].

Acknowledgments. We wish to thank Matteo Poropat, developer of LibroGame-Creator, and Mauro Longo for their valuable insight. Also, many thanks to Federico Bianchini, Poropat and Longo for providing the reference GameBooks used to test and to validate the prototype. We also thank the anonymous reviewers for their valued feedback.

References

1. Bilic, L., Ebner, M., Ebner, M.: A voice-enabled game based learning application using Amazon's echo with Alexa voice service: a game regarding geographic facts about Austria and Europe. Int. J. Interact. Mob. Technol. (iJIM) **14**(03), 226–232 (2020). https://onlinejour.journals.publicknowledgeproject.org/index.php/i-jim/article/view/12311. Number: 03
2. Carstensdottir, E., et al.: Progression maps: conceptualizing narrative structure for interaction design support. In: Proceedings of the 2020 CHI Conference on Human Factors in Computing Systems, CHI 2020, pp. 1–13. Association for Computing Machinery, New York (2020). https://doi.org/10.1145/3313831.3376527
3. Compton, K., Kybartas, B., Mateas, M.: Tracery: an author-focused generative text tool. In: Proceedings of International Conference on Interactive Digital Storytelling, vol. 9445, pp. 154–161 (2015). https://doi.org/10.1007/978-3-319-27036-4_14
4. Filimon, M., Iftene, A., Trandabăţ, D.: Bob - a general culture game with voice interaction. Procedia Comput. Sci. **159**, 323–332 (2019). https://doi.org/10.1016/j.procs.2019.09.187. http://www.sciencedirect.com/science/article/pii/S1877050919313699
5. Frank Horror, Small Basket Studios: Eye of the Elder Gods (2018). https://www.eyeoftheeldergods.com/
6. Juul, J.: A Clash between Game and Narrative, February 1999. https://www.jesperjuul.net/thesis/
7. Longo, M., Malaspina, Poropat, M.: Scrivi la tua avventura! Dalle storie a bivi ai librogame. Work On Color Edizioni (2019)
8. Mateas, M., Stern, A.: Towards integrating plot and character for interactive drama. In: Dautenhahn, K., Bond, A., Cañamero, L., Edmonds, B. (eds.) Socially Intelligent Agents: Creating Relationships with Computers and Robots. Multiagent Systems, Artificial Societies, and Simulated Organizations, pp. 221–228. Springer, Boston (2002). https://doi.org/10.1007/0-306-47373-9_27
9. McKee, R.: Story: style, structure, substance, and the principles of screenwriting. Harper Collins (1997)
10. Nascimento, T.H., et al.: Using smartwatches as an interactive movie controller: a case study with the bandersnatch movie. In: 2019 IEEE 43rd Annual Computer Software and Applications Conference (COMPSAC), vol. 2, pp. 263–268, July 2019. https://doi.org/10.1109/COMPSAC.2019.10217. ISSN 0730-3157
11. Ong, T., Leggett, J.J.: A genetic algorithm approach to interactive narrative generation. In: Proceedings of the Fifteenth ACM Conference on Hypertext and Hypermedia, HYPERTEXT 2004, pp. 181–182. Association for Computing Machinery, New York, August 2004. https://doi.org/10.1145/1012807.1012856
12. Poropat, M.: LibroGameCreator, July 2020. http://www.matteoporopat.com/librogame/libro-game-creator-3/
13. Riedl, M.O., Stern, A.: Believable agents and intelligent story adaptation for interactive storytelling. In: Göbel, S., Malkewitz, R., Iurgel, I. (eds.) TIDSE 2006. LNCS, vol. 4326, pp. 1–12. Springer, Heidelberg (2006). https://doi.org/10.1007/11944577_1

14. Sali, S., Mateas, M.: Using information visualization to understand interactive narrative: a case study on Façade. In: Si, M., Thue, D., André, E., Lester, J.C., Tanenbaum, J., Zammitto, V. (eds.) ICIDS 2011. LNCS, vol. 7069, pp. 284–289. Springer, Heidelberg (2011). https://doi.org/10.1007/978-3-642-25289-1_31
15. Young, R.M., Riedl, M.: Towards an architecture for intelligent control of narrative in interactive virtual worlds. In: Proceedings of the 8th International Conference on Intelligent User Interfaces, IUI 2003, pp. 310–312. Association for Computing Machinery, New York, January 2003. https://doi.org/10.1145/604045.604108

Conversational Agents to Promote Children's Verbal Communication Skills

Fabio Catania[1(✉)], Micol Spitale[1,2], Giulia Cosentino[1], and Franca Garzotto[1]

[1] Politecnico di Milano, Milano, Italy
fabio.catania@polimi.it
[2] IBM Italy, Milan, Italy

Abstract. The fundamentals of verbal communication skills are developed during childhood, and existing studies pinpoint the benefits of stimulating language and expression skills from an early age. Our research is a preliminary evaluation of conversational technology to support this process. In this paper, we describe the design process of a speech-based conversational agent for children, which involved a Wizard-of-Oz empirical study with 20 primary school children aged 9–10 y.o. in order to identify the design guidelines for the automated version of the system. Our agent is called ISI, is integrated into a web application and exploits oral and visual interaction modes. ISI enables children to practice verbal skills related to the description of a person's physical characteristics. It provides opportunities for them to learn and use words and linguistic constructs. Also, ISI permits to develop their body awareness and self-expression (when describing their self) or the attention to "the other" (when describing someone else). ISI engages users in a speech-based conversational flow composed of two main repeated steps. It talks to the children and stimulates them with questions about a specific part of their body (e.g., "What color is your hair?"). When the users describe the required feature adequately, ISI provides a cheerful real-time visual representation of the answer; otherwise, it provides hints.

Keywords: Conversational technology · Natural language visualization · Children · Language learning · Learning

1 Introduction

Verbal communication is the foundation of relationships and is essential for learning, playing, and social interacting [17]. Early oral communication skills are developed during childhood [48]. Children learn how to convey information, needs, and feelings in a more effective way [13] by acquiring words and linguistic constructs of the language.

Previous studies proved that individuals differ in how they learn [53] and that various stimuli can support children in enhancing verbal communication capabilities and learning a language [10]. The VAK model [4] identifies three learning modalities:

© Springer Nature Switzerland AG 2021
A. Følstad et al. (Eds.): CONVERSATIONS 2020, LNCS 12604, pp. 158–172, 2021.
https://doi.org/10.1007/978-3-030-68288-0_11

- Visual learning, that exploits graphs, charts, maps, diagrams, pictures, paintings, and other kinds of visual stimulation;
- Auditory learning, that depends on listening and speaking;
- and Kinesthetic learning, that requires gestures, body movements, and object manipulation to process new information.

The strengths of each learning modality show up independently or in combination [3]. Generally, learners appear to benefit most from visual and mixed modality presentations, for instance, using both auditory and visual techniques. A review study [1] concluded that visual stimulation improves learners performance in the following areas:

- Retention. Learners remember and recall information better when it is represented and learned both visually and verbally;
- Reading comprehension. The use of visual stimulation helps to improve the reading comprehension of learners;
- Learning achievement. Learners with and without learning disabilities improve achievement across content areas and grade levels;
- Critical thinking. When learners use visual stimuli during learning, their critical thinking skills are enhanced.

In addition, according to [38], visual aids are used for various aspects in the teaching-learning process, and practicing teachers are often led to believe that "the more visuals, the better".

Our research concerns Computer-Aided Language Learning [47], i.e., language learning and communication skills training with the help of a machine. Our final goal is to investigate the use of an intelligent interface combining visual and auditory stimuli for children to improve their verbal communication skills.

We present ISI, an Italian speech-based conversational agent (CA) for children that exploits oral and visual communication modes. A conversational agent is a dialogue system able to interact with a human through natural language [14]. ISI enables children to practice verbal skills related to the description of a person's physical characteristics. In this way, ISI offers opportunities for children to learn and practice with words and linguistic constructs. Also, it permits to develop their body awareness and self-expression (when describing their self) or the attention to *the other* (when describing someone else).

The name ISI stands for "Io Sono Io", that is the Italian version of "I am me". This name takes inspiration from the German book "Das kleine Ich bin ich" [33] that supports children to answer the question "Who am I?" Furthermore, in Italian, ISI is pronounced in the same way as the English word "easy", that perfectly fits with the principles underlying the system:

- it is simple to use for children;
- it facilitates and trains communication skills and self-knowledge.

This paper not only contributes in exploring conversational technology merged with Natural Language Visualization for support learning, but also provides interesting design insights for conversational technology for children.

Indeed, in this paper, we describe the process of designing ISI: we implemented a Wizard-of-Oz version of the agent, and we conducted a preliminary empirical study with 20 primary school children aged 9–10 y.o. to identify effective design guidelines for the application.

Assessing the potential of ISI as a teaching tool is beyond the scope of this paper and will be analyzed in the future by exploiting an automated version of ISI. Here, we addressed the following research questions:

- "Is a system with the characteristics of ISI usable by children?"
- "Is a system like ISI engaging?"

2 Related Works

The rapid and continuous improvements in the field of Artificial intelligence are making spoken and written Conversational Technologies smarter, leading to new forms of collaboration with humans and new application areas [19]. Voice-based conversational agents (e.g., Apple's Siri, Amazon's Alexa, Google Assistant) are progressively getting more embedded into people's lives due to their intuitive, easy-to-use natural language human-computer interface: according to [24], 46% of United States adults use them in their daily routines.

From literature, we know some conversational agents specific for teaching and supporting the learning process. They are called Pedagogic Conversational Agent (PCA) and can be defined as smart systems that interact with the student in natural language, assuming the role of an instructor, a motivator, a student, or a companion. They are cheaper than human tutors and can exploit adaptive learning technology in order to meet the needs of each student [15].

There are PCAs for different targets – e.g., for children and adults – and for various topics that range from math to literature [27]. For children, one of the most common uses of PCAs is language teaching and practice. For example, [34] describes embodied agents offering language challenges to children. Also, Baldi is a tutor who guides students through a variety of exercises designed to teach vocabulary and grammar, to improve speech articulation, and to develop linguistic and phonological awareness [35]. In [11], an animated CA, named Marni, interacts with children to teach them to read and learn from the text. In [51], it is proposed the use of Pedagogic Conversational Agents to develop computational thinking in children. Hayashi [26] proposed multiple PCAs to support collaborative learning in children, and highlighted how multiple PCAs can implement roles yielding different types of suggestions. In [25], the authors implemented an intelligent virtual environment with many Embodied Conversational Agents, for improving speaking and listening skills of non-native English language learners. Finally, [50] reports about CAs to engage children in book reading activities and to create oral stories in a highly interactive manner.

Concerning design, there are several sets of established guidelines for Graphical User Interfaces (GUIs) (e.g., [40]) and Tangible User Interfaces (e.g., [54,55]) for children, but the ones for Conversational User Interfaces are few and not universally accepted. Indeed, previous studies have already explored commercial and non-commercial CAs for children both for play [2,16,43] and learning [35,52], but without finding specific guidelines. Besides Nielsen, [41] who defined ten heuristics to test the usability of any interfaces, Moore and Arar [36] made the first attempt to suggest some guidelines for designing a conversational interaction experience for generic users and contexts. Also, Murad et al. [39] summarized some design guidelines to support researchers in solving issues related to usability and learning of hands-free speech interfaces.

To the best of our knowledge, so far, there is no conversational application teaching or enabling the practice of self-description and body parts learning for children with a Natural Language Visualization support system.

3   ISI

ISI is a tool for teachers and caregivers to make primary-school children practice with turn-taking and language constructs, and words related to the description of a person's physical characteristics, colors, and positions. Also, ISI allows children to develop their body awareness and self-expression (when describing themself) or the attention to *the other* (when describing someone else). It can be used autonomously, both in primary school and at home. Its design is grounded on the VAK model [4] for which the combination of visual and auditory stimuli improves the children learning.

ISI is a goal-oriented, domain restricted and Italian speaking conversational agent. It is integrated into a web application and enables both vocal and visual interaction with the user through the screen, the microphone, and the speakers of the device (both standalone and mobile). ISI engages children in a speech-based conversational flow composed of two main repeated steps. First, it talks and stimulates them with questions about a specific part of their or someone else's body. Questions can be about color (e.g., "What color is your hair?"), size (e.g., "How big is your nose?"), and position (e.g., "Where's the mole?"). Second, if users describe the required feature adequately, ISI shows a cheerful real-time visual representation of the answer; otherwise, it provides hints and feedback. The strength of ISI lies in exploiting an original Natural Language Visualization software module to associate expressions describing a person's physical appearance with an avatar produced in real-time using Bitmoji's API [49]. ISI provides real-time feedback, and support children through a dual visual and auditory stimulation, as defined in the VAK model [4].

ISI's GUI (see Fig. 1) is very basic since the screen represents just a support channel compared to the speech that is the primary interaction channel. The app shows a box in the middle of the screen where it visualizes in real-time the avatar as the user described it so far. During the experience, ISI provides the user of visual feedback about its status (idle - Fig. 1 -, listening, or speaking) to help her/him to handle the interaction and to understand the system better. Also, the system displays a digital button to be clicked by the user before and after speaking, respectively, to trigger the system and to let it stop listening (i.e., to express the concepts "It is my turn" and "It is your turn"). The button was designed to be visible and intuitive to touch, using a color (yellow) in contrast with the background (light blue). Pushing the button implies a tangible interaction: its use is typical in GUI and requires the user to be able to point beyond pressing. Today's most popular CAs are triggered when they perceive a keyword or a short utterance spoken by the user; this phrase is universally known as a *wake word* (e.g., "OK Google" for Google Assistant, "Alexa" for Alexa, and "Hey Siri" for Siri). CAs stop listening when they recognize a pause that marks the end of the person's speech. This allows people to use CAs even when their hands and gaze are busy. We opted for pressing the button as *wake* and *sleep* action because we hypothesized that this method could promote the sense of agency and increase children's subjective awareness of being in control of the interaction [8]. Besides, this approach was already used for children (just as wake action) [6]. The motivations for having the same commands to wake up and put to sleep the system are the following: we have the vision that future conversational technologies will become more and more accessible and will be widely used even by children with special communication needs, and according to the theory of *partner-perceived communication* [12,30], the predictability and repetitiveness of the sequences makes it possible to better give meaning to them even for those children with complex communication needs.

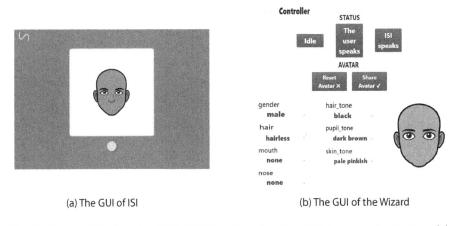

(a) The GUI of ISI   (b) The GUI of the Wizard

Fig. 1. On the left side the GUI of ISI waiting for the child to press the button (a); On the right side the GUI of the Wizard (b) (Texts are translated into English as a matter of paper readability) (Color figure online)

4   Wizard of Oz Experimentation

To study on the field the usability of ISI by children and their engagement while interacting with the agent, we conducted a Wizard of Oz experiment. Indeed, the participants interacted with a prototype of ISI that they believed to be autonomous, but that actually spoke and performed thanks to an unseen human being in a second room (i.e., the Wizard).

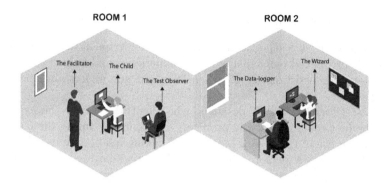

Fig. 2. Wizard of Oz experiment evaluation setting

4.1   Participants

We recruited 20 Italian speaking children aged 9 to 10 (11 girls and 9 boys) from the primary school of Cornaredo (MI, Italy). We have chosen this sample since they had already studied in school how to describe themselves, and consequently, we supposed they had the linguistic capabilities to accomplish in autonomy the self-description task interacting with the agent. From a survey by the teachers, we know that subjects were familiar with technology and computers through computer-classes at school. None of them said she/he had interacted with any conversational agents (e.g., Google, Siri, Alexa, and Cortana) previously. We are aware that all over the world many children deal with conversational technologies in their every-day life since conversational interfaces are spreading more and more in the people's homes [20]. However, this trend is slower in Italy (13% of penetration compared to other places - for example, to 24% of United States), and therefore our sample is closely representing the children of our country [9].

All participants provided us an informed consent signed by their parents.

4.2   Setting

The study was conducted during a summer campus in a primary school. This location was chosen to let children feel as comfortable as possible in a familiar space to them. The setting of the experiment was split into two separate rooms (see Fig. 2):

- Room 1. There was a touch-screen PC on a desk and a chair in front of it;
- Room 2. There was the research team, who could listen to the participant in the Room 1, speak to her/him, and observe her/his gestures through a connected laptop.

In addition to children, people involved in the study were:

- *The Facilitator*: A teacher who managed the experiment at the forefront in Room 1, introduced participants to the experience and helped them in case of requests for assistance (e.g., when they did not understand the task to complete);
- *The Test Observer*: A UX designer, who silently observed the experiment from the first room identifying problems and concerns during the interaction (e.g., in the use of the digital button) and taking qualitative notes;
- *The Data-logger*: A person collecting quantitative data (e.g., the number of errors and help requests of participants) from the second room;
- *The Wizard*: A trained person, who spoke with the children following a rigid script and simulating being a computer. This means that, for example, he did not respond when the user did not comply with the digital button interaction protocol (i.e., pressing the button before and after speaking). The Wizard controlled the system by using a web interface connected via the WebSocket API [37]. From the page shown in Fig. 1 the Wizard could remotely change the app status (idle, speaking, or listening) and the physical characteristics of the avatar displayed on the user's web page. The Wizard's voice was altered by using the Web Audio API to sounds more like a robot.

4.3   Procedure

Participants spontaneously showed up one at a time to play with ISI as single players. The Facilitator welcomed them in the classroom and invited them to sit down in front of the laptop. Afterward, she explained the participants of the coming experience and provided them with instructions about the wake and sleep action to use to trigger the system (i.e., pushing the digital button on the screen before and after speaking). When instructions were clear, the session started. The agent welcomed the children by saying, "Hello! My name is ISI. Today, we are going to create your avatar. Let's play together!" and asked her/him eight standardized questions: "What's your name?", "Are you a boy or a girl?", "What color is your skin?", "What color are your eyes?", "How big is your nose?", "How long is your hair?", "What color is your hair?", and "How big is your mouth?". Children described themselves, and every time they responded to a question, they saw the visual representation of the feature described directly on the avatar in the GUI. At every step, ISI prompted them, "Do you like your avatar as it is now?". If the answer was negative, ISI removed the last feature added and repeated the last question (allowing the children to change their avatar aspect).

During the whole experiment, the Test Observer and the Data-logger took note. If the participant did not understand what ISI said, she/he could directly ask the system to repeat any time, or she/he could reach out to the Facilitator. At the end of the session, ISI showed the final avatar to the participant and thanked her/him for playing. The Facilitator asked the child to fill out a smile-o-meter with 5 levels about the likeability of the game. We opted for the smile-o-meter since it was proved to be a valid toolkit to measure children's engagement [46].

4.4   Data Collected

During the empirical study, the Data-logger took notes about the number of occurrences that each participant asked for help to the Facilitator about the interaction modality, and the number of errors made by each participant during the session. In the context of this study, an error is when children did not respect the interaction protocol, i.e., when they spoke before or without pressing the button, or when they pressed the button but did not speak. We calculated the variable n_{help} as the number of user's requests for help about the interaction mode during the session. n_{error} is defined as the number of errors committed by the participant while interacting with ISI divided by the number of dialogue exchanges. The Facilitator collected data about the likeability by the user with a 5 levels smile-o-meter. *liker* is the child's evaluation score voted in the questionnaire (from 1 to 5) at the end of the interaction.

Besides, we automatically stored the timestamps of some relevant events for each conversational step (i.e., when the user started/stopped speaking, when the user pushed the button, and when ISI started/stopped speaking). From the timestamps, we measured the following variables:

- the interval of time during which the child was speaking ($t_{durationspeak}$),
- the time difference between the end of ISI's speech and the user pressing the button on the screen ($t_{interact}$),
- the time difference between the child pressed the button, and she/he started to speak ($t_{startspeak}$),
- and the time elapsed between the last word spoken by ISI and the first word spoken by the child ($t_{turntaking} = t_{startspeak} + t_{interact}$).

In addition to quantitative data, during the empirical study, we also collected some qualitative data. The Observer looked at the child interacting with ISI and wrote down observations about comments aloud by participants and the Facilitator, questions from subjects to the Facilitator, requests for help to complete the self-description task, reactions, gestures [5], and behavior of participants during the experience, usability issues (e.g., difficulties interacting with the application due to the use of the button or to participant's pronunciation defects), breaking points in the conversation.

5   Results and Discussion

5.1   Results

In Table 1, there is a recap of the measured variables computed on the collected data. We are conscious that the homogeneity of our population in terms of age (they were all 9 to 10 years old) leads to significant and reliable considerations about the target, but we are also aware that data analysis is less generalizable. We start reporting results from the analysis of the timing of turn-taking between children and ISI. From literature, we know that adults take split second between conversational turns (on average, between 0–200 ms). When it comes to having dialogues with young children, the turn-taking slows down [28]. Different children need different amounts of time to take a turn, but on average, they need 5–10 s [21]. We compared the timing data of our sample with the general population.

A single sample t-test was conducted to determine if a statistical significance exists between the time elapsed before speaking of our sample and the benchmark population in human-human conversations ($\mu_0 = 7.5$ s) [21]. Our null hypothesis is that the sample mean is equal to the population mean. Children interacting with ISI took much more time ($M = 5.09$ s, $SD = 3.90$ s) for starting the interaction (i.e., pushing the button) compared to the conventional children population, $t(19) = -2.78$, $p = .00$; on the other hand, they took much similar amount of time to start speaking ($M = 6.71$ s, $SD = 3.94$ s) compared to our benchmark value, $t(19) = -0.89$, $p = .18$.

Another single sample t-test was conducted to determine if a statistical significance exists between the duration of the child's turn of the empirical sample and the benchmark in human-human interactions ($\mu_0 = 2$ s) [21]. Children speaking with ISI takes less time to end their turn ($M = 1.6$ s, $SD = 0.4$ s) compared to the conventional children population, $t(19) = -4.65$, $p = .00$.

On average, children did not make many errors ($M = 0.15$, $SD = 0.37$), and they barely asked for help about the interaction mode ($M = 0.45$, $SD = 0.76$) during the session with ISI. Besides, they enjoyed playing with ISI as the questionnaire results revealed ($M = 4.2$, $SD = 0.83$).

The observations by the Observer are used as a starting point for identifying ISI's design insights described in the next section.

Table 1. Wizard of Oz experimental study: the variable obtained from the quantitative data about the children sample

Quantitative variable	Average (M)	Standard deviation (SD)
$t_{startspeak[s]}$	5.09	3.88
$t_{interact[s]}$	1.62	0.79
$t_{turntaking[s]}$	6.71	3.94
$t_{durationspeak[s]}$	1.60	0.62
n_{help}	0.45	0.76
n_{error}	0.15	0.37
$liker$	4.2	0.83

5.2   Discussion: Lessons Learned

From the results of the Wizard-of-Oz study, we elicited a set of lessons learned that could be applied to enhance the usability and engagement of ISI, and that may be useful for any conversational agent for children's learning.

The Ease of ISI's Multimodal Interaction – The time spent by children to start speaking with ISI during each conversational step is consistent with the literature's corresponding value in human-human interaction. This result suggests that the mixed interaction paradigm (speech, tangible, and visual) can be considered user-friendly and straightforward for this target group and could be applied to conversational agents for children in general. This result is also in line with what is described in the guidelines of Conversation design by Google [23], which claims that conversational interfaces are intrinsically multi-modal. Intuitiveness and ease of interaction are also supported by the low number of errors committed by children and the low number of times they asked for help about the interaction modality. As future work, pushing the button on the screen could be compared with other wake actions. A recent study [8] compared different actions to find out how effective they are as wake and sleep ones for children who want to interact with a conversational agent. Their results suggest that the physical button is the most appropriate solution for this target group, which opens new directions in the design of interaction affordances of CAs for children.

ISI as a Game with a Purpose – The smile-o-meter's results showed that children liked to play with ISI. Findings are in line with the positive feeling of the *Facilitator* and the *Test Observer* about the ISI-child conversational experience. We conclude that ISI has the potential to interact with children. Conversational agents need to be explored more for this population for different goals (e.g., learning, engagement, assistance). As a limitation of the study, we are aware that children tend to provide positive ratings to evaluation scales like smile-o-meter [46]. However, smile-o-meter is still an adequate tool for an easy and attractive method of scoring an opinion, especially with older children [45]. Future studies with ISI will exploit more general survey methods [45]. Also, the Again – Again table and the Fun Sorter will be used to rank specific features of the agent [45].

ISI's effectiveness for training their linguistic and communication skills is not verified, yet, and will be explored in the next study. We hypothesize that, if translated into various languages, ISI could help children to learn new languages interactively. Also, in a school environment, where socializing among peers is significant, ISI could enable the interaction with the classmates while playing in multiplayer mode.

ISI as a Self-explorative Tool for Elementary School Children – During the experimentation, the Observer took note of various requests for help by children to the *Facilitator* regarding their physical appearance in order to answer to ISI's questions. We drew two conclusions on this datum. On the one hand, the app is well-tailored around the target user, providing children an occasion to practice their self-description skills and to have a moment of reflection on their physical appearance. On the other hand, ISI lacks a tool to help children in the self-description process since users had to ask the *Facilitator* for the information they were seeking. This consideration leads naturally to the necessity of providing the user of hints (visual and/or auditory) about the different options she/he can select from while describing her/his physical appearance; for example, the range of hair colors that can be opted. Additionally, it could be interesting to insert a *mirroring canvas* in the GUI of the application, centered on the exploration of the physical appearance by the user. Multi-modal support in interactive interfaces is suggested even in [42].

Speech-to-Text to Support the Interaction – During the experiment, the Wizard was able to understand the user even in non-optimal conditions (e.g., when the user was speaking looking away or when there was an external noise). While designing the automated version of ISI (and conversational agents in a broad sense), it would be important to take into account that Automatic Speech Recognition and Understanding would not be as straightforward as for humans. Indeed, there are many studies about speech-to-text performance evaluation both in typical laboratory settings (quiet environment, wideband, and read speech) [32] and in various non-standard and adverse situations and we know from those studies that machine performance degrades below that of humans in noisy situations – whatever noise we consider. For example, there are automatic transcription evaluations in noisy environments [29] (e.g., traffic, crowd), with foreign accents [18], with children's voice tone [44], with emotional speech [7], and with subjects presenting disfluencies in speech and with deaf and hard-of-hearing people [22].

To overcome this drop in performance, we recommend ISI to provide a real-time transcript of the conversation on the screen as evidence of what it understands. In this way, users would have a better understanding of the behavior by the system. Also, ISI should ask very targeted and scoped questions so that users could answer them briefly (ideally with one single word) and thus help the transcription by the system. Finally, for older children, ISI could also provide text-based interactions and prevent any speech-to-text misunderstanding.

The Potential of Natural Language conversations of ISI – Designing the GUI with the clickable button gave the children a sense of control [31], and they quickly understood how to interact with ISI. During the conversation, the graphical explanation of the system status was relevant to letting the children know exactly when it was time to listen and speak. We recommend conversational designers to take this functionality into account for every conversational agent for children, as system status visibility is also encouraged in Nielsen's 10 usability heuristics for user interface design [41]. We noticed that children were positively engaged in speaking with ISI, and they were surprised by the fact that ISI called them by their name. Moreover, we observed that they felt comfortable as the agent used a familiar tone with them. This suggests us to put children's needs, capabilities, and behavior first and attempt to design the conversation on how they react. And this applies to all conversational agents for children and not just to ISI. For example, in our case, it could be useful to add more positive feedback as "Good job!", to engage them to go on with the gamified experience and make the conversation more natural and fluid. In this regard, it may be interesting to investigate the introduction of an avatar that reflects ISI and leads the children through the experience, examining children's perception and how they adapt the way they interact with the agent.

6   Conclusion and Future Works

This paper aims at exploring the usage of ISI, a speech-based conversational agent that enables children to practice verbal skills through natural language visualization. For this purpose, we ran a preliminary empirical study involving 20 primary school children. From this study, we learned the ease of multi-modal interaction for children and the potential of conversational technologies like ISI for this target group. The contribution of this paper is twofold:

- we described the design process to develop a conversational technology merged with a speech-to-image system that supports children in learning, and we tested its usability and the engagement produced;
- we reported the lessons we learned concerning our agent because we believe that they could be useful ever while designing other conversational agents for children to support the learning.

Our research brings up a few limitations. First, in our study, we involved just children within a restricted range of ages since we wanted them to be able to accomplish the self-description task easily. On one side, it was the right choice because all the children managed to complete the self-description task with the agent without any significant problems. On the other hand, this choice limits the generalization of our results to a broader children's age. To overcome this problem, in our future work, we will introduce different difficulty levels, and we will extend the research to a broader population. Second, so far, we tested only the Wizard-of-Oz version of ISI, and we reported the lessons we learned based on this first experience. However, we are conscious of the differences concerning the conversational skills of an automatic version of ISI compared to our human Wizard, and we know these differences could severely affect the conversational interaction with children. Unfortunately, we could not run an additional empirical study to validate the automated version of ISI because of the pandemic. We will do it as soon as it is possible.

Finally, this research opens up many questions that we want to address in our future studies. First, we will investigate whether a system like ISI that combines Conversational Technology and Natural Language Visualization can be a valid tool for children for improving communication skills – such as lexicon, expressions and sayings, observance of the dialogue timing, and prosody. Then, we would like to focus on the application of ISI as a tool for children to learn a foreign language. Also, we want to analyze if a technology like ISI can be an effective tool for children to improve their self-knowledge, self-awareness, and self-acceptance.

Acknowledgements. This work is partially funded by EIT Digital - Project LETSSAY "Conversational Technology for Speech and Language Therapy".

References

1. Graphic Organizers: A Review of Scientifically Based Research. The Institute for the Advancement of Research in Education at AEL (2003)
2. Al Moubayed, S., Lehman, J.: Toward better understanding of engagement in multiparty spoken interaction with children. In: Proceedings of the ACM ICMI 2015 (2015)
3. Barbe, W.B., Milone, M.N.: What we know about modality strengths (1981)
4. Barbe, W., et al.: Teaching Through Modality Strengths: Concepts and Practices (1979)
5. Begany, G., et al.: Factors affecting user perception of a spoken language vs. textual search interface: a content analysis. Interact. Comput. **28**, 170–180 (2015)
6. Benveniste, S., et al.: Designing improvisation for mediation in group music therapy with children suffering from behavioral disorders. In: Proceedings of the IDC 2009 (2009)
7. Catania, F., et al.: Automatic speech recognition: Do emotions matter? In: 2019 IEEE International Conference on Conversational Data and Knowledge Engineering (2019)
8. Catania, F., et al.: What is the best action for children to "wake up" and "put to sleep" a conversational agent? a multi-criteria decision analysis approach. In: Proceedings of the 2nd Conference on Conversational User Interfaces. ACM (2020)
9. Celi: Voice assistants: Celi's research reveals the habits of Italians (2019). shorturl.at/gvCS6
10. Coffield, F., et al.: Learning styles and pedagogy in post 16 education: a critical and systematic review (2004)
11. Cole, R., et al.: How marni teaches children to read. Educational Technology (2007)
12. Costantino, M.A.: Costruire libri e storie con la CAA: gli IN-Books per l'intervento precoce e linclusione. Erickson (2011)
13. Council, N.R., et al.: From Neurons to Neighborhoods: The Science of Early Childhood Development. National Academies Press, Washington, D.C. (2000)
14. DeepAI: Conversational agent (2019). shorturl.at/gsADL
15. Doswell, J.T.: Pedagogical embodied conversational agent. In: IEEE ICALT 2004 (2004)
16. Druga, S., et al.: Hey google is it ok if i eat you?: initial explorations in child-agent interaction. In: IDC Conference (2017)
17. Eğeci, İ.S., Gençöz, T.: Factors associated with relationship satisfaction: importance of communication skills. Contemp. Family Ther. **28**, 383–391 (2006)
18. Eskenazi, M.: Using automatic speech processing for foreign language pronunciation tutoring: some issues and a prototype. Lang. Learn. Technol. **2**(2), 62–76 (1999)
19. Forbes: How artificial intelligence is making chatbots better for businesses, May 2018. shorturl.at/koFU2
20. Gartner: 25% of customer service operations will use virtual customer assistants by 2020 (2018). www.gtnr.it/2MHVDG3
21. Garvey, C., Berninger, G.: Timing and turn taking in children's conversations. Discourse Process. **4**, 27–57 (1981)
22. Glasser, A.: Automatic speech recognition services: deaf and hard-of-hearing usability. In: The 2019 CHI Conference on Human Factors in Computing Systems (2019)
23. Google: What is conversation design? (2019). shorturl.at/byJL9

24. Hassani, K., Lee, W.S.: Visualizing natural language descriptions: a survey (2016). www.pewrsr.ch/2l4wQnr. Accessed 16 Oct 10 2019

25. Hassani, K., et al.: Design and implementation of an intelligent virtual environment for improving speaking and listening skills. ILE **24**, 252–271 (2016)

26. Hayashi, Y.: Multiple pedagogical conversational agents to support learner-learner collaborative learning: effects of splitting suggestion types. CSR **54**, 246–257 (2019)

27. Kerry, A., Ellis, R., Bull, S.: Conversational agents in e-learning. In: Allen, T., Ellis, R., Petridis, M. (eds.) Applications and Innovations in Intelligent Systems XVI, pp. 169–182. Springer, London (2009). https://doi.org/10.1007/978-1-84882-215-3_13

28. Levinson, S.C., Torreira, F.: Timing in turn-taking and its implications for processing models of language. Front. Psychol. **6**, 731 (2015)

29. Li, J., et al.: An overview of noise-robust automatic speech recognition. IEEE/ACM Trans. Audio Speech Lang. Process. **22**, 745–777 (2014)

30. Light, J., Drager, K.: AAC technologies for young children with complex communication needs: state of the science and future research directions. AAC **23**, 204–216 (2007)

31. Limerick, H., et al.: Empirical evidence for a diminished sense of agency in speech interfaces (2015)

32. Lippmann, R.P.: Speech recognition by machines and humans. Speech Commun. **22**, 1–15 (1997)

33. Lobe, M., Fritsch, R.: Das Kleine Ich Bin Ich Und Das Kleine Hokuspokus. Jumbo Neue Medien (2012)

34. Massaro, D.W.: Embodied agents in language learning for children with language challenges. In: Miesenberger, K., Klaus, J., Zagler, W.L., Karshmer, A.I. (eds.) ICCHP 2006. LNCS, vol. 4061, pp. 809–816. Springer, Heidelberg (2006). https://doi.org/10.1007/11788713_118

35. Massaro, D., et al.: A multilingual embodied conversational agent. In: Proceedings of the 38th HICSS Annual Hawaii International Conference on System Sciences (2005)

36. Moore, R.J., et al.: Conversational UX design. In: ACM CHI 2017 (2017)

37. Mozilla: Websocket. shorturl.at/KMS27 (2019). Accessed 03 Feb 2020

38. Mueller, G.A.: Visual contextual cues and listening comprehension: an experiment. Mod. Lang. J. **64**, 335–340 (1980)

39. Murad, C., et al.: Design guidelines for hands-free speech interaction. In: Proceedings of the 20th International Conference on Human-Computer Interaction with Mobile Devices and Services Adjunct (2018)

40. Nielsen, J.: UX Design for Children (Ages 3–12). Nielsen Norman Group (2010)

41. Nielsen, J.: 10 usability heuristics for user interface design. NNG **1**(1) (1995)

42. Oviatt, S.: Ten myths of multimodal interaction. Commun. ACM **42**(11), 74–81 (1999)

43. Park, H.W., et al.: Telling stories to robots: the effect of backchanneling on a child's storytelling. In: HRI 2017 (2017)

44. Potamianos, A., et al.: Automatic speech recognition for children. In: Fifth European Conference on Speech Communication and Technology (1997)

45. Read, J.C., MacFarlane, S.: Using the fun toolkit and other survey methods to gather opinions in child computer interaction. In: IDC 2006, New York, NY, USA (2006)

46. Read, J.C., et al.: Endurability, engagement and expectations: measuring children's fun (2002)

47. Sanjanaashree, P., et al.: Language learning for visual and auditory learners using scratch toolkit. In: CCI International Conference (2014)
48. Schmidt, C.R., Paris, S.G.: The development of verbal communicative skills in children. In: Advances in Child Development and Behavior, vol. 18. Elsevier (1984)
49. Snap: Libmoji (2018). wwww.github.com/matthewnau/libmoji
50. Sun, M., et al.: Collaborative storytelling between robot and child: a feasibility study. In: Proceedings of the 2017 Conference on Interaction Design and Children (2017)
51. Urrutia, E.K.M., et al.: A first proposal of pedagogic conversational agents to develop computational thinking in children. In: TEEM Conference (2017)
52. Wiggins, J., et al.: Conversational UX design for kids: toward learning companions. In: Proceedings of the Conversational UX Design CHI 2017 Workshop (2017)
53. Willingham, D.T., et al.: The scientific status of learning styles theories. Teach. Psychol. **42**, 266–271 (2015)
54. Xu, D.: Tangible user interface for children-an overview. In: Proceedings of the UCLAN Department of Computing Conference (2005)
55. Xu, D.: Design and evaluation of tangible interfaces for primary school children. In: Proceedings of the 6th International Conference on Interaction Design and Children (2007)

Chatbots for Customer Service

More than FAQ! Chatbot Taxonomy
for Business-to-Business Customer Services

Antje Janssen[(⊠)] [iD], Davinia Rodríguez Cardona[iD], and Michael H. Breitner[iD]

Information Systems Institute, Leibniz Universität Hannover, Königsworther Platz 1, 30167
Hannover, Germany
{janssen,rodriguez,breitner}@iwi.uni-hannover.de

Abstract. Chatbots are becoming increasingly important in the customer service
sector due to their service automation, cost saving opportunities and broad customer satisfaction. Similarly, in the business-to-business (B2B) sector, more and
more companies use chatbots on their websites and social media channels, to
establish sales team contact, to provide information about their products and services or to help customers with their requests and claims. Customer relations in the
B2B environment are especially characterized by a high level of personal contact
service and support through expert explanations due to the complexity of the products and service offerings. In order to support these efforts, chatbots can be used
to assist buying centers along the purchase decision process. However, B2B chatbots have so far only been marginally addressed in the scientific human-computer
interaction and information systems literature. To provide both researchers and
practitioners with knowledge about the characteristics and archetypal patterns of
chatbots currently existing in B2B customer services, we develop and discuss a
17-dimensional chatbot taxonomy for B2B customer services based on Nickerson
et al. [1]. By classifying 40 chatbots in a cluster analysis, this study has identified
three archetypal structures prevailing in B2B customer service chatbot usage.

Keywords: Chatbot taxonomy · Business-to-Business · Customer services

1 Introduction

Especially in B2B segments, customer care is seen as an essential part of any business service or product commercialization, while often being one of the most resource-intensive
units within a business [2–4]. Customer service priorities are driven by the expectation
of a simple and fast service, which must be as personalized and individualized as possible [2]. To remain competitive, organizations are currently investing heavily in digital
and innovative self-service customer care solutions [3, 5]. In this context, chatbots offer
enormous savings potential in customer care effort and costs through service automation
[3]. In recent years, due to the further development of natural language processing and
machine learning, chatbots are being increasingly used in application areas within the
customer service sector, such as claim diagnosis or replacement provision [2]. Even in
the B2B sector, which is often characterized by long decision-making processes and
complex products and services, chatbots are becoming extensively popular. Although

© Springer Nature Switzerland AG 2021
A. Følstad et al. (Eds.): CONVERSATIONS 2020, LNCS 12604, pp. 175–189, 2021.
https://doi.org/10.1007/978-3-030-68288-0_12

single articles focusing on specific aspects and use cases of B2B customer service chatbots have been published [6–8], this does not reflect the theoretical and practical level in which a growing number of companies are discovering chatbots as a communication channel for themselves. What is much more lacking is an overview of how chatbots are used in B2B customer service in practice and what functions and characteristics they have. A taxonomy can help both practice and research to identify utilization possibilities as well as serve as a foundation for B2B chatbot research. Hence, we address the following research questions (RQ):

RQ1: Which conceptually grounded and empirically validated design elements for B2B customer service chatbots exist?
RQ2: Which archetypes can be empirically deduced for B2B customer services chatbots?

To answer the RQ1, we develop a chatbot taxonomy for B2B customer services by following the research approach of Nickerson et al. [1]. The taxonomy is developed in four iterations based on scientific literature about customer service chatbots and on empirical data obtained through the classification of 40 real-world B2B chatbots. To answer RQ2 and to show the status quo, we additionally perform a cluster analysis to identify B2B customer service chatbot archetypes. This is followed by a discussion of the results, including recommendations, implications, and limitations before the conclusions.

2 Chatbot Literature for Customer Services

Customer service is defined as the supply of information, help and support to the customers of an enterprise [9, 10]. Due to their efficiency, cost reduction and automation potential, chatbots as a self-service channel in customer service have received widespread attention, in both research and practice [3, 5]. Sangroya et al. [2] consider chatbots in the role of an intermediary between a customer and a customer care ecosystem with several services in that the chatbot interacts with the customer, identifies the needs, requirements, and emotions of the user. The chatbot as a controlling agent conducts a dialogue with the customer in order to detail certain subtasks by asking questions and performs the tasks for the customer by deciding which channel in the customer care environment is suitable for examining the request [2]. Essential drivers of dialogues with customer service chatbots are the users' questions, efficient and concise answers of the chatbots and the opportunity to be connected to a human employee if the dialogue is not satisfactory [5]. In principle, chatbots are not intended to replace the human customer service employee, rather chatbots are seen as the assistance of a human employee contributing to efficiency and effectiveness by prioritizing requests, answering automatically and processing subtasks before transferring or escalating to a human employee [3]. This handling is also called tiered approach [9]. Since the customer usually enters into a dialogue with the chatbot with a problem or a task, the dialogue with customer service chatbots is usually user-driven and designed for short-term [10]. Due to an increasing demand and usage of technology-based self-service channels for customer service purposes in practice [5], several scientific articles have been published dealing with quality aspects (e.g., [5]) communication styles (e.g., [11, 12]), user requirements (e.g., [3, 9]) and design aspects (e.g., [4, 13]) of chatbots in the customer service sector.

Traditional marketing distinguishes between business-to-customer (B2C) markets, where companies market their products and services to individual private consumers, and B2B markets, where companies sell their products and services to other businesses, often involving several people, also called buying centers, into the process, which in turn influences the use of communication channels and the communication itself [14]. Referring to the chatbot environment, however so far, only sporadically articles exist about the use of customer service chatbots in the B2B sector. Damnjanovic [8] has sketched application areas of chatbots along the B2B customer acquisition processes focusing on the interaction and co-existing of automated services and salespeople. According to the researcher, the role is to provide information to the potential customers and collect data about the potential customers for salespeople [8]. In the awareness and interest phase of a B2B sales funnel, chatbots can give the potential customers more detailed information about the desired offers, as well as create awareness and interest for the products and offerings of the organization, while first information about potential customers, their speech patterns and preferences can be collected for the company [8]. Whereas in the conversion and qualification phase as well as in the closing phase, the focus lays on proving the potential customer with detailed and personalized information and offers, which is delivered merely by sales representatives on basis of the information collected through the interaction with the chatbot [8]. Gnewuch et al. [6] focused on presenting insights from developing a B2B chatbot for a service provider in the energy industry. Rossmann et al. [7] focused on developing a performance measurement model by comparing results of a hotline and a chatbot in a B2B manufacturing context. These are however only very specific use cases and the use of customer service chatbots in the B2B area has not yet been sufficiently considered [6]. An article, offering a holistic view of B2B customer service chatbots in form of a taxonomy is missing.

Several chatbot taxonomies have been published in the scientific literature in recent years, but most of them have carried out a general analysis of chatbots (e.g., [15]) or classified specific areas such as collaborative work (e.g., [16]) or platforms for conversational agent development (e.g., [17]). Følstad et al. [10] developed a chatbot classification by concentrating on two typology dimensions "duration of relation" and "locus of control" while classifying 57 chatbots within the customer support and three further domains. Feine et al. [18] concentrated on building a taxonomy of social cues of conversational agents focused on verbal, visual, auditory and invisible aspects. Janssen et al. [15] developed a chatbot taxonomy classifying 102 domain-specific chatbots within 17 dimensions while focusing on the perspectives intelligence, interaction and context. During development, the authors aimed to examine chatbots from the most wide-spread application areas, which they in turn classified into six application domains. 21% of the sample was classified into the characteristic e-customer service and 48% of these e-customer service chatbots were assigned to the archetype "utility expert chatbot" [15].

In summary, it can be concluded that there are already some chatbot taxonomies, which provide insights into customer service chatbots. However, all chatbot taxonomies lack the focus B2B customer service specifications. Since we believe that there are further specific characteristics as well as application scenarios where chatbots are used in B2B sector, the goal is to develop a taxonomy that represents the characteristics of chatbots for B2B customer services.

3   Research Design, Methodology, and Results

3.1   Taxonomy Development Procedure

In order to develop a taxonomy of design elements for B2B customer service chatbots, we followed the framework of Nickerson et al. [1, p. 340]. According to Nickerson et al. [1], a taxonomy (T) consists of a set of dimensions with each dimension (D_i) having its own subset (k_i) of characteristics $(C_{i,j})$. One dimension must consist of at least two characteristics. Each object classified according to the taxonomy must have exactly one characteristic of each dimension, not more or less. Nickerson et al. [1] illustrate the former conditions with the following formula:

$$T = \left\{ D_i, i = 1, \ldots, n \,|\, D_i = \left\{ C_{ij}, j = 1, \ldots, k_i; k_i \geq 2 \right\} \right.$$

The applied taxonomy development framework comprises seven iterative steps. First, a meta-characteristic must be set for the taxonomy, meaning the focus of the taxonomy must be defined. In this case the meta-characteristic are the design elements for B2B customer service chatbots, i.e., the socio-technical features defining the structural and functional composition of B2B customer service chatbots. Second, a set of ending conditions must be determined, since the process is iterative, without predefined ending conditions the development of a taxonomy can be an infinite process. In this case the ending condition chosen correspond to all the objective and subjective ending conditions proposed by Nickerson et al. [1, p. 344]. Posteriorly, in line with Nickerson et al. [1] two viable approaches can be used for the creation of the taxonomy: empirical-to-conceptual or conceptual-to-empirical. These approaches can be applied on an alternating basis until the adopted ending conditions are met and therefore, the development process of the taxonomy can be regarded as finished.

To integrate the extant theoretical knowledge in the field of chatbots and empirical findings related to real-world B2B service chatbots, we adopted a conceptual-to-empirical approach to begin the taxonomy development process. Accordingly, we performed a literature review and the findings thereof were used for the deductive conceptualization of the dimensions and characteristics for an initial taxonomy of potential relevant dimensions and characteristics. Subsequently, we adapted this initial taxonomy through an iterative empirical analysis of a total set of 40 existing B2B chatbots in customer service. A list of the examined chatbots for the taxonomy development is aggregated in Table A.1 in online appendix (http://bit.ly/Supplementary_Material). After four iterations, we complied with all ending conditions (see Table 1) and achieved a final taxonomic structure. Below we delineate the actions conducted in each iteration.

3.2   Iteration 1

In this iteration, following a conceptual-to-empirical approach, a first taxonomic structure was conceptualized using the knowledge derived from a review of the scientific literature on chatbots in customer service. The scope of the literature review included the databases of AISeL, IEEE Xplore, SpringerLink, ACM, and JSTOR. We applied the search string ("chatbot" OR "conversational agent") AND ("customer service" OR

Table 1. Compliance with the adopted ending conditions

Iteration 1	Iteration 2	Iteration 3	Iteration 4	Ending conditions
				Subjective ending conditions (Nickerson et al. [1])
		•	•	Mutually exclusive: no object has two different characteristics in a dimension
		•	•	Collectively exhaustive: each chatbot has at least one characteristic in each dimension
			•	Concise: dimensions and characteristics are limited
	•	•	•	Robust: sufficient number of dimensions and characteristics
			•	Comprehensive: identification of all (relevant) dimensions of an object
•	•	•	•	Extendable: possibility to easily add dimensions and characteristics in the future
		•	•	Explanatory: dimensions and characteristics sufficiently explain the object
				Objective ending conditions (Nickerson et al. [1])
	• (5)	• (12)	• (23)	All chatbots (or a representative sample) were analyzed
			•	No object was merged or split
		•	•	At least one object assigned to each characteristic
			•	No new dimensions or characteristics were added
			•	No dimensions or characteristics were merged or split
•	•	•	•	Every dimension is unique
•	•	•	•	Every characteristic within the dimension is unique
		•	•	Every combination of characteristics is unique

"customer support") within the aforementioned databases that yielded a total of 565 articles within the five databases. Thereby, by reading title and abstract, and applying backward, forward and similarity search, we identified a total of 14 relevant articles providing features and functions of chatbots in customer service which were used as a basis for the creation of the first dimensions and characteristics. Most of ending conditions were not fulfilled in this iteration because of its conceptual nature (see Table 1).

The first iteration resulted in 18 dimensions and 53 mutually exclusive characteristics drawn from the literature as detailed in Table 2.

Table 2. Taxonomy dimensions conceptualized from the literature

Dimension	[3]	[4]	[5]	[8]	[9]	[13]	[19]	[20]	[21]	[22]	[23]	[24]	[25]	[26]
D_1 Business integration			•											•
D_2 Access to business data							•							
D_3 Dialogue structure	•	•				•		•			•			
D_4 Conversation beyond Q&A interaction			•							•				•
D_5 Data policy	•													
D_6 Handoff to human agent	•				•				•		•	•		
D_7 Small talk		•							•				•	•
D_8 Features presentation							•							
D_9 Conversational memory							•	•	•					
D_{10} Human-like avatar					•									
D_{11} Content related service						•								
D_{12} Account related services						•								
D_{13} Account authentication						•								
D_{14} Requests													•	
D_{15} Question personalization			•					•					•	
D_{16} Customer service orientation												•		
D_{17} User assistance design										•				•
D_{18} Context management						•								

3.3   Iteration 2

In the second iteration, an empirical-to-conceptual approach was chosen and a first random sample of 5 chatbots for B2B customer service (see Table A.1 in online appendix, http://bit.ly/Supplementary_Material) presented in chatbots conferences (e.g., [27]) were examined to adapt the conceptual dimensions and characteristics abstracted in the first iteration. Based on the empirical analysis of chatbots, first we eliminated the dimensions that were found to be not relevant for describing the set of analyzed chatbots (i.e. D_4, D_8, D_9, D_{12}, D_{17}, D_{18}). The former dimensions have been described in the literature, however they could not be confirmed in the empirical review. For example, socio-technical features as the presence of conversational memory in chatbots has been described in the literature (see e.g., [19–21]), but was not present in any of the chatbots examined. Furthermore, we added to the initial taxonomy 4 empirically identified dimensions of chatbots in B2B customer service, composed in the following manner: *service/product information = {no, yes}; success stories = {no, yes}; book/show a demo = {no, yes}; and career information = {no, yes}.* Since all ending conditions were not achieved, an additional iteration was required.

3.4   Iteration 3

Subsequently, we conducted a further empirical-to-conceptual approach. For this purpose, we additionally examined 12 chatbots from the B2B customer service (see Table A.1 in online appendix). The chatbots were drawn from chatbot databases (e.g., [28]), websites of large and medium-sized B2B companies and customer lists from chatbot providers. In this iteration, we identified 6 new dimensions allocating 14 new characteristics as follows: *industry classification = {financial services industry, manufacturing industry, marketing industry, software industry}; pricing = {no, yes}; support question/ticket = {no, yes}; callback request = {no, yes}; billing details = {no, yes}; user management = {no, yes}.* Given the similar nature of the new identified function-related dimensions, we merged the dimension of *book/show a demo, callback request* into an overarching dimension named *action request*, and similarly, the dimensions of *support question/ticket, billing details, user management* were consolidated into a wide-ranging dimension designated as *service request.* Likewise, the dimensions of service/product information and success stories were found to be redundant and were therefore merged. Furthermore, 5 new characteristics were added to the dimensions of account authentication (i.e., $C_{i,j}$ *optional*); action request (i.e., $C_{i,j}$ *both, none*); service request (i.e., $C_{i,j}$ *multiple, none*) to increase their descriptive power. After that the final conditions were checked again. Since new dimensions were identified and new characteristics were added, all ending conditions have not yet been satisfied in this iteration.

3.5   Iteration 4

Since not all ending conditions were fulfilled in the previous iteration, we performed an additional empirical-to-conceptual iteration. For this purpose, a larger random sample consisting of 23 chatbots from the B2B customer service were examined (see Table A.1 in online appendix). The examined chatbots identified through and assessment focused on blogs providing B2B chatbot use cases or comparing and rating chatbots or chatbot platforms. In this iteration, no new dimensions and characteristics of B2B customer service chatbots could be identified, as well, no dimensions or characteristics were eliminated, merged or split. Hence, after this iteration all objective and subjective ending conditions proposed by Nickerson et al. [1] were fulfilled and the taxonomy development process was completed. The final chatbot taxonomy for B2B customer services consisting of 17 dimensions and 45 characteristics is presented in Table 3, along with the distribution of the characteristics identified within the sample of 40 classified B2B customer service chatbots.

Table 3. Final chatbot taxonomy for B2B customer services

Dimensions D_i	Characteristics $C_{i,j}$ (% distribution)		
D_1 Industry classification	$C_{1,1}$ Financial services industry (5%)	$C_{1,2}$ Manufacturing industry (22%)	
	$C_{1,3}$ Marketing industry (10%)	$C_{1,4}$ Software industry (63%)	
D_2 Business integration	$C_{2,1}$ No (68%)	$C_{2,2}$ Yes (32%)	
D_3 Access to business data	$C_{3,1}$ No (90%)	$C_{3,2}$ Yes (10%)	
D_4 Dialogue structure	$C_{4,1}$ Predefined (48%)	$C_{4,2}$ Open (15%)	$C_{4,3}$ Both (37%)
D_5 Data policy	$C_{5,1}$ Not provided (65%)	$C_{5,2}$ Provided (35%)	
D_6 Handoff to human agent	$C_{6,1}$ Not possible (12%)	$C_{6,2}$ Possible (88%)	
D_7 Small talk	$C_{7,1}$ Not possible (80%)	$C_{7,2}$ Possible (20%)	
D_8 Human-like avatar	$C_{8,1}$ No (90%)	$C_{8,2}$ Yes (10%)	
D_9 Content related service	$C_{9,1}$ Content advertisement (70%)	$C_{9,2}$ Content consumption (30%)	
D_{10} Account authentication	$C_{10,1}$ Not required (63%)	$C_{10,2}$ Optional (12%)	$C_{10,3}$ Required (25%)
D_{11} Question personalization	$C_{11,1}$ None (12%)	$C_{11,2}$ FAQ (50%)	
	$C_{11,3}$ Personalized account questions (30%)	$C_{11,4}$ Highly personalized questions (8%)	
D_{12} Customer service orientation	$C_{12,1}$ Knowledge-oriented (53%)	$C_{12,2}$ Task-oriented (47%)	
D_{13} Company information	$C_{13,1}$ No (70%)	$C_{13,2}$ Yes (30%)	
D_{14} Service/product information	$C_{14,1}$ No (15%)	$C_{14,2}$ Yes (85%)	
D_{15} Pricing	$C_{15,1}$ No (80%)	$C_{15,2}$ Yes (20%)	
D_{16} Action request	$C_{16,1}$ Book/show a demo (8%)	$C_{16,2}$ Callback request (32%)	
	$C_{16,3}$ Both (35%)	$C_{16,4}$ None (25%)	
D_{17} Service request	$C_{17,1}$ Support question /ticket (32%)	$C_{17,2}$ Billing details (3%)	$C_{17,3}$ User management (3%)
	$C_{17,17}$ Multiple (10%)	$C_{17,5}$ None (52%)	

To ease interpretation and increase the explanatory power of the taxonomy, we describe the characteristics that may not be self-explanatory in the Appendix Table 5. For example, the dimensions D_{16} action request and D_{17} service request describe respectively the functional actions or service inquires related to customer service elements present in the analyzed chatbots (e.g., pricing, user management).

To assess the inter-coder reliability of our results, a random sample of 8 chatbots was again classified by all authors involved in the coding process and, subsequently, the quality of the inter-coder agreement was evaluated using the kappa coefficient of Fleiss [29]. As a result, a kappa coefficient of 0.64 was obtained, which indicates a substantial strength of inter-coder agreement [30].

4   Findings and Chatbot Archetypes

To identify which clusters are represented within our dataset, we applied the Ward [31] algorithm that calculates the distances between all elements of our dataset [32]. The Ward algorithm has the advantage that it can be used without having to specify a certain number of clusters in advance, as opposed to, e.g., the K-means or K-medois algorithms, which are non-hierarchical [15]. However, in the scientific literature it is recommended to combine hierarchical algorithms and non-hierarchical partitioning algorithms to unite the advantages of both algorithm types [33]. Using the dendogram obtained by means of the Ward algorithm, we have graphically determined the number of archetypes based on the distances between the groupings (see Fig. 1). Within the dendogram (see Fig. 1), a first splitting is visible on the height of 2.1, followed by a split at approximately 1.75 and 1.5. Therefore, we investigated the possibility of three and four archetypes using the partitioning K-means algorithm before deciding on three archetypes based on the content-related plausibility.

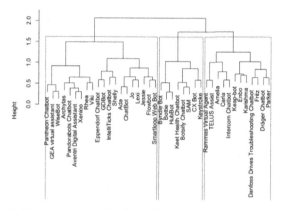

Fig. 1. Dendogram visualization of the conducted Ward clustering

Table 4 shows the distributions of the characteristics in the three archetypes, which we named *lead generation chatbot* (archetype 1, n = 8), *aftersales facilitator chatbot* (archetype 2, n = 10) and *advertising FAQ chatbot* (archetype 3, n = 22). These archetypes are intended to guide chatbot developers as an orientation to identify relevant attributes within the development based on their customer service purposes within B2B business.

The **lead generation chatbot archetype** contains chatbots from software industry that are aimed at actively generating leads by encouraging users to book demos and/or provide their contact details (e.g., business email address or company name) to be called back by human employees. These task-oriented chatbots are characterized by having a predefined dialog structure guiding the user without small talk to an action. While some chatbots in this archetype have the sole function of collecting the customer's contact data (e.g., Botsify chatbot), other chatbots ask specific questions to assess the appropriate sales executive depending on the customer's needs (e.g., Keet Health chatbot). On the other hand, the **aftersales facilitator chatbot archetype** includes task-oriented chatbots that offer more personalized dialogues by asking the user for requirements, such as the number of employees working on the CRM system (e.g., Carla Chatbot), before providing the appropriate product and service information or offering a request. These chatbots are characterized by content consumption trough asking personalized

Table 4. Results of the k-means cluster analysis

	Label	Lead generation chatbot	Aftersales facilitator chatbot	Advertising FAQ chatbot
	Archetype	1	2	3
	n	8	10	22
Industry classification	Financial services industry	0%	10%	5%
	Manufacturing industry	0%	50%	18%
	Marketing industry	0%	10%	14%
	Software industry	100%	30%	64%
Business integration	No	75%	40%	77%
	Yes	25%	60%	23%
Access to business data	No	88%	70%	100%
	Yes	13%	30%	0%
Dialogue structure	Predefined	88%	20%	45%
	Open	0%	40%	9%
	Both	13%	40%	45%
Data Policy	Not provided	38%	60%	77%
	Provided	63%	40%	23%
Handoff to human agent	Not possible	0%	20%	14%
	Possible	100%	80%	86%
Small talk	Not possible	100%	60%	82%
	Possible	0%	40%	18%
Human-like avatar	No	100%	70%	95%
	Yes	0%	30%	5%
Content related service	Content advertisement	75%	0%	100%
	Content consumption	25%	100%	0%
Account authentification	Not required	50%	60%	68%
	Optional	0%	20%	14%
	Required	50%	20%	18%
Question personalization	None	50%	0%	5%
	FAQ	0%	20%	82%
	Personalized account questions	38%	70%	9%
	Highly personalized questions	13%	10%	5%
Customer service orientation	Knowledge-oriented	0%	0%	95%
	Task-oriented	100%	100%	5%
Company information	No	100%	60%	64%
	Yes	0%	40%	36%
Service/product information	No	38%	10%	9%
	Yes	63%	90%	91%
Pricing	No	100%	60%	82%
	Yes	0%	40%	18%
Action request	Book/show a demo	25%	0%	5%
	Callback request	25%	40%	32%
	Both	50%	20%	36%
	None	0%	40%	27%
Service request	Support question/ticket	13%	40%	36%
	Billing details	0%	0%	5%
	User management	0%	10%	0%
	Multiple	0%	40%	0%
	None	88%	10%	59%

Due to rounding inaccuracies, the sum of a column in a dimension is not always exactly 100%

| 0% | 10% | 20% | 30% | 40% | 50% | 60% | 70% | 80% | 90% | 100% |

questions. Thereby, they are intended to execute a task by giving the user support for example when the account operator profile is locked (e.g., Intercom chatbot) or when "motor won't start" (e.g., Danfoss Drives Troubleshooting Chatbot). Lastly, the **advertising FAQ chatbot archetype** contains knowledge-oriented chatbots that have the goal of advertising products and services, for which the chatbots answer standard FAQs within the dialog, whereby some of them linking articles on the website (e.g., Eppendorf Chatbot) or embedding videos (e.g., ChatBot).

5 Discussion, Implications, Recommendations, Limitations, and a Further Research Agenda

To answer the research questions, we developed a chatbot taxonomy for B2B customer services, classified 40 chatbots and identified three archetypes. The taxonomy and the analysis of the examined chatbots reveal several implications and limitations, which are discussed and from which twelve research directions (RD) are derived below.

The empirical analysis of the 40 chatbots shows that 88% of the B2B chatbots for customer services offer the possibility to contact a human agent (D_6), in contrast to the results of other taxonomic studies such as Janssen et al. [15], where only 20% of the considered chatbots from various application areas offered this possibility. While handoff is seen as a highly important topic in research [3, 9, 21] the empirical result shows that customer contact is also extremely important in the B2B sector and products and services often require explanation. Much more, chatbots are used to generate leads by offering action requests (65%) through callback requests or demo booking (D_{16}). This is so far that in 25% of the chatbots it is necessary to enter contact data (D_{10}), like the business email address, before the chatbot dialogue is continued. It is noticeable that the scientific literature mainly prescribes the use of chatbots in the first stages of the sales funnel [6–8]. However, the chatbot taxonomy shows that 48% of the B2B chatbots also offer service requests (D_{17}) in the form of, e.g., support ticket creation and are therefore also used after the purchase is completed. But billing details (3%) or user management (3%) are rarely provided within the dialogue, which can be adapted by further companies. Further research can examine the use of chatbots in different levels along the sales funnel (RD1). Additionally, it is recommended to investigate what information the customers expect from a chatbot at the different phases of the customer journey and across diverse industries (RD2). The feature of information personalization also requires closer examination. Taking a look on the sample, access to business data (D_3) is not present in 90% of the chatbots considered. This topic holds great potential for B2B sector, as there are often extremely specific requirements that often necessitate a batch size of 1. A possible personalization may also require the provision and adherence to a data policy (D_5), to which 35% referred. In further research, it is of theoretical and practical value to examine the trade-off between the degree of personalization (e.g., custom responses) and data privacy concerns relating to, e.g., B2B customer data obtained during the interaction (RD3), which must be compared to results of the explorative interview-based study on trust in B2C customer service chatbots conducted by Følstad et al. [30]. While some chatbot researchers emphasize the importance of small talk in customer service [4, 22, 25], in the B2B sector little emphasis is placed on the presence of this capability, as only 20% of chatbots were capable of small talk (D_7). However, this also supports the generic marketing communication attribute described B2C markets are rather characterized by emotionality and B2B companies ascribe rationality to their customers [14], which in turn influences the content aspects of communication. Our results show that the distinction between B2B and B2C use of chatbots exists in practice and must also be reflected in research (RD4). On the other hand, it also shows that classic B2B marketing characteristics, such as rationality in decision-making, are also adopted by companies in the chatbot environment. However, quantitative studies can contribute to identify the critical factors, as well as the causal relationships between them, in order to provide further insights into the underlying differences (e.g., in view of the intention to use, functional expectations or shifting motivations) among B2B and B2C chatbots (RD5) from the user's point of view. It is also interesting to examine the way B2B customers communicate with a chatbot (RD6) and the expectations of B2B users regarding socio-emotional behavior and social cues (RD7) using cross-industry cases.

To answer RQ2, we identified three currently existing archetypes. The lead generation (archetype 1) and advertising FAQ (archetype 3) chatbot archetypes are mainly located in the pre-purchase step whereas with different emphases. While archetype 1 aims to collect customer information for further personal contact, archetype 3 focuses on providing information to stimulate buying interest. Chatbots in the aftersales facilitator chatbot archetype (archetype 2), on the other hand, have also the functionalities of giving information about products and services but completely content consumption and customer oriented. In addition, these chatbots have also the possibility to help the customers after the purchase with requests or claims and act therefore much more as facilitators. Since we believe that the functionalities of a chatbot should not stop with the purchase but should be completely focused on the users' demands we see great potential for archetype 2 which is why it should be explored more closely in the further research (RD8).

Due to the lack of availability of B2B literature, we almost exclusively used scientific literature from the general chatbot customer service to develop the taxonomy. Hence, building on the extant literature in the field of chatbots, we have contributed to present a foundation to further B2B chatbot research. Hence, it is useful to do a further conceptual-to-empirical iteration when this area has been further researched (RD9). Furthermore, only chatbots that can be accessed externally were tested. Whereas, chatbots that are publicly accessible but require authentication or naming of the business email address or other personal data within the dialogue were included (D_{10}). Under certain circumstances, the inclusion of internal chatbots from B2B customer service, which require a more company-bound login, can lead to different results as they can have more access to business data or more personalization (RD10). The B2B customer service chatbots were tested in July and August 2020. The deployment, adoption, and skills of chatbots are evolving rapidly, so it makes sense to repeat the empirical-to-conceptual step in further research to identify further dimensions and characteristics that can be used to spot emerging trends (RD11) as well as to conduct an evaluation with researchers and practitioners to verify the applicability of the taxonomy (RD12).

6 Conclusions

We developed a taxonomy of chatbots for B2B customer services and thus elaborated these B2B specific characteristics. In addition to the conducted literature research, 40 B2B customer service chatbots were empirically analyzed and classified. Within four iterations a final taxonomy was developed which contains 17 dimensions and 45 characteristics. We discovered that chatbots from the B2B customer service predominantly give detailed information about services and products, unfortunately, mostly without having access to business data, but offer the possibility to get in contact with a human employee. However, there are major differences between these chatbots in terms of customer service orientation and content related services which is why three archetypes were identified.

Appendix

See Table 5.

Table 5. Definitions of taxonomy dimensions and underlying conceptual bases

Dimension D_i	Definition
D_1 Industry classification	Describes the industry to which the company offering the B2B chatbot service belongs
D_2 Business integration	Describes whether the chatbot is supported by integrated product or customer databases [5, 26]
D_3 Access to business data	Describes whether the chatbot has access to non-public business data and uses it to enhance its responses [19]
D_9 Content related service	Describes whether the chatbot provides only commercial content on products or services, or enable the user to acquire them [13]
D_{10} Account authentication	Describes whether the chatbot requires the authentication of the user by means of a business email address or username and password to begin the interaction [13]
D_{11} Question personalization	Describes the degree of response customization of the chatbot, e.g., the capacity of the chatbot to tailored highly personalized questions require information obtained through the interaction with the user [8, 20, 25]
D_{12} Customer service orientation	Describes whether a chatbot is primarily oriented to provide information or to perform a task [24]
D_{16} Action request	Describes the functional actions related to customer service that the chatbot is able to perform [25]
D_{17} Service request	Describes the functional service inquires related to customer service elements present in the chatbots [25]

References

1. Nickerson, R.C., Varshney, U., Muntermann, J.: A method for taxonomy development and its application in information systems. Eur. J. Inf. Syst. **22**(3), 336–359 (2013). https://doi.org/10.1057/ejis.2012.26
2. Sangroya, A., Saini, P., Anantaram, C.: Chatbot as an intermediary between a customer and the customer care ecosystem. In: Proceedings of 9th International Conference on Management of Digital EcoSystem, pp. 128–133 (2017)
3. Corea, C., Delfmann, P., Nagel, S.: Towards intelligent chatbots for customer care - Practice-based requirements for a research agenda. In: Proceedings of 53rd Hawaii International Conference of System Sciences, pp. 5819–5828 (2020)
4. Cui, L., Huang, S., Wei, F., Tan, C., Duan, C., Zhou, M.: Superagent: A customer service chatbot for E-commerce websites. In: Proceedings of 5th Annual Meeting of the Association for Computational Linguistics, pp. 97–102 (2017)
5. Gnewuch, U., Morana, S., Maedche, A.: Towards designing cooperative and social conversational agents for customer service. In: Proceedings of the International Conference on Information Systems (2017)
6. Gnewuch, U., Heckmann, C., Morana, S., Maedche, A.: Designing and implementing a B2B chatbot: Insights from a medium-sized service provider in the energy industry. In: Proceedings of 14th International Conference Wirtschaftsinformatik (2019)
7. Rossmann, A., Zimmermann, A., Hertweck, D.: The impact of chatbots on customer service performance. Springer International Publishing (2020). https://doi.org/10.1007/978-3-030-51057-2_33
8. Damnjanovic, V.: Entry market strategy for weaver chatbot using the digital B2B model. In: Proceedings of International Conference on Artificial Intelligence: Applications and Innovations, pp. 40–43 (2019)
9. Følstad, A., Skjuve, M.: Chatbots for customer service: User experience and motivation. In: Proceedings of ACM International Conference on Conversational User Interface (2019)
10. Følstad, Asbjørn., Skjuve, Marita, Brandtzaeg, Petter Bae: Different chatbots for different purposes: towards a typology of chatbots to understand interaction design. In: Bodrunova, Svetlana S., et al. (eds.) INSCI 2018. LNCS, vol. 11551, pp. 145–156. Springer, Cham (2019). https://doi.org/10.1007/978-3-030-17705-8_13
11. Hewitt, T., Beaver, I.: A case study of user communication styles with customer service agents versus intelligent virtual agents. In: Proceedings of the SIGdial 2020 Conference, pp. 79–85 (2020)
12. Xu, A., Liu, Z., Guo, Y., Sinha, V., Akkiraju, R.: A new chatbot for customer service on social media. In: Proceedings of Conference on Human Factors in Computing Systems, pp. 3506–3510 (2017)
13. Hwang, Shinhee., Kim, Beomjun, Lee, Keeheon: A data-driven design framework for customer service chatbot. In: Marcus, Aaron, Wang, Wentao (eds.) HCII 2019. LNCS, vol. 11583, pp. 222–236. Springer, Cham (2019). https://doi.org/10.1007/978-3-030-23570-3_17
14. Reklaitis, K., Pileliene, L.: Principle differences between B2B and B2C marketing communication processes. Manage. Organ. Syst. Res. **81**(1), 73–86 (2019). https://doi.org/10.1515/mosr-2019-0005
15. Janssen, A., Passlick, J., Rodríguez Cardona, D., Breitner, M.H.: Virtual assistance in any context: a taxonomy of design elements for domain-specific chatbots. Bus. Inf. Syst. Eng. **62**(3), 211–225 (2020). https://doi.org/10.1007/s12599-020-00644-1
16. Bittner, E., Oeste-Reiß, S., Leimeister, J.M.: Where is the bot in our team? Toward a taxonomy of design option combinations for conversational agents in collaborative work. In: Proceedings of the 52nd Hawaii International Conference on System Sciences. Proceedings of Hawaii International Conference on System Sciences (2019)

17. Diederich, S., Brendel, A.B., Kolbe, L.M.: Towards a taxonomy of platforms for conversational agent design digital nudging view project chatbots and gamification view project. In: Proceedings of 14th International Conference on Wirtschaftsinformatik, pp. 1100–1114 (2019)

18. Feine, J., Gnewuch, U., Morana, S., Maedche, A.: A taxonomy of social cues for conversational agents. Int. J. Hum Comput Stud. **132**, 138–161 (2019). https://doi.org/10.1016/j.ijhcs.2019.07.009

19. Feine, J., Adam, M., Benke, I., Maedche, A.: Exploring design principles for enterprise chatbots: an analytic hierarchy process study. In: Proceedings of 15th International Conference on Design Science Research in Information Systems and Technology (2020)

20. Følstad, A., Skjuve, M., Brandtzaeg, P.B.: Different chatbots for different purposes: towards a typology of chatbots to understand interaction design. In: Bodrunova, Svetlana S., et al. (eds.) INSCI 2018. LNCS, vol. 11551, pp. 145–156. Springer, Cham (2019). https://doi.org/10.1007/978-3-030-17705-8_13

21. Herrera, A., Yaguachi, Lady, Piedra, N.: Building conversational interface for customer support applied to open campus an open online course provider. In: Proceedings of 19th International Conference on Advanced Learning Technologies, pp. 11–13 (2019)

22. Johannsen, F., Leist, S., Konadl, D., Basche, M., De Hesselle, B.: Comparison of commercial chatbot solutions for supporting customer interaction. In: Proceedings of 26th European Conference on Information Systems (2018)

23. Kvale, K., Sell, O.A., Hodnebrog, S., Følstad, A.: Improving conversations: lessons learnt from manual analysis of chatbot dialogues. In: Følstad, A., et al. (eds.) CONVERSATIONS 2019. LNCS, vol. 11970, pp. 187–200. Springer, Cham (2020). https://doi.org/10.1007/978-3-030-39540-7

24. Li, F.L., et al.: AliMe assist: an intelligent assistant for creating an innovative E-commerce experience. In: Proceedings of International Conference on Information and Knowledge Management, pp. 2495–2498 (2017)

25. Michaud, L.N.: Observations of a new chatbot: drawing conclusions from early interactions with users. IT Professional **20**(5), 40–47 (2018)

26. Sousa, D.N., Brito, M.A., Argainha, C.: Virtual customer service: building your chatbot. In: Proceedings of ACM International Conference of ICBIM, pp. 174–179 (2019)

27. Chatbots Life: The Chatbot Conference - AI, Chatbots, Virtual Assistants and Voice, https://www.chatbotconference.com/. Accessed 27 Aug 2020

28. Chatbots.org: Chatbot Reviews, Community & News, https://www.chatbots.org/. Accessed 30 Aug 2020

29. Fleiss, J.L.: Measuring nominal scale agreement among many raters. Psychol. Bull. **76**(5), 378–382 (1971). https://doi.org/10.1037/h0031619

30. Landis, J.R., Koch, G.G.: The measurement of observer agreement for categorical data. Biometrics **33**(1), 159–174 (1977). https://doi.org/10.2307/2529310

31. Ward, J.H.: Hierarchical grouping to optimize an objective function. J. Am. Stat. Assoc. **58**(301), 236–244 (1963)

32. Gimpel, H., Rau, D., Röglinger, M.: Understanding FinTech start-ups – a taxonomy of consumer-oriented service offerings. Electron. Markets **28**(3), 245–264 (2018). https://doi.org/10.1007/s12525-017-0275-0

33. Balijepally, V., Mangalaraj, G., Iyengar, K.: Are we wielding this hammer correctly? A reflective review of the application of cluster analysis in information systems research. J. Assoc. Inf. Syst. **12**(5), 375–413 (2011)

Customer Service Chatbots: A Qualitative Interview Study into the Communication Journey of Customers

Margot J. van der Goot[1]([⊠]) [iD], Laura Hafkamp[2], and Zoë Dankfort[2]

[1] Amsterdam School of Communication Research (ASCoR), Nieuwe Achtergracht 166, 1018 WV Amsterdam, The Netherlands
m.j.vandergoot@uva.nl
[2] Ruigrok Netpanel, Silodam 1A, 1013 AL Amsterdam, The Netherlands

Abstract. The current qualitative interview study describes the communication journey of customers who wish to contact companies, and their evaluation of chatbot communication within this journey. Interviews were conducted with a sample (N = 24) that was varied in terms of gender, age, educational level and household composition. Experiences with nine customer service chatbots were included. The analysis focuses on three stages in the journey: first, customers' prior expectations when contacting a company; second, their experiences during chatbot conversations, and third, their final conclusions about under which conditions customer service chatbots should be implemented, and the consequences of chatbot communication for customers' company perceptions. Implications for research and practice are discussed.

Keywords: AI · Chatbots · Company perceptions · Customer service · Qualitative interview study · User experience

1 Introduction

Developments in AI fundamentally alter how companies communicate with their customers [9]. Particularly in customer service, chatbots are increasingly implemented [7, 11, 12]. Customers who need information or who want to complain can type their questions in a dialogue screen (often looking like a chat interface), and receive answers in natural language. The essential characteristic of this type of communication is that, although the answers are automatically generated, the conversation is made to resemble a dialogue between humans [7]. Since this is a novel way of interacting with a company, the question arises how customers experience these conversations, and how this communication affects their company perceptions. The current qualitative interview study aims to shed light on these issues by describing the communication journey of customers who wish to contact companies, and their evaluation of chatbot communication within this journey. The analysis focuses on three stages in the journey: first, customers' prior

© Springer Nature Switzerland AG 2021
A. Følstad et al. (Eds.): CONVERSATIONS 2020, LNCS 12604, pp. 190–204, 2021.
https://doi.org/10.1007/978-3-030-68288-0_13

expectations when contacting a company; second, their experiences during chatbot conversations, and third, their final conclusions about under which conditions customer service chatbots should be implemented, and the consequences of chatbot communication for customers'company perceptions.

The current analysis is most closely related to recent qualitative work that also focused on users' perceptions of customer service chatbots [5, 6, 13]. As Følstad and Skjuve noted, thus far, research providing insights in user experiences and motivations regarding customer service chatbots has been severely limited. The present analysis extends the previous qualitative studies in at least two ways. First, previous studies have already shown that the prime motivation for the use of customer service chatbots is to get their (simple) customer queries answered in a fast and convenient matter [6, 13]. The present study takes this as given, and provides further context to this motivation by showing how communication with customer service chatbots is embedded in customers' communication journey with a company. Second, compared to the interview study in which customers were interviewed after their chatbot use of two specific companies [6], the present study encompasses more variation. The current study uses nine chatbots, of both profit and non-profit organizations. The chatbots are also varied in terms of humanlike characteristics. Moreover, whereas the strength of Følstad and Skjuve's study was that it approached people who actually used the two chatbots, the present study takes the approach of inviting a wider variety of people. The current sample includes both people who use customers service chatbots as well as people who are rather unwilling to use them.

By doing so, this study provides further insight into real-life experiences customers have with existing chatbots, thus providing necessary context to experimental work that investigates effects of -particularly- humanlike cues on persuasion outcomes and company perceptions [2, 9, 10]. The study also provides guidance to companies that are faced with the challenge of implementing chatbot technology for their customer service. Although much has been written about how to design and scale chatbots, it remains important to look at chatbot communication through customers' eyes.

2   Background

This section showcases what previous academic research has already shown about the three stages in the communication journey that we focus on in the current study.

2.1   Customers' Prior Expectations of Communication with a Company

Previous qualitative work has shown that the primary reason for customers to enter a conversation with a customer service chatbot is to get their (simple) customer queries answered in a fast and convenient manner [3, 5, 6, 13]. This implies that the key to succesful chatbot communication in customer service is that the queries are answered in a correct and fast way. This makes sense, but in real life this motivation is embedded in the broader journey of communicating with a company. Therefore, the current qualitative interview study sets out to describe what the expectations are that customers have when contacting a company, and what the position is of chatbot communication within the journey.

In addition to this main motivation for using customer service chatbots, research has shown that the mood people are in may determine their experiences during the chatbot conversation. Particularly, Hadi found that customers who entered the chat in an angry emotional state reported lower satisfaction with the chat when it was humanized compared to when it was not. This in contrast to non-angry customers for whom humanization could actually enhance their customer satisfaction [9]. This suggests that we need to know more about the states that customers are in when they enter a conversation with a customer service chatbot. Therefore, the current study asks:

RQ1: What do customers expect from communication with a company, how do they use customer service chatbots within this communication journey, and what moods are they in when they start a chatbot conversation?

2.2   Customers' Experiences During Chatbot Conversations

Once customers decide to use a chatbot, the question arises what the conversation features are that optimize their user experience. The design aspect that received most attention in design education as well as in academic research is the humanization of chatbots [6, 7]. Humanizing chatbots can be done by adding anthropomorphic cues such as a name, persona, and by using a conversational language style with dialogical cues [8].

Quite some experimental studies have manipulated specific anthropomorphic cues in chatbots to assess the effects of such cues [2, 8, 9]. For instance, Araujo investigated whether anthropromorphic design cues influenced perceptions about the chatbot as well as company-related outcomes [2]. He found that humanlike language or a name were sufficient to increase the perception of the agent as being humanlike. This experiment also showed that the usage of humanlike cues had a significant influence on the emotional connection customers felt with the company. Thus the study found some initial evidence that chatbots with humanlike cues can have a positive effect on relationship building. However, Hadi found that the outcomes of humanizing chatbots depend on customer characteristics, but also on the specific service context. Specifically she found that humanization of the chatbot indeed improved customer satisfaction, but not when customers were angry [9].

It is relevant to place this humanization in the broader context of the overall user experience during a chatbot conversation. In the aforementioned qualitative study, Følstad and Skjuve found that customers experienced humanization and language style as less important than whether they received help with their enquiries [6]. Therefore, qualitative research is called for to further delve into the question of what role humanization plays in the user experience. The present study does this by asking the following question:

RQ2: What are the most important characteristics of customers' experiences with customer service chatbots? And, more specifically, how do they experience the humanization of these chatbots and their language style?

2.3 Overall Evaluations of Customer Service Chatbots and Company Perceptions

The aforementioned qualitative studies provided some preliminary insights in how customers overall evaluate the implementation of chatbots for customer service. Følstad and Skjuve concluded that customers have quite realistic expectations of what customer service can and can not do [6]. However, these studies did not specifically look into relations between perceptions of the chatbot's performances and company perceptions.

Some previously mentioned experimental studies did look into the effects of (specifically) humanizing chatbots on company perceptions. Araujo found initial evidence that humanlike cues can have a positive impact on the emotional relation that customers feel with a company. However, such effects were not found for attitudes towards the company [2]. Also, as said, Hadi found that these effects of the humanization of chatbots on evaluations of the company depend on the emotional state customers are in [9]. The current study builds on this previous qualitative and experimental work by asking:

RQ3: What are customers' final conclusions about under which conditions customer service chatbots can be implemented, and what are the consequences of chatbot communication for customers' company perceptions?

3   Method

3.1 Interviews

The qualitative interview study was approved by the Ethics Review Board of the first author's university, and the interviews were conducted by ISO-certified research agency Ruigrok Netpanel. The idea for this study came from the first author, and the other two authors are researchers/interviewers employed by Ruigrok Netpanel. Each interview was conducted by one of these two interviewers, whereas the other two researchers were present in the adjacent observation room and discussed the ongoing interview to check whether there were any additional questions that needed to be asked. The interviews took place on three days in November 2019, on two locations in the Netherlands (Amsterdam and Amersfoort). All interviews were conducted in Dutch, lasted one hour, and participants signed a consent form prior to the interview. All interviews were video recorded, and transcribed verbatim.

Interview Guide. The interview guide was developed by the three researchers, and was slightly adjusted between the three days. The interview guide consisted of an introduction and three topics. The introduction was mainly an introduction of the agency, the collaboration with the university, and contained some guidelines regarding how the interview would work, but did not yet contain information regarding the specific interview topic. The first topic focused on communication with companies. The interviewer asked whether the interviewee had contacted companies before, in what type of situations, for what type of questions, through what types of communication channels, and with what expectations. We also wanted to know whether interviewees spontaneously mentioned chatbots; therefore the interviewer did not mention chatbots, virtual agents etc. in any way here. The responses to these questions are used to answer RQ1.

After this first topic, the interviewee was asked to interact with one of the chatbots that we preselected. The second topic pertained to their experiences during this specific chatbot conversation. First, the questions were open-ended and did not yet pertain to specific characteristics of the conversation. The interviewer asked "what did you just do?", "what happened here", "how did it go", and "to what extent do you have the feeling that you are helped?". This enabled us to answer the first part of RQ2.

Subsequently, the interviewer aimed to gain insight in the experiences with the anthropomorphic cues and the language style, which is the second -more specific- part of RQ2. The interviewer first probed into what the interviewee thought he/she was communicating with, by asking "what is behind this?", "how would you describe it?", "what happens on the other side"?, and also "what do you base this on?" The interviewer also asked to what extent the interviewee experienced this chatbot conversation as communication, and what this way of communicating tells them about the company. This last question helped us in answering RQ3 which focuses on company perceptions. After these questions, the interviewee was invited to use a second chatbot that we assigned to them, and subsequently they answered a shortened version of topic two for this second conversation.

The third and last topic tapped into the final evaluations regarding the implementation of chatbot conversations, and thus related to RQ3. The interviewer reminded interviewees of the expectations that they mentioned in the first topic, and asked about the extent in which the chatbot conversations during the interview fulfilled these expectations. Relatedly, the interviewer probed into how the conversation ideally should have been. The interviewer also asked about future uses of customer service chatbots: would they use them again, and if yes, what would they use them for, and in which types of moments. We also asked for what types of companies, and for what types of questions they think chatbots are appropriate.

Selection of Chatbots. We selected nine customer service chatbots that together showed variation on two dimensions: first, chatbots for profit as well as non-profit organizations were selected, and second, chatbots with humanlike characteristics versus chatbots with more robotlike characteristics were selected. We ensured that we had two humanlike chatbots for profit organizations, two humanlike chatbots for non-profit organizations, etc. All chatbots were available on the companies' websites. For each chatbot, we prepared a scenario with a question that the chatbot was able to answer, and one that the chatbot was not able to answer. Prior to each interview, we assigned two chatbots to the interviewee based on their customer characteristics to ensure that they would use a chatbot of a company that they would contact in real life.

3.2 Sample

Research agency Ruigrok Netpanel coordinated the selection of the interviewees, with the help of ISO-certified agencies specialized in respondent recruitment. The interviewees received a monetary compensation for their participation, in line with the normal procedures of Ruigrok Netpanel. Interviewees were not allowed to have participated in qualitative research in the six months before the interview. A selection criterion was that the interviewee should have experience with contacting companies.

We ensured that the sample of interviewees (N = 24) was varied in terms of gender (male N = 12; female N = 12), age (18-25 years N = 5; 26-35 years N = 15; 36–45 years N = 5; 46–65 years N = 5; 65–78 years N = 4), educational level (low N = 8; middle N = 8; high N = 8) and household composition.

3.3 Data Analysis

First, the two authors working for the research agency wrote a research report (in Dutch, available upon request) in a way that is typically employed by research agencies. They summarized the main findings for each of the three research questions, and illustrated these with numerous quotes. Subsequently, the first author analyzed the interviews, taking the research report as a starting point. All interview transcripts were uploaded in the computer program Atlas.ti. In Atlas.ti, she conducted open coding, a procedure commonly used as the first step in the Grounded Theory Approach [4]. She read the interviews closely, line-by-line, and -for each research question- added codes. After going through the interviews, she wrote the current result section. The contents of the result section are in line with the research report, but the section does include some additional insights, such as the paragraph on the effort that customers need to put into communication with a customer service chatbot (RQ2).

4 Results

Based on the interviews, this section describes the communication journey of customers who wish to contact companies, and the evaluation of chatbot communication within this journey.

4.1 Customers' Prior Expectations of Communication with a Company

RQ1 asked about customers' expectations and moods prior to starting a conversation with a customer service chatbot. The starting points for interviewees' communication journeys with companies were -obviously- their questions or complaints. The interviewees expressed clear expectations of companies. Of utmost importance is getting their question answered or complaint addressed. This needs to be done fast (directly, within a few hours, for some questions a few days could be fine). They want to be taken seriously, and they want to be helped in a friendly manner. Sometimes it is needed that the customer is addressed with his/her name, that there is continuity over the course of several contacts, and in case of problems empathy is required. Interviewees expressed that sometimes they come into such conversations in a bad mood, even angry, for instance because they need an arrangement because they can not pay a bill; products or internet/phone connections do not work, or a package did not get delivered.

So what are the modes of communication through which these expectations can be fulfilled? And -importantly- are chatbots among these? Interviewees indicated that they first search for information online, and in case additional contact is necessary they rely on calling, e-mail or chat. In terms of preferred modes of communication, we can distinguish "phone callers" and "typers". "Phone callers" are interviewees who emphasized human contact, hearing someone's voice, being able to ask follow-up questions and talking back and forth to come to an answer. Talking to a person makes it more direct and honest, and one immediately gets an answer. One can also express frustrations. The disadvantages of calling are the waiting times, that call center agents sometimes work with sale scripts, and that it is not available 24/7."Typers" were the interviewees who preferred e-mailing or live chat (i.e., chatting with a human being). They indicated that they sometimes feel less comfortable with talking on the phone, and that they feel the need for having the information in writing for later referral. An additional advantage is multitasking: being able to send a mail or chat message while being at work. It is relevant to note that also being in contact with someone through live chat can be experienced as personal and having enough human touch. As interviewee 16 (female, 36 years, management assistant) said: "as long as it is a human being".

Within this interview context of openly discussing how one prefers to contact companies, nine interviewees mentioned chatbots (and more mentioned them later in response to the chatbots in the interviews). Reasons for using chatbots were: finding information (comparing the function of chatbots to Google), being able to contact the company outside of office hours, and getting through to a live chat.

Several interviewees spontaneously described problems with chatbots, expressing mild frustration to clear anger. They expressed a lack of confidence in chatbots' abilities. Chatbots do not understand their questions and keep asking "do I understand you correctly?". Interviewee 16 described coming across chatbots when the live chat is closed in the evening: "and then you also have chatbots, but there you really do not get anywhere, so then I rather send an e-mail. Yeah, [with chatbots] you type a question, but they cannot give you a clear answer because it is such a robot of course".

Based on their negative expectations with chatbot interactions in real-life, some interviewees already started the chat during the interview with "oh no, not a chatbot!". For instance interviewee 7 (female, 29 years, cook) had already indicated her frustration with previous chatbots. Starting the chat, she exclaimed "this is clearly such a robot, I don't like it". Several interviewees expressed that normally they would avoid using chatbots, and rather wait "till Monday" to have a phone call or send an e-mail.

4.2 Customers' Experiences During Chatbot Conversations

RQ2 asked about the most important characteristics of customers' experiences with chatbot conversations, and asked specifically about their perceptions of the humanization of these chatbots and their language style. During the interviews, interviewees used two customer service chatbots (without us saying that these were chatbots). In the user experiences during the interviews, four elements stood out.

Prerequisite: Receiving Adequate Help. As expected, the main prerequisite for a positive evaluation of the conversations was that the interviewee felt that he/she had received adequate help. To exemplify such positive experience:

> He [the chatbot] immediately gave a lot of information. As I just mentioned, that is what I really like. That I do not have to probe further. And even though it is digital, it is very friendly. It is more than enough information for me, so it really

helped me. [...] I would give it a 10. Nothing is missing. (Interviewee 3: male, 19 years, student)

This interviewee said that this chat met his expectations, and that he prefers a robot "because you get the answers and you get them fast". Even though this interviewee judges this chat as "perfect", he does not see chatbot communication as sufficient enough to function as a stand-alone mode of communication. According to him, communication with a human is still required in case of problems, for instance when a package has not been delivered.

What interviewees particularly appreciated was that some chatbot conversations helped to filter information or that the chatbot provided links where the interviewee could find the information. As an interviewee positively noted: "Nice! Saves some searching". Interviewee 16 said: "It was fine, clear, right information". As mentioned, she had had negative experiences with chatbots before and had indicated that she would not use them. This chatbot conversation went fine, but did not erase her negative expectations "ok, this was fine, but I don't know what would have happened if the question would have been more complicated". In other words, despite of this positive experience, she was still expecting negative experiences to come.

In quite some cases, the chatbot did not meet the requirement of answering the question satisfactorily. The interviews clearly showed us how this leads to quite some frustration. Interviewee 1 (male, 64 years, human resources) almost started screaming:

I want to stop; I don't get an answer. This was my first question, then I get this [shows answer]. Then I pose the second question, and I get: 'thanks for your response, with your input I can improve myself'. I want to scream: 'no, I was looking for something else!' The biggest problem here is that I do not get an answer to my question, so I want to stop this [...] In my perception this just does not work: how precise can I be?

Effort. The interviews clearly revealed that it takes quite some effort for customers to use chatbots. This is partially related to the just described situation of not getting an answer, but there are also other ways in which customers are putting in effort when using chatbots.

Starting the chatbot conversation, some interviewees were wondering and estimating whether this chatbot would actually be able to answer their question. Some of them thought that for simple questions it may work, but not for more complicated questions. After considering this, they are making an effort to formulate the question in such way that they think the system will be able to understand it. Some say: "you need to use the right key words". A complication here is that chatbots currently available do not all operate the same way: some indeed work best with key words as input, whereas others instruct the user to type full sentences like in human-human conversations.

It was quite common that, after typing the question, the chatbot did not come back with a relevant answer, and the interviewee needed to reformulate the question, sometimes several times. As the above-mentioned angry interviewee 1 expressed: "I already tried to ask the same question twice; now I would have to formulate it a third time; I am not going to do that". In case there is no alternative for the company (i.e., the customers needs this specific company) and/or there is no other means of contacting the company (e.g. late at night), one feels convicted to keep trying to get an answer even when one does not feel like it. When in the end the result is still unsatisfactory, some interviewees sighed: "see, this is what I mean, this all takes time, and now I would have to find another way of finding the information". These efforts sometimes trigger prior negative experiences with chatbots. For instance interviewee 2 (male, 30 years, train driver), who did not mention chatbots during the first topic, said:

> See, and then I am sitting at home and it annoys me. Then I think 'guys!' Often it does not work, or it is too slow, or indeed -that happened to me too- then it says 'I do not understand it, can you formulate it differently'. Yeah, and that takes time, and you just don't feel like that.

Simulation of Human Touch. An essential feature of chatbot communication is that it can appear humanlike due to anthropomorphic cues and its conversational nature. At the end of their interviews, two interviewees still thought they had been exchanging messages with human beings. Although interviewee 9 (female, 78, retired) still thought this, she did start doubting it during the course of the interview: "I HOPE it is a person!". She was not completely out of touch with technological possibilities, but expressed concerns about her digital literacy related to her age: "I do have Instagram, to stay in touch with the children. But I don't know whether young people understand how difficult it is for us [older people]".

All other interviewees (sooner or later) were aware that they were using a chatbot, although they used many different names for it (a chatbot, chatbox, robot, computer, system, digital assistant, virtual assistant, algorithms, etc.). As interviewee 1 said: "I communicated with a computer, not with a lady Nina". Also for these interviewees there was confusion sometimes, especially in the beginning of the conversations, and especially about whether it was a live chat (i.e. chatting with a human being) or a chatbot. Interviewees concluded that it was a chatbot predominantly with the help of the following cues: the responses came very fast, the responses were too similar, and their question was not understood. As one said: "You hope that it is a real agent, but the answers show that it is a robot". Interviewee 4 (female, 40 years, operations manager) also expressed disappointment:

> When you see the name 'Billy', you think it is a person. Also for me, although I do think that it is a virtual assistant. The first association is that it is a real human, and then the disappointment is bigger when you do not get anywhere [with getting the question answered]

Interviewees typically saw the conversation as a automated chat with a *simulated* human touch to it. The word "simulated" is important here. They expressed that with dialogical cues ("Hello, how can I help you today?"), a name, an icon or a picture of a human face, they make it seem that you talk to a real customer service agent. As interviewee 3 explained about the icon:

That is just a picture to make it seem as humanlike as possible [...] The same applies to the name probably; they want to make it look human. Giving it a name, an icon, in order for you to feel like you are communicating with a human being.

Opinions about this type of simulation varied. Some said the liked it and thought it was nice: "yeah, it is a bit more cozy". Interviewee 8 (male, 46 years, male nurse) said:

Often you have this with such chat, that they have given it a name. I like that more. Then it looks more like 'oh, you are not talking to a virtual assistant, you are talking to something with a name. Then it's more personal.

Others said they do not care about this simulation. As interviewee 2 said: "Names I do not care about that much, but I do want to know: do I speak to a robot or... I do not even know what it is called.. an automated thing".

And yet others were outrightly annoyed by the simulation and saw it as counter-productive. These interviewees saw it as a tricks and as a sign that the company was not taking them seriously. They became even more negative when their query was not answered. Interviewee 7 said about chatbot Iris (with name and cartoonlike icon): "Ha-haha, that is Iris, robot Iris! They do this to make it look more personal, to give the impression that you are chatting with someone. I do not care that much; I don't really look at it". But later she turned much more negative: "Well, Iris, with the friendly smil-ing icon: probably they did this to make it look more personal. But they really made a mistake here. Because it is a very distant robot. And inefficient too".

Language Style. One of the essential aspects of chatbot development is conversational design. Interviewees typically responded to our question about the chatbot's language style by saying something about whether the style was formal versus informal. More specifically, they often mentioned the use of "u" versus "je", which are the two nouns in Dutch to say "you" in a formal versus more informal way. Related to the communication expectations mentioned above, they also judged whether the conversation was friendly enough. In most cases, interviewees were fine with the style. As interviewee 3 noted:

For example the questions 'how can I help you', 'let's see what we have got': just very clear, very friendly. Not too blunt, answers are nicely elaborate. Also important that in the end he asks 'is there something else I can do for you?', those kinds of things. Then you see that it comes across as very friendly.

However, some interviewees expressed their discontent with informal language. Interviewee 5 (female, 64 years, management assistant) said: "the use of 'jij' every-where, I think it is too informal, but there is nothing we can do about it, we just have to accept it". Sometimes such opinions are related to a specific company, for instance "the Douane [i.e., customs] should say 'u'" (interviewee 6, female, 52 years, front office employee).

4.3   Overall Evaluations of Customer Service Chatbots and Company Perceptions

RQ3 tapped into customers' final conclusions about under which conditions customer service chatbots can be implemented, and into the consequences of chatbot communica-tion for customers'company perceptions. On the positive side, interviewees concluded that chatbots have the potential to be helpful for certain purposes. Chatbots were considered to be good at helping with searching information. Some interviewees applaud the speed, and the 24/7 availability. Interviewee 2 said: "at least it points you in the right direction; now I do not have to search on the website. I fill out a word –'inboedelverzekering' ['contents insurance']- I get some information, I can click on it, so that was fast". This can be seen as a type of service, although they also say it is not always sufficient. Overall, interviewees were pretty clear that chatbots can be helpful for general and simple questions: it is perceived as a type of frequently asked questions, but presented in another way. If working well, it could also serve as a type of filtering, before being transferred to human agent. Some expressed understanding that the trend towards the use of chatbots and related technologies is inevitable, but that it needs to be improved.

However, interviewees were unified in that chatbots can not function as a stand-alone mode of communication, and that it can *not* replace human communication. As interviewee 5 said: "it will never meet the expectations, because it is not a human being, it will remain standard texts". Chatbots can not answer all questions. Moreover, a human being can discuss with customers, can probe, and such conversation is more personal. Especially for personal and/or complex questions interviewees deem chatbots not useful because empathy is lacking. For instance interviewee 6 said that when she asks for money back, she wants to be comforted by a human being. Relatedly, interviewees mentioned that for certain companies and organizations, such as the police, hospitals and health care providers, chatbots are not suitable because these companies deal with personal situations. As interviewee 3 explained about contacting a doctor: "such issues most likely influence your body or your personal situation, so then I would prefer to have personal contact with a doctor versus via the chat".

Company Perceptions. So what do these experiences tell the interviewees about the companies? On the positive end, some interviewees saw the companies as innovative. Some also saw it as a service for customers. However, interviewees typically thought that the implementation of chatbots was done more for the company itself than for the customers. As interviewee 8 said:

> It looks they wanted to do it as cheap as possible. They did not pay attention to making it a bit nicer. Either they did not make an effort to find out how that could be done, or they did not come up with the right ideas to make it nicer.

A recurring thought in the interviews was that the primary reason for companies to use chatbots is to save costs. Their reasoning is that chatbots replace employees and that this saves money. As interviewee 1 expressed: "This is cost cutting, I know that, because that is also why I lost my last job".

Some interviewees were also surprised about how bad the technology still is, especially when one had higher expectations of the level of innovation of a particular company. For instance, interviewee 7 had high expectations of the chatbot of a particular company, and was negatively surprised that this chatbot was not able to answer her question: "with the [name of another company], I kind of have and old-fashioned feeling, but with [name of company] you think: it is a very large company, everything will function well there".

The effort that it takes customers to use the chatbot, and the frustration, can contribute to negative statements about a company. The above-mentioned angry interviewee 1: "what do you want to achieve with this mister [name company]? Maybe in their eyes it is customer friendly: 'we help our customers'. Oh really? Come and use it yourself".

5 Discussion

In the following sections, we will highlight the main findings for each of the three stages in the communication journey that customers have with companies. For each stage we will connect the findings to previous and future research, and outline the practical learnings. After this, we will describe some limitations of the current study and present additional suggestions for future research.

5.1 Customers' Prior Expectations of Communication with a Company

The current interview study showcases the expectations that customers have, and the moods that customers are in, when starting conversations with customer service chatbots. This is important because previous research taught us that the state that customers are in when they begin a chatbot conversation plays a role in how they experience the chat [9].

Our interviews reveal that the main priority of customers is -obviously- to receive help with their customer query: their questions need to be answered; information needs to be provided, and their complaints need to be addressed. This has to be done fast, in a friendly manner. Some customers come into the conversation frustrated or angry. This may not only be because of the nature of their question or complaint, but -importantly- also because of previous interactions with chatbots (of other companies) that did not go well. For future experimental research, this implies that angry or frustrated participants need to be included in the sample, or that participants need to be brought in such state prior to the conversation.

In terms of practical recommendations, these findings imply that it is of utmost importance that developers take into account that there may be quite some resistance on the side of customers to overcome. Companies need to use the information they have about the states of their customers. Automated sentiment analysis will grow more sophisticated in the future and may make it possible to detect the mood that a specific customer is in when starting the chat. However, it needs to be kept in mind that interviewees expressed that in case of anger, frustration or fear (e.g. when not being able to pay the bills), empathy from fellow human beings is called for.

5.2 Customers' Experiences During Chatbot Conversations

In the four aspects of user experiences that we found, we see a similar hierarchy as described by Følstad and Skjuve [6]: for customers, receiving adequate help is much more important than the humanization of the chatbot or the language style. Our finding that users have to put in quite some effort seems to deviate slightly from findings from previous qualitative work [6]: our interviewees seem to express more frustrations and anger about chatbots' functioning. This disparity is most likely due to the fact that our sample included interviewees who were rather unwilling to use a chatbot, whereas the previous study [6] "only" included interviewees who actually had chosen to use a chatbot. Moreover, our finding is in line with other types of research that displayed quite some issues and errors in the current generation of customer service chatbots [7, 11, 12].

With the first practical recommendation we echo previous work: the top priority should be to help customers in a sufficient and efficient way. Currently it still occurs too often that a customer does not find what he/she is looking for. The experience should be as seamless as possible to avoid (further) fuelling of frustrations. Placing a chatbot online early in its development may be useful for data collection and scaling the chatbot. However, looking at it through an individual customer's eyes, one needs to realize that this scaling approach can lead to quite some effort and frustration on the individual level.

Another issue is the simulation of human touch. Some users may indeed find it entertaining, or on an unconscious level it may trigger positive responses. However, it also needs to be realized that it can be problematic, both from a business perspective, as well as from an ethical perspective. The current interviews showed that humanization may also backfire: users can see it as an unwanted trick or as deception. Hadi's research implied that this is specifically the case when customers are angry when coming into the chat [9], and the current interview study illustrated that customers are indeed angry and frustrated at times. From an ethical perspective, it is problematic that some users trust the information because they incorrectly think they are communicating with a human being. This means that transparency is called for. It seems to become the social norm that a chatbot should be identified in the introduction section as a chatbot, or virtual agent, but the interviews illustrate that quite some users overlook such disclosure.

5.3 Customers' Overall Evaluations and Company Perceptions

In line with previous qualitative work [6], we found that some customers have specific ideas about what chatbots currently can and can not do. However, they still end up disappointed with the results. Thus, it is important that developers have a clear view of what the purpose of a specific chatbot is, and this should be communicated as clearly as possible to the user. Providing users with more guidance regarding the queries a chatbot can help with may be useful.

In terms of company perceptions, the interviews showed that the implementation of chatbots is currently quite a risky adventure for companies. Although some interviewees related the chatbot to the innovative character of the organization, it was common that they saw it as a result of cost-cutting. Also, interviewees typically thought the implementation of chatbots was done more for the company itself than for the customers. In terms of an organization's image, it is relevant to consider whether these are the associations that one would want to trigger.

5.4 Limitations and Future Research

The focal point of the current analysis was the communication journey that customers have with a company, and a chatbot's place in it. This means that there are specific elements in the user experiences that call for more in-depth analyses; in particular the responses to the anthropomorphic cues require a more detailed look. The link between certain chatbot perceptions (e.g., seeing it as a search engine versus expecting answers to more complex questions) and ways of communicating with the chatbot (e.g. using only key words, or typing natural sentences) should also be explored.

By definition, after a qualitative study, quantitative follow-up studies are required. Surveys and experiments are needed to further investigate the relations between mood states prior to the chatbot conversation, and subsequent user experiences. Also the role of humanization within the overall user experience needs to be disentangled more fully. This work should also delve into the relations between demographics (such as age, gender, and educational level) and chatbot perceptions [1].

For all research into user experiences of chatbot communication goes that the findings are bound to a particular point in time, due to continuous improvements and AI developments. However, we do think that some of the experiences outlined in the current study will remain important for research and practice for quite some time.

Acknowledgements. This study was partially funded by *Logeion*, the Dutch association for communication professionals.

References

1. Araujo, T., ter Hoeven, C., van Zoonen, W.: Automated 1-2-1 communication. In: SWOCC. Stichting Wetenschappelijk Onderzoek Commerciële Communicatie (SWOCC), vol. 77 Amsterdam (2019)
2. Araujo, T.: Living up to the chatbot hype: the influence of anthropomorphic design cues and communicative agency framing on conversational agent and company perceptions. Comput. Hum. Behav. **85**, 183–189 (2018). https://doi.org/10.1016/j.chb.2018.03.051
3. Brandtzaeg, P.B., Følstad, A.: Why people use chatbots. In: Kompatsiaris, I., et al. (eds.) INSCI 2017. LNCS, vol. 10673, pp. 377–392. Springer, Cham (2017). https://doi.org/10.1007/978-3-319-70284-1_30
4. Charmaz, K.: Constructing Grounded Theory: A Practical Guide Through Qualitative Analysis. Sage, London (2006)
5. Følstad, A., Nordheim, C.B., Bjørkli, C.A.: What makes users trust a chatbot for customer service? an exploratory interview study. In: Bodrunova, Svetlana S., et al. (eds.) INSCI 2018. LNCS, vol. 11193, pp. 194–208. Springer, Cham (2018). https://doi.org/10.1007/978-3-030-01437-7_16
6. Følstad, A., Skjuve, M.: Chatbots for customer service: user experience and motivation. In: Proceedings of the 1st International Conference on Conversational User Interfaces, pp. 1–9. ACM, New York (2019). https://doi.org/10.1145/3342775.3342784
7. Gnewuch, U., Morana, S., Maedche, A.: Towards designing cooperative and social conversational agents for customer service. In: Proceedings of the 38th International Conference on Information Systems (ICIS) (2017)
8. Go, E., Sundar, S.S.: Humanizing chatbots: the effects of visual, identity and conversational cues on humanness perceptions. Comput. Hum. Behav. **97**, 304–316 (2019). https://doi.org/10.1016/j.chb.2019.01.020
9. Hadi, R.: When humanizing customer service chatbots might backfire. NIM Market. Intell. Rev. **11**(2), 30–35 (2019)

10. Ischen, C., Araujo, T., Voorveld, H., van Noort, G., Smit, E.: Privacy concerns in chatbot interactions. In: Følstad, A., et al. (eds.) CONVERSATIONS 2019. LNCS, vol. 11970, pp. 34–48. Springer, Cham (2020). https://doi.org/10.1007/978-3-030-39540-7_3

11. Rese, A., Ganster, L., Baier, D.: Chatbots in retailers' customer communication: how to measure their acceptance? J. Retail. Consum. Serv. **56**, 102176 (2020). https://doi.org/10.1016/j.jretconser.2020.102176

12. Sheehan, B., Jin, H.S., Gottlieb, U.: Customer service chatbots: anthropomorphism and adoption. J. Bus. Res. **115**, 14–24 (2020). https://doi.org/10.1016/j.jbusres.2020.04.030

13. van der Goot, M.J., Pilgrim, T.: Exploring age differences in motivations for and acceptance of chatbot communication in a customer service context. In: Følstad, A., et al. (eds.) CONVERSATIONS 2019. LNCS, vol. 11970, pp. 173–186. Springer, Cham (2020). https://doi.org/10.1007/978-3-030-39540-7_12

Understanding the User Experience of Customer Service Chatbots: What Can We Learn from Customer Satisfaction Surveys?

Knut Kvale[1]([⊠]) [iD], Eleonora Freddi[1] [iD], Stig Hodnebrog[2] [iD], Olav Alexander Sell[2] [iD], and Asbjørn Følstad[3] [iD]

[1] Telenor Research, Fornebu, Norway
knut.kvale@telenor.com
[2] Telenor Norway, Fornebu, Norway
[3] SINTEF, Oslo, Norway

Abstract. Understanding and improving user experience is key to strengthening uptake and realizing the potential of chatbots for customer service. In this paper, we investigate customer satisfaction surveys as a source of insight into such user experience. A total of 5,687 customer satisfaction reports on users' interactions with a customer service chatbot, and the corresponding chatbot interactions, are analyzed. The findings demonstrate that customer satisfaction reports are closely associated with the degree to which the problems motivating users' chatbot interactions are resolved. Furthermore, the findings show substantial variation in the performance of different chatbot intents in terms of customer satisfaction and problem resolution. This implies that user experience varies substantially depending on the problems motivating users to interact with the chatbot. Finally, we identify key characteristics of the intents associated with particularly high or low customer experience, suggesting paths towards efficient improvement of chatbot user experience. Based on the findings, we point to key implications for theory and practice and suggest directions for future research.

Keywords: Chatbot · User experience · Customer satisfaction

1 Introduction

Customer service is a major chatbot application domain. Chatbots may be low-threshold channels for information and support, serving as a cost-effective and accessible supplement to manual customer service. In a recent report, Gartner [13] predicts that about one-third of the surveyed companies deploy or have near-future plans of deploying conversational platforms in customer service, and that such deployment will substantially increase operational efficiency. However, the same report also predicts that there will be substantial turnover in such conversational platforms, and that a number of older chatbot applications will be abandoned. This suggests that, while potential benefit of chatbots for customer service is high, there is substantial risk of failure.

© Springer Nature Switzerland AG 2021
A. Følstad et al. (Eds.): CONVERSATIONS 2020, LNCS 12604, pp. 205–218, 2021.
https://doi.org/10.1007/978-3-030-68288-0_14

User experience is a key determinant of successful implementation of chatbots for customer service [5]. While an increasing number of service providers are offering customer service through chatbots, user uptake has been found to lag behind [12]. In response, substantial research and practitioner effort have been spent on strengthening user experience for chatbots in general [24], and for customer service in particular [19, 28]. Research and practitioner guidelines suggest an at times bewildering range of potential drivers of chatbot user experience, but at the same time, there seems to be a shortage of advice for how to strengthen it. Hence, service providers might find it challenging to prioritize and guide chatbot development and improvement initiatives.

In this context, we present a study that provides insights from a systematic application of customer satisfaction surveys to understand chatbot user experience. We asked a sample of users of a chatbot for customer service (N = 5,687) to report (a) their satisfaction with the chatbot interaction and (b) the degree to which the problem motivating their interaction had been resolved. The survey data was analyzed with regard to information on the actual user conversations, specifically on the chatbot intents triggered as part of the interaction.

The findings strongly suggest that problem resolution is highly important for a better user experience in chatbots for customer service. Furthermore, the findings indicate that the user experience depends on the quality of the support provided through the specific intents triggered in an interaction. Accordingly, a user's perception of the chatbot is shaped by the type of problem he or she want to get resolved. In particular, customers were found to have a more positive experience when the chatbot provided concrete and detailed support, guiding the user closer to problem resolution, for example, by drawing on integrations with back-end systems for user information and transactions on behalf of the user.

The findings contribute to the current body of knowledge on chatbot user experience, demonstrating the importance of efficient and effective problem resolution. They also provide implications for practice, suggesting how customer satisfaction data may be used to improve the user experience in existing chatbots for customer service.

2 Background

In this section, we present the background concerning chatbots for customer service, chatbot user experience, and – finally – customer satisfaction, its relation to user experience, and how customer satisfaction surveys are used in research and industry to assess and improve service quality.

2.1 Chatbots for Customer Service

Chatbots are increasingly important for customer service. A recent CapGemini report [32] finds that, in retail banking and insurance, 49% of the top 100 organizations employ chatbots. In consumer products and retail, the corresponding number is 23%. In response to the current interest, there is a wide range of available chatbot platforms for customer service [13], such as IBM Watson, IPsoft, Microsoft Bot Framework, Nuance, and boost.ai.

The increased interest in chatbots over the last few years is motivated by users and service providers' uptake of chat platforms, as well as by improved language processing capabilities due to advances in artificial intelligence and machine learning [7]. In particular, enhanced access and availability of chat-based customer service, as well as cost-efficiency and upgraded user experiences, have increased service providers' engagement in chatbot for customer service [27]. Users are reported to appreciate the opportunity for immediate and low-threshold access to support provided by chatbots for customer service [6]. However, chatbots for customer service have also been found to entail challenges concerning, for example, the ability to correctly predict users' intents and a lack of capabilities for handling complex requests [11].

Key components of chatbots for customer service include language processing and intent handling, exception handling, context awareness, analytics, and integration with back-end systems [13]. Users typically enter their requests as free text messages, often in conjunction with the option of selecting predefined answer alternatives through buttons or quick replies. The user requests that the chatbot may recognize and respond to are typically structured in intent hierarchies, where language processing techniques and machine learning models are employed to predict user intents on the basis of the users' free text input [30]. As soon as an intent is correctly predicted, the chatbot often provides the user with navigation support to move within the intent hierarchy. For example, if a chatbot predicts user requests corresponding to an intent on invoicing, the chatbot may ask users if they want to see an invoice, ask about a particular invoice, or pay an invoice. These options are meant to facilitate easy navigation in the intent hierarchy.

Chatbots for customer service typically need to support a large number of request types. For example, chatbots in the banking sector may require several thousand intents to cover a sufficient breadth of user requests [9]. A larger number of intents widens chatbot coverage, but also increases the potential for false positives, that is, responses which do not adequately address the user request [10]. Establishing and maintaining the needed intent hierarchies in chatbots for customer service is demanding [19]. The key parts of this work are to identify needed intents, create content and actions associated with intents, and train machine learning models to improve intent prediction.

2.2 Chatbot User Experience

Following the surge of interest in chatbots, chatbot user experience has recently become a topic and focus of substantial research. User experience is a complex construct, including factors such as pragmatic quality, hedonic quality, aesthetic appeal, and goodness [20]. In the international standard of human-centered design, ISO 9241-210 [18], user experience is defined as users' perceptions and responses from use and anticipated use including "emotions, beliefs, preferences, perceptions, physical and psychological responses, behaviours and accomplishments" (p. 3).

Because of the complexity of the construct, user experience is investigated from a wide range of perspectives and in consideration to a large number of determinants. This holds both for chatbots in general and for chatbots for customer service in particular. General chatbot user experience has been, for example, studied from the perspectives of pragmatic and hedonic quality [8], social presence [21] and anthropomorphism [23]. Furthermore, chatbot user experience has been investigated as determined by chatbot personality [31], chatbot gender [22], human likeness [3], and conversational design [14].

User experience of customer service has been shown to depend on effectiveness and efficiency in problem resolution [5] but also on factors such as expectation management [26], courtesy and friendliness [16], and responding adequately to the customer's mood or tone of voice [17]. This varied set of factors affecting user experience is reflected also in research on chatbots for customer service. Here, user experience has been studied in relation to factors such as trust [25], user emotion and rapport [28], anthropomorphism, and social presence [1]. User experience for customer service chatbots has been found to be determined by such factors as types of dialogue scripts [28] and conversational repair [10], as well as information quality, system quality, and service quality [34]. However, industry reports suggest that users' main reasons for not using chatbots for customer service include chatbots not being sufficiently skilled for complex requests and challenges concerning interpretation and goal achievement [6, 11]. This may imply that the user experience of chatbots for customer service is likely to be strongly determined by the chatbot's ability to provide accessible help. Likewise, motivations for using chatbots in general have been found to be strongly determined by pragmatic motivations [2].

2.3   Customer Satisfaction, User Experience, and Service Improvement

Given the broad variety of user experience perspectives and measurements available, it will be important for service providers to identify those that are of particular relevance for continuous improvement of chatbot implementations [19].

To provide insight into users' perceptions of service interactions, a much used measurement in the service industries is customer satisfaction surveys [4]. In such surveys, users report their satisfaction with a brand, a service, or particular service interactions. Temkin [33] finds that 85% of surveyed companies measure customer satisfaction at the level of interactions. Customer satisfaction reports linked to particular service interactions, while not direct measures of the entire user experience construct, are likely to reflect the overall perceived quality of the user experience. That is, low customer satisfaction scores may indicate poor user experience, while high customer satisfaction scores indicate good user experience. However, satisfaction scores alone cannot provide insight into the details of the user experience [29].

Customer satisfaction has been shown to substantially covary with company performance and with other customer feedback measures [4]. Previously, customer satisfaction was typically measured with multi-item instruments, but studies such as that of Van Doorn et al. [35] have shown that single-item satisfaction measures have similar performance to that of multi-item measurements.

Customer satisfaction surveys also have a substantial impact more generally on service organizations, and in particular on service improvement. For transactional interactions, customer satisfaction surveys have been found to outperform other experience-oriented measurements in terms of organizational impact [33].

3   Research Questions

Motivated by the current state of the art, we acknowledge the need to strengthen insight into the key determinants of user experience in chatbots for customer service. The prominence of customer satisfaction assessment in the service literature suggests that this may be a viable approach towards such insight. Hence, our research objective is to investigate what we can learn about chatbot user experience from customer satisfaction surveys. Drawing on the presented background, three research questions are of particular relevance:

RQ1. How is the user experience of chatbots for customer service affected by whether or not users' problems are resolved?
RQ2. How is the user experience of chatbots for customer service affected by the kind of problem for which users seek help?
RQ3. What characterizes intents associated with positive and negative user experiences in chatbots for customer service?

Through RQ1, we investigate the degree to which problem resolution impacts the user experience in chatbots for customer service. While a broad range of drivers may impact user experience in customer service chatbots, the literature suggests that problem resolution is likely to have a substantial impact [6, 11]. Furthermore, it is relevant to investigate potential variation in user experience depending on the character of the problem and how problem resolution is implemented through related chatbot intents (RQ2). Finally, given such variation in user experience across different user problems, it is important to explore the characteristics of the problems and associated intents to identify potential underlying causes of this variation (RQ3).

4   Method

To address the research questions, we conducted a study analyzing data on customer satisfaction, problem resolution, and customer interaction with a running chatbot for customer service. In our analysis addressing RQ1, we compared customer satisfaction scores for different levels of problem resolution in the chatbot interaction. To shed light on RQ2, we compared customer satisfaction scores for chatbot interactions with different intents triggered. Investigating RQ3, we analyzed and compared the characteristics of chatbot interactions associated with high customer satisfaction scores with interactions associated with low customer satisfaction scores.

In the following, we first present the chatbot for which the customer satisfaction data were gathered as well as the different data sets included in the analysis. We then detail the analyses conducted in response to the three research questions respectively.

4.1   The Customer Service Chatbot

This study was conducted by analyzing data gathered from *Telmi*, a chatbot employed by the international telecom provider Telenor. The chatbot complements the company's customer service in its Norwegian operation. Telmi is provided as a separate channel for customer service, in addition to self-service on the Telenor customer website and smartphone app, phone-based support, and assistance through social media platforms such as Facebook and Twitter.

The chatbot provides help and information in response to user free text input. The user intents are predicted on the basis of language processing through machine learning models. The chatbot is capable of predicting more than 2,700 intents structured in intent hierarchies. When an intent is identified, the dialogue can evolve by the user choosing among buttons with predefined answer alternatives or by interpreting further free text input within the context of the previous intents.

The chatbot is offered to users who log into the customer website as well as to anonymous users. It can help users by answering frequently asked questions, but it can also provide personalized information and conduct transactions associated with tasks, such as getting PUK codes, ordering and activating a SIM card, getting details on data spending, ordering extra data packages, and blocking a subscription. The chatbot was implemented in the first half of 2019 and has since been in continuous improvement and development. Intents have been added and updated; training of machine learning models has been improved, and support for more personalization has been provided through application programming interfaces (APIs) to back-end business systems.

4.2   The Data Sets

Customer Satisfaction Survey. To assess and improve the chatbot, feedback from users was gathered through a customer satisfaction survey. All users interacting with the chatbot received invitations to respond to the survey provided that (a) the user was logged into a customer website or application when using the chatbot, and (b) the user had not responded to similar surveys during the last three months. In the period february 26–may 31, 2020, n = 5,687 users responded to the survey, constituting a response rate of 18% of those receiving the invitation. In total, 14,8381 customers used Telmi in the analyses period, either on the open web or as logged in customers. Hence, the 5,687 customers only represented 4% of the total number of conversations.

In the customer satisfaction survey, users reported on their recent interaction with the chatbot. Primarily, they were asked to report their "satisfaction with the interaction with Telmi" on a five-point scale (1 = very dissatisfied; 5 = very satisfied). Furthermore, the customers were asked to disclose the degree to which their problem was resolved at the time of responding to the survey (fully resolved, partially resolved, not resolved). In addition, the survey contained questions about factors that are not treated in this study, such as how easy or difficult the users found the problem resolution, details on failure to resolve problems, expectations of the chatbot, and whether they had sought to solve the problem through other means of support.

Chatbot Interaction Data. Data from the users' interactions with the chatbots are stored in a way that protects the users' privacy, while allowing to combine the interaction data with the satisfaction survey data. here, data which may contain personal information are handled in accordance with the European Union's General Data Protection Regulation (GDPR) and deleted within the defined retentions schedule. However, predicted intents, chatbot responses, and timestamps are stored.

Thus, for each interaction, it is possible to include in the analysis the time of the inter-action, the number of triggered intents, the specific triggered intents, and the chatbot's associated responses. These data provide valuable information for training and improve-ment of the chatbot, as it is possible to identify interactions leading or not leading to relevant support, as well as to analyze the different intents or combinations of intents with regard to user reports of satisfaction and problem resolution.

4.3 The Analyses

On the basis of the combined data sets for the users' self-reports (the customer satisfaction survey) and the users' interactions (chatbot interaction data), we conducted analyses to investigate the three research questions.

Impact of Problem Resolution on User Experience (RQ1). In line with Temkin [33], user experience was operationalized as customer satisfaction. Clearly, customer satisfac-tion is not a direct measure of the entire user experience construct – as this encompasses, for example, users' emotional responses – but it is to be seen as reflecting user experience. Therefore, customer satisfaction will be a useful proxy for investigating whether the user experience was positive or negative. In particular, we compared customer satisfaction for users with different levels of self-reported problem resolution (fully resolved, par-tially resolved, unresolved). Comparisons among the levels of problem resolution were conducted as descriptive analyses and one-way analyses of variance (ANOVA).

Impact of the Kind of Problem for Which Users Seek Help (RQ2). The problem for which users seek help was operationalized as the specific user intent predicted by the chatbot based on users' free text requests. all intents with more than 40 observations in the data set were included, except for intents concerning social interaction (e.g., greetings and pleasantries), requests for escalation to human support, error recovery (e.g., fallback responses to user requests without a certain intent prediction), and two intents that had recently been reworked. An observation refers to a single interaction between a user and the chatbot. The included intents were compared on the basis of customer satisfaction scores. Comparisons were conducted as descriptive analyses and one-way ANOVA.

Characteristics of Intents Associated with Positive and Negative User Experience (RQ3). The most frequently predicted intents were sorted into groups according to the level of customer satisfaction. The intents associated with particularly low or high levels of satisfaction were investigated with regard to their common characteristics. The investigation was conducted in an open-ended analysis by three of the AI trainers working with improving and maintaining the Chatbot.

5 Results

In this section, we present the findings associated with each of the three research questions consecutively.

5.1   Problem Resolution Impacts User Experience (RQ1)

To investigate the impact of problem resolution on user experience, we compared customer satisfaction scores for chatbot interactions associated with different levels of self-reported problem resolution. The findings suggest that problem resolution strongly impacts user experience. Among users responding that the problem had been fully resolved, 97% reported positive customer satisfaction (score 4 or 5 – satisfied or very satisfied). However, among users reporting the problem to be unresolved, 4% gave a positive customer satisfaction score. Among users disclosing partial problem resolution, 55% reported positive customer satisfaction. Details are provided in Fig. 1.

One-way ANOVA with self-reported problem resolution as an independent variable and customer satisfaction as a dependent variable showed significant differences among the groups with no problem resolution ($M = 1.66, SD = 0.87$), partial problem resolution ($M = 3.52, SD = 0.90$), and full problem resolution ($M = 4.55, SD = 0.63$), ($F(2, 13310) = 10951, p < 0.000$). The effect size of the differences was large ($\omega^2 = 0.62$).

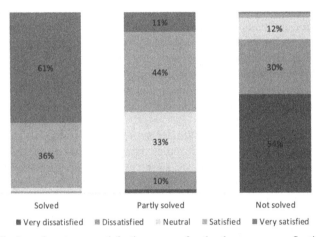

Fig. 1. Distribution of customer satisfaction scores for the three groups reflecting full, partial, and no problem resolution

5.2   User Experience Varies Substantially for Different Kinds of Problems (RQ2)

To investigate the impact of the users' type of problem on user experience, the different kinds of problems were operationalized as the distinct predicted intents in the chatbot – where each intent corresponds to a particular problem area and level of detail – and user experience was operationalized as customer satisfaction.

The analysis was run on the 22 most frequently observed intents. Customer satisfaction was found to vary substantially among the different intents, as shown in Table 1. Customer service scores are provided for the five high-scoring intents and the five low-scoring intents. In this table, we also include details on the proportion of users' self-reported problem resolution.

To investigate the significance of the variation in the customer service scores, a one-way ANOVA was conducted with the four most frequently observed intents (Problems internet, Invoice question, Update smart card, TV) as independent variables and customer satisfaction score as the dependent variable ($F(3, 878) = 20.81, p < 0.000$).

Table 1. Examples of most frequently observed chatbot intents with corresponding customer satisfaction scores and proportion of users reporting problem resolution. The examples include the five high-scoring and the five low-scoring intents out of the 22 intents in the analysis.

Predicted intent	% reporting problem resolved	Customer satisfaction score		% positive (Customer satisfaction 4 or 5)
		Mean	SD	
Forgot PIN code	65%	3.65	1.49	70%
PUK code	42%	3.56	1.51	62%
Cancel subscription	44%	3.14	1.61	56%
Activate SIM card	49%	3.36	1.71	53%
Update smart card TV	40%	3.28	1.54	52%
Help with router	3%	2.03	1.12	13%
Invoice question	5%	1.96	1.09	11%
Help with e-mail	0%	1.7	0.99	10%
Help with TV decoder	2%	1.62	1.03	9%
Error in invoice	1%	1.89	1.02	7%

5.3 Varying Characteristics for Intents Associated with Positive and Negative User Experience (RQ3)

To explore possible systematic variations in the characteristics of intents associated with positive and negative user experience respectively, intents with particularly high and low scores were investigated by three chatbot AI trainers.

As a starting point for this investigation, it was noted that high-scoring intents were also those for which the highest proportion of users reported the problem to be fully resolved. Moreover, it was noted that high-scoring intents were those that cover specific and concrete issues with a simple-to-understand answer that actually solves the problem. For example: If a customer asks "Please update my smart card" and the chatbot answers "Sure. Press confirm to update."

For low-scoring intents, it was found that intents typically aim to deal with too many situations, thereby not being sufficiently concrete and specific. One example is "Problem with internet," which covers a wide range of possible issues and has multiple possible directions intended to support the user. The risk is that the user does not always understand the nature of the problem and, therefore, often ends up in an information loop.

The scores for the remaining 12 intents cover the entire range of values from high-scoring to low-scoring intents and so it is harder to draw insightful conclusions across these – hence, our analysis is limited to the high and low scoring intents.

In conclusion, intents that provide concrete and relevant help bringing the user closer to problem resolution will generate a good user experience, whereas generic responses to issues that the user does not fully grasp will likely generate a poor user experience.

6 Discussion

The presented study provides insight in response to gaps in the current knowledge, as well as implications of theoretical and practical relevance. We first discuss the findings for each research question relative to the state of the art. We then detail key implications of the findings, and finally, we address limitations of our study and suggest venues for future research.

6.1 User Experience Insights from a Customer Satisfaction Survey

The analysis of customer satisfaction data, combined with data on problem resolution and the evaluation of the characteristics of the most used intents in the chatbot, provides relevant insights into the three research questions.

Problem Resolution is Likely a Key Determinant of User Experience in Chatbots for Customer Service (RQ1). While user experience is certainly a broader construct than customer satisfaction, measures of satisfaction may indicate whether or not a service interaction has generated a positive or negative user experience. Our finding that problem resolution is strongly associated with customer satisfaction suggests that solving the user's case is a highly important determinant of user experience. Previous research has indicated that a broad range of factors, such as trust, user emotion, and anthropomorphism, may impact user experience of chatbots for customer service [1, 25, 28]. Nevertheless, our findings concerning the impact of problem resolution resonate with the previous research on general chatbots [2], where it has been shown that most users have pragmatic motivations for utilizing chatbots – that is, chatbots are typically used because they are seen as an easy and convenient means for users to achieve their goals. Furthermore, chatbots' ability to provide support, training or help has been found to be highly important for user experience for general chatbots [8]. Thus, it is not surprising that problem resolution may strongly predict user experience. Our findings also shed light on this relationship in chatbots for customer service. Moreover, we find the strength of the relation between problem resolution and user experience to be noteworthy. In particular, our results highlight that nearly all users with their problem resolved reported to be satisfied, whereas nearly no customers with unsolved problem gave positive scores. These findings suggest to service providers that whether or not a chatbot for customer service actually resolves a problem – or contributes to it being solved – may be decisive for user experience.

User Experience Varies Depending on the Users' Specific Problems (RQ2). Chatbots differ from other interactive systems, such as customer websites, by providing less information with regard to their capabilities and the opportunities they offer for the user [30]. Because of this, the limited interaction between the user and the chatbot will likely be decisive for the user experience [15]. For example, in the case of a service inquiry, the content and user value provided through the few messages exchanged between the chatbot and the user during the interaction could play a key role in the overall experience. Due to the limited content offered to all users in a chatbot – as opposed to website interaction where broader ranges of content are presented to all users – different users may experience the chatbot very differently. our study findings clearly suggest the importance of the users' problem for the user experience in the chatbot. For some problems, associated with one set of user intents, customer satisfaction scores are consistently high. For other issues, associated with other user intents, customer satisfaction is consistently low. Based on these results, it seems fair to assume that the overall design of the chatbot is less important to user experience than the actual support the user receives when triggering a particular intent. This is a highly interesting finding for service providers as it proposes a concrete means to improve user experience – by prioritizing improvements for intents with relatively low customer satisfaction scores.

Specificity in Problem Resolution May Determine the User Experience Associated with Certain Intents (RQ3). The AI trainer analysis of the intents associated with particularly high or low customer satisfaction scores further served to detail the insight that problem resolution is of key importance to user experience in customer service chatbots. It is noteworthy that intents associated with high customer satisfaction scores are those that provide concrete and direct support for the user towards problem resolution. Typically, such direct assistance is due to the chatbot drawing on information about the user from back-end systems or conducting transactions for the users directly following the user's request. Conversely, intents associated with low customer satisfaction scores were typically either presenting too generic information, not sufficiently adapting to the user's situation, or supporting problem areas that are inherently complex and bewildering to users. These findings are useful both to understand variation in user experience for one and the same chatbot and to guide practical upgrade of chatbots. Moreover, it highlights the kind of improvement efforts that are most likely to lead to an enhanced user experience.

6.2 Implications for Theory and Practice

Our study findings hold several implications for theory and practice. We see the following as having particular relevance:

Implications for Theory. The findings serve to extend and strengthen current theory on chatbots to specifically chatbots for customer service.

1. **The primacy of pragmatic quality.** In the theory of user experience, addressing both pragmatic and hedonic quality is seen as equally salient [20]. However, while hedonic quality – for example, in the form of stimulation and identity – is important to chatbots for customer service, pragmatic quality – in particular, goal achievement – is of primary importance in state of the art for chatbots.

2. **User experience as a consequence of the particular interaction.** Whereas user experience assessments are often seen as concerning the entire application or user interface [14], it may be relevant to consider user experience on a task level for customer service chatbots. This bears resemblance to the interaction effects between the task and chatbot personality found in previous research [22].

Implications for Practice. The findings also hold important implications for practical design and implementation of chatbots for customer service.

1. **Targeted improvement of chatbot intents**. Customer satisfaction surveys have substantial potential in guiding chatbot improvement and maintenance. Specifically, identifying and reworking intents that are widely used but score low on satisfaction will be important to address.
2. **Prioritization of problem resolution**. To strengthen user experience in customer service chatbots, it will be beneficial to prioritize helping users to take the concrete steps needed towards problem resolution rather than providing general information. It is likely that offering personalized help and support by drawing on data from back-end systems will be required in this regard.

6.3 Limitations and Future Work

The presented study, while providing valuable insights into user experience for customer service chatbots, also has important limitations. First, the study focuses on one chatbot within a specific market. While we assume that the findings may be generalizable also to chatbots for customer service in other markets, it is advisable to test this assumption. Hence, for future work, we foresee studies including a broader range of chatbots and markets.

Second, the study is limited to relying on customer satisfaction as the only measurement of customer experience. While valuable as a reflection of good or poor user experience, this measurement does not provide needed nuance for the customer experience construct. Thus, for future work, we anticipate studies combining customer satisfaction surveys with other measurements of relevance for user experience. Furthermore, we foresee qualitative user experience studies to gain insight into how different levels of problem resolution and different intents impact user experience.

Finally, the study is limited in that it does not include satisfaction measures for different channels. Such additional measures would have enabled cross-channel comparison and, thereby, an assessment of the relative satisfaction with the chatbot channel – something that would be relevant both for theory and practice. Cross-channel comparison clearly is a relevant topic for future work.

In spite of the limitations, the study encourages further use of customer satisfaction surveys as a means to understand user experience in chatbots for customer service. Such surveys may provide new theoretical insight and will also have benefits for practice given the widespread uptake of customer satisfaction surveys within service providers.

Acknowledgements. The work of the four first authors was supported by Telenor Research and Telenor Norway. The work of the fifth author was supported by the Research Council of Norway through research grant no. 270940.

References

1. Araujo, T.: Living up to the chatbot hype: the influence of anthropomorphic design cues and communicative agency framing on conversational agent and company perceptions. Comput. Human Behav. **85**, 183–189 (2018). https://doi.org/10.1016/j.chb.2018.03.051
2. Brandtzaeg, P.B., Følstad, A.: Why people use chatbots. In: Kompatsiaris, I., et al. (eds.) INSCI 2017. LNCS, vol. 10673, pp. 377–392. Springer, Cham (2017). https://doi.org/10.1007/978-3-319-70284-1_30
3. Ciechanowski, L., Przegalinska, A., Magnuski, M., Gloor, P.: In the shades of the uncanny valley: an experimental study of human–chatbot interaction. Future Gener. Comput. Syst. **92**, 539–548 (2019)
4. De Haan, E., Verhoef, P.C., Wiesel, T.: The predictive ability of different customer feedback metrics for retention. Int. J. Res. Mark. **32**(2), 195–206 (2015)
5. Dixon, M., Freeman, K., Toman, N.: Stop trying to delight your customers. Harv. Bus. Rev. **88**(7/8), 116–122 (2010)
6. Drift: The 2018 State of Chatbots Report. Technical Report, Drift (2018). https://www.drift.com/blog/Chatbots-report/
7. Følstad, A., Brandtzæg, P.B.: Chatbots and the new world of HCI. Interactions **24**(4), 38–42 (2017)
8. Følstad, A., Brandtzaeg, P.B.: Users' experiences with chatbots: findings from a questionnaire study. Qual. User Exp. **5**, 1–4 (2020)
9. Følstad, A., Skjuve, M.: Chatbots for customer service: user experience and motivation. In: Proceedings of the 1st International Conference on Conversational User Interfaces, Paper no. 1. ACM, New York (2019)
10. Følstad, A., Taylor, C.: Conversational repair in chatbots for customer service: the effect of expressing uncertainty and suggesting alternatives. In: Følstad, A., Araujo, T., Papadopoulos, S., Law, E.-C., Granmo, O.-C., Luger, E., Brandtzaeg, P.B. (eds.) CONVERSATIONS 2019. LNCS, vol. 11970, pp. 201–214. Springer, Cham (2020). https://doi.org/10.1007/978-3-030-39540-7_14
11. Forrester Consulting: Human vs. machines: how to stop your virtual agent from lagging behind. Technical report, Forrester Consulting (2017). https://www.amdocs.com/blog/place-digital-talks-intelligent-minds/aia-humans-vs-machines-how-to-stop-your-chatbot-from-lagging-behind
12. Forrester: The six factors that separate hype from hope in your conversational AI journey. Technical report, Forrester (2018). https://www.forrester.com/report/The+Six+Factors+That+Separate+Hype+From+Hope+In+Your+Conversational+AI+Journey/-/E-RES143773
13. Gartner: Market guide for virtual customer assistants. Technical report, Gartner (2019) https://www.gartner.com/en/documents/3947357/market-guide-for-virtual-customer-assistants
14. Go, E., Sundar, S.S.: Humanizing chatbots: the effects of visual, identity and conversational cues on humanness perceptions. Comput. Human Behav. **97**, 304–316 (2019)
15. Hall, E.: Conversational Design. A Book Apart, New York (2018)
16. Hocutt, M.A., Bowers, M.R., Donavan, D.T.: The art of service recovery: fact or fiction? J. Serv. Mark. **20**(3), 199–207 (2006)
17. Hu, T. et al.: Touch your heart: a tone-aware chatbot for customer care on social media. In: Proceedings of CHI 2018, paper no. 415. ACM, New York (2018)

18. ISO: Ergonomics of human–system interaction — Part 210: Human-centred design for interactive systems. International Standard. ISO, Geneva (2010)

19. Kvale, K., Sell, O.A., Hodnebrog, S., Følstad, A.: Improving conversations: lessons learnt from manual analysis of chatbot dialogues. In: Følstad, A., et al. (eds.) CONVERSATIONS 2019. LNCS, vol. 11970, pp. 187–200. Springer, Cham (2020). https://doi.org/10.1007/978-3-030-39540-7_13

20. Law, E.L.C., Van Schaik, P.: Modelling user experience–an agenda for research and practice. Interact. Comput. **22**(5), 313–322 (2010)

21. Luria, M., Reig, S., Tan, X.Z., Steinfeld, A., Forlizzi, J., Zimmerman, J.: Re-embodiment and co-embodiment: exploration of social presence for robots and conversational agents. In: Proceedings of the 2019 on Designing Interactive Systems Conference, pp. 633–644 (2019)

22. McDonnell, M., Baxter, D.: Chatbots and gender stereotyping. Interact. Comput. **31**(2), 116–121 (2019)

23. Morana, S., Gnewuch, U., Jung, D., Granig, C.: The effect of anthropomorphism on investment decision-making with robo-advisor chatbots. In Proceedings of ECIS 2020 (2020)

24. Moore, R.J., Arar, R.: Conversational UX Design: A Practitioner's Guide to the Natural Conversation Framework. ACM, New York (2019)

25. Nordheim, C.B., Følstad, A., Bjørkli, C.A.: An initial model of trust in chatbots for customer service—findings from a questionnaire study. Interact. Comput. **31**(3), 317–335 (2019)

26. Palmer, A.: Customer experience management: a critical review of an emerging idea. J. Serv. Mark. **24**(3), 196–208 (2010)

27. PwC. Bot.Me: a revolutionary partnership. How AI is pushing man and machine closer together. Consumer Intelligence Series, PwC (2018). https://www.pwc.com/it/it/publications/assets/docs/PwC_botme-booklet.pdf

28. Sands, S., Ferraro, C., Campbell, C., Tsao, H.Y.: Managing the human–chatbot divide: how service scripts influence service experience. J. Serv. Manag. (2020). https://doi.org/10.1108/JOSM-06-2019-0203

29. Schaffer, E., Lahiri, A.: Institutionalization of UX: A Step-by-Step Guide to a User Experience Practice, 2nd edn. Addison-Wesley, Upper Saddle River (2013)

30. Shevat, A.: Designing bots: Creating conversational experiences. O'Reilly Media, Sebastopol (2017)

31. Smestad, T.L., Volden, F.: Chatbot personalities matters. In: Bodrunova, S.S., et al. (eds.) INSCI 2018. LNCS, vol. 11551, pp. 170–181. Springer, Cham (2019). https://doi.org/10.1007/978-3-030-17705-8_15

32. Taylor, M.P. et al.: Smart talk: How organizations and consumers are embracing voice and chat assistants. Technical report, Capgemini SE (2019). https://www.capgemini.com/wp-content/uploads/2019/09/Report---Conversational-Interfaces_Web-Final.pdf

33. Temkin, B.: The state of CX metrics, 2017. Technical report, Qualtrics XM Institute (2017). https://www.qualtrics.com/xm-institute/state-of-customer-experience-metrics-2017/

34. Trivedi, J.: Examining the customer experience of using banking chatbots and its impact on brand love: the moderating role of perceived risk. J. Internet Commer. **18**(1), 91–111 (2019)

35. Van Doorn, J., Leeflang, P.S., Tijs, M.: Satisfaction as a predictor of future performance: a replication. Int. J. Res. Mark. **30**(3), 314–318 (2013)

Author Index

Printed in the United States
By Bookmasters